Acclaim for Paul Clemens's

Made in Detroit

"An honest and bracing account not only of mutual mistrust across the color divide, but also of the peculiar Rust Belt pride that kept whites and blacks locked together, even as the city collapsed around them."
—*The New Yorker*

"Hilarious and sobering, trenchant and swaggering, and always wonderfully well-written."
—*Detroit Free Press*

"A richly detailed, often funny story about living in a tight-knit ethnic enclave inside an otherwise black city."
—*Publishers Weekly*

"Bold and brutally honest. . . . [Clemens] exposes the cultural conditions that have transformed [Detroit] over the past few decades."   —*The Washington Post Book World*

"Insightful. . . . [A] blunt cry from the heart."
—*The Wall Street Journal*

Made in Detroit

[A South of 8-Mile Memoir]

Paul Clemens

Anchor Books

A Division of Random House, Inc.

New York

FIRST ANCHOR BOOKS EDITION, OCTOBER 2006

Copyright © 2005 by Paul Clemens

The Library of Congress has cataloged the Doubleday edition as follows:
Clemens, Paul, 1973–
Made in Detroit : a south of 8-Mile memoir / by Paul Clemens.—1st ed.
p. cm.
1. Clemens, Paul, 1973—Childhood and youth. 2. Whites—Michigan—
Detroit—Biography. 3. Detroit (Mich.)—Biography. 4. Detroit (Mich.)—
Race relations. I. Title.
F574.D453C58 2005
305.809'0977434'092—dc22
[B] 2005041327

Anchor ISBN-10: 1-4000-7596-3
Anchor ISBN-13: 978-1-4000-7596-6

Book design by rlf design

www.anchorbooks.com

Printed in the United States of America
10 9 8 7 6 5 4 3 2 1

In memory of E.J.K.

1978–2000

No other city in America, no other city in the Western world has lost the population at that rate. And what's at the root of that loss? Economics and race. Or should I say, race and economics.

—Coleman A. Young, Mayor of Detroit, 1974–1994, on the city's abandonment

What does a writer need most? When I ask this question, I think of my father.

—Bernard Malamud

Author's Note

In the following pages some names have been changed and some identifying details altered or obscured. Given these small deviations, the following may be read as a novel. God knows I would have preferred to have written one. But I have tried to be as factually accurate as memory and decency allow. In this, I have been aided by the very shortcoming that prevented this book from being fiction in the first place: I'm lousy at making things up.

—P. C.

Made in Detroit

Right to Go Left

*P*AUL, PAUL, GET UP, GET UP." This is my mother, shaking me awake around three in the morning on a midsummer night in 1989. Before being poked in the ribs I had been sleeping with the violent soundness of a sixteen-year-old boy and so had not, in my upstairs bedroom, heard the noise—a gunshot blast—that had awakened my parents downstairs. Me, turning away: "What the hell, Ma?" Her, pulling back the sheet: "Paul, you've got to go after your dad." Me, sitting up: "Jesus—what for?" "Some guys just shot out the windows to our truck. Your dad went after them. They have a *gun*. Get up." "Christ. Where're my running shoes?"

Ever the organized housewife, even at the witching hour, she already had them in her hands, and as I too had the drill down cold by this point—such things tended to happen quite a bit in our corner of Detroit—I sleepily grabbed for the baseball bat that leaned against my bedpost for just such a purpose. The bat was an aluminum Easton, thirty-two inches in length and weighing twenty-nine ounces, with a barrel, according to the bat's red lettering, two and a half inches in diameter: the B5 Magnum. The model name struck me as an unfortunate misnomer, as it was not, in fact, a gun, which would have been more appropriate to the occasion. A gun was what my dad had—and so did the guys we were chasing. On my bedpost hung a rosary blessed, in Rome, by Pope Pius XII, which I ritually ran my fingers over before falling asleep. I did so for a second time before running downstairs.

Though on past occasions I had had to give futile chase on foot, I was able, by sixteen, to hop in the car that I'd recently purchased with a combination of parental help and house painting money, my previous summer's earnings. I drove slowly at first, headlights off, stopping briefly in intersections to look up and down the dark side streets. After a minute or two of searching, I caught a glimpse a couple blocks up— toward 8 Mile Road—of the getaway car, which went streaking by. On its back bumper, with my father behind the wheel, was the chase car. They were both, I guessed, going about seventy, in cars not manufactured to go much faster: four-cylinder imports, theirs from Japan, my father's from Europe. But my father, who had raced go-carts, dune buggies, and dragsters for most of his adult life, was by far the better driver, able to get the most out of the little five-speed that was used, by and large, by my mother to run errands.

My father had amazed me throughout my childhood with his ability to spin 360s in icy intersections—it had something to do, I noticed, with violently jerking up the parking brake—and he remains the only person I know able to shift his way from first through fifth without his foot once touching the clutch. "It's how the European rally drivers do it," he once told me. "They never use their left foot. Their right heel is on the brake, and the ball of their right foot is on the accelerator." "But how do you know when you can shift that way?" "Without using the clutch to disengage the gears, you mean? Oh, you can hear it when the gears mesh." Car performance, and upkeep, was everything to this man. When he purchased a new car (new to us, I mean: we bought used cars), the first thing my father did was pull out the air conditioner. All those damn things did was use up gas, drain off power, and make it more or less impossible to work on the engine when something went wrong, stuck, as air conditioners were, smack in the middle of significantly more important components. "This is Michigan," he'd always say. "Eight months out of the year you don't need air conditioning anyway."

Whom to obey, where opinion diverges: Mom or Dad? My mother was always fond of pointing out that *things,* as she would have it, were replaceable, but that *people* were not. You can always buy another (blank), but you could never, *never* replace (so-and-so). This was Mom's theory, often stated, and the reason that she'd awakened me in the first place: to be sure to bring her irreplaceable husband home alive. But my father's stance, which went stoically unstated, because self-evident, was somewhat different and, oddly enough, of a piece with that of my favorite philosopher at the time, who sang in that summer's inescapable song—"You can have anything you want, but you better not take it from me." That night, I sided with the old man and Axl. Instead of concentrating my efforts on calling off the chase, whatever that would've entailed, I joined in the pursuit, baseball bat—*check*—by my side. Despite many, much better incentives to rejoin the battle, these summer car chases, perhaps half a dozen in all, would be my farewell to vigilantism, that unfairly criminalized response to widespread criminality.

What with his white T-shirts, wiry build, and messy sideburns, my father looks, in family photo albums from the mid-to-late seventies, like every other young father of that era—which is to say, like Bruce Springsteen on the back cover of *Darkness on the Edge of Town.* Ten years later he had softened only slightly. Blessed with a helpful disposition and familiar with his hometown's every last alleyway, he could happily discuss directions in Detroit until doomsday. "Now remember," he said to many visitors over the years, as they put on their coats to leave, "at 8 Mile, there, you're gonna have to go right to go left." The phrasing of these directions was revealing of his worldview. Life is a list of things you *have* to do; one of these, on the major surface streets of Detroit, is to go right to go left.

This phenomenon is the so-called Michigan left, that traffic quirk that forces one, on busy boulevards particularly, to turn right initially in order to go left eventually. If you were to drive north on Kelly Road, an eastern divider between city and suburb, and wanted to turn left onto 8 Mile Road, the city's northern boundary, you would not, upon approaching the intersection, get into the left-hand turn lane, for the simple reason that there is no left-hand turn lane. There is a right-hand turn onto 8 Mile only, and those who would have liked to go left must employ the hairpin turnaround on the boulevard's far side, a full four lanes over, which occurs immediately after making the turn off of Kelly.

A good deal more than just two streets converge at this intersection. If you had continued going east along 8 Mile instead of doubling back, you would quite quickly have entered into Grosse Pointe, the old, well-to-do suburb to the east of the city, along the banks of Lake St. Clair. You would, too, have remained in Wayne County, the oldest in Michigan, for which the city of Detroit—settled, three centuries back, by the French—is the county seat. By taking the turnaround to the westbound side of 8 Mile you enter Macomb County, the working-class suburban enclave that, more than twenty years after first achieving national fame, still finds itself, every four years, beloved of pollsters and trackers of voting patterns.

At the time of the Iranian hostage crisis, the gas shortages, and the Olympics boycotts, Macomb County was considered a national political trendsetter, an area in which large numbers of ethnic Catholics and unionized blue-collar workers decided to vote against Jimmy Carter in the 1980 presidential election. Such voters would later be labeled Reagan Democrats—would, in fact, constitute a "movement," and the movement's epicenter was said to be located five blocks to our north, in Macomb County, which began (the past tense is important here) with the suburb of East Detroit. The suburb was not to be confused with the east *side* of Detroit, where we lived; it was a separate entity entirely, like East St. Louis. The residents of East Detroit voted in the early 1990s to change the town's name to Eastpointe, hoping that some of the sheen from Lakeshore Drive might rub off on their suburb, composed almost entirely of Muffler Men and collision shops, by simple virtue of no longer having the syllables *de-troit* in its name.

I knew that the guys with the gun would be headed to the west side, which meant that they would go to 8 Mile, which meant that, sooner or later, they would need to go right to go left. I knew too that my father, the most tenacious man I've ever met, would tail them every inch of the way. So I switched on my headlights, said a short prayer, and headed straight for 8 Mile, doing my best, in my little American four cylinder, to beat them to the anticipated spot.

It worked. Ten seconds later they went whizzing by, first the totally outclassed criminals, who would never shake the driver behind them, and then my father, revving the little Renault for all it was worth. The two cars were drifting, in tandem, to the far side of 8 Mile, preparing to take the turnaround that would direct them back toward the west. Knowing that I had no hope of catching them by following that path, I went left to go right—against the flow of what, hours before sunrise, was the nonexistent traffic. When I came out of the turnaround the criminals' car, which I was now facing, came to a stop, as did my father's car behind them.

What now? It will be interesting, I remember thinking, to see how this one shakes out. It was three in the morning, and we were three cars at a dead stop on the (then) East Detroit side of 8 Mile, with one of us—me—facing the wrong way. Come on, fellas, wouldn't it be better to settle this on our home turf, on the Detroit side? What next, we all drive east, to Grosse Pointe, where they *really* didn't want to be bothered with this shit at three a.m.? I would gladly have gotten out of their way if I could have secured a promise, then and there, that they would use the next turnaround to return to Detroit, where we all belonged.

Such a promise proved unnecessary. A few seconds later they panicked and plowed their little Japanese import over the curb of the median, slipping and sliding across the grassy island between the eastbound and westbound sides of the boulevard. After briefly bottoming out on the descent, sending sparks skyward, they tore back down the Detroit side street that I'd driven up only moments before. Unwilling to inflict similar damage to our own cars, my father and I took the next turnaround, and the guys with the gun took the opportunity to disappear back inside Detroit's northeast corner, the streets of which I knew much, much better than the back of my hand.

We drove around slowly for a bit, looking left and right at intersections, and eventually drifted south toward St. Jude Church on 7 Mile, where my father had gone to grade school and where our family still went to Mass. We always sat in the church's western alcove at Sunday services, in the pew directly behind the votive candles; my sister and I spent the majority of each service picking at melted wax, which burnt our fingertips before it cooled and hardened, blissfully unaware that the flames in front of us had been lit by those in various stages of despair. During Saturday-evening services in the fall and winter your fingers might grow cold gripping your songbook, but look at the light of the low sun reflecting off the stained glass; forget, for a second, about the spiderwebs in the upper reaches of the ceiling, and take a minute to appreciate the acoustics in the place; ignore the stiffness in your joints, and the lack of padding on the kneelers (the result of half a century's penitence), and acknowledge that your Savior suffered far worse, and in far less pleasant surroundings.

I hadn't lit a candle or even offered up a prayer entirely free of cursing, but St. Jude, the patron saint of the lost cause, answered my petition that night: there, up ahead, was the criminals' car, abandoned now, having evidently crashed into the parked Crown Regal on the corner. We would later hear that the car wasn't even theirs, but had been stolen earlier that evening from a house several blocks away. But still: the sight of that totaled car looked, to my sixteen-year-old eyes, like victory—for my father, for me, and for what I can only call, waxing euphemistic, our way of life.

It was a victory that would prove short-lived. The next summer, the car in which I'd challenged those criminals to a game of chicken would be stolen from our driveway, and because, like an attentive mother, I could recognize in my sleep the sound of my car's squeaky belts, its automotive wake-up cries, I got to the window in time to see it pull away. By no means a particularly nice car, it was, as my high school locker partner once put it, not without some appeal in an urban center.

Though the process was certainly cumulative, gathering momentum over the years and crimes, this event's aftermath capped, for me, the odd position of being white in a city that wasn't white any longer— a city where, when your car was stolen and a black Detroit cop happened, several hours later, to arrive on the scene, the quizzical look you were given said, "What are you *doing* here?"—as if, at seventeen, I were a doddering British farmer, stubbornly tending land in a country I insisted on calling Rhodesia.

To hell with this place, I remember thinking. Accompanying this, however, was another thought, this one hinting at the dawning of what I now realize to be a stage-one literary sensibility: I've got *material*.

What I hadn't realized at seventeen was that the words at my disposal didn't exactly do justice to the situations they sought to describe: not specific enough here, not accurate enough there, and in many instances entirely misleading. My Detroit experience was through-the-looking-glass on a basic linguistic level: those persons frequently identified as "minorities" were, in fact, the majority inhabitants of the city. Those persons often described as "disempowered" were, in fact, in power: the mayor, the chief of police, the city council. ("The 'powers that be' be black," as I explained to those not from these parts.) East Detroit became Eastpointe, even as it began to resemble more and more the city whose name it had discarded, and many of the stores on the Detroit side of Mack Avenue came up with wholly inappropriate names, calling themselves Grosse Pointe Furniture Refinishing, Grosse

Pointe Cleaners, Grosse Pointe Day School, Pointe Towing, Pointe Nails, and The Pointe After, a sports collectibles store. When you were giving directions and told someone that he needed to turn left onto 8 Mile Road, you began, straight out of the box, by telling him to turn right. This, no one would dispute, was some kind of semantically confusing city, and so getting at the truth of my material—in words with meanings that slipped and slid like a stolen getaway car—would be no easy matter.

There was, too, the disconnect of being white in a society in which this is seen as an "entitled" status but having been born and raised in late-twentieth-century Detroit, where whiteness entitled one to nothing at all. I recall watching a news program on race in America in which a grade school teacher lectured to an integrated, adult studio audience on the insidiousness of stereotyping. Her claim to expertise was a classroom experiment in which an arbitrary group of students—blue-eyed children, say—would be ostracized as inferior. I remember her instructing the white audience members on the ways in which they'd benefited from the systematic oppression of the blacks seated around them. Racial prejudice, you see: she was *against* it.

I started to laugh. I couldn't help it. This parade of moral simpletonism was more than I could take. But my father, who sat on the couch alongside me, stayed serious. "No, no, she has a point," he said, his tone gently scolding. He had, by this time, taken a poorly paid position as a draftsman for the Detroit Public Lighting Department, where his boss was black, and where his whiteness did him no favors whatsoever on qualifying and promotional exams. "Why, by now," he said, "I must have stopped every black person in Detroit, at one time or another, and *demanded* they shine my shoes."

The best description of Detroit in twentieth-century literature comes from Louis-Ferdinand Céline's *Journey to the End of the Night*, published in the early 1930s and, in its sophisticated French fashion, quite possibly the most pessimistic novel ever written. After leaving behind World War I battlefields, Paris slums, and malarial African jungles, Céline's restless narrator makes his way to the Motor City, to work in the Ford factory. At the beginning of the first Detroit chapter he says, in an observation yet to be improved upon: "It was even worse than everywhere else."

Céline had visited the city at its incontestable peak. Detroit was then the fourth-largest city in America and seemed poised to go higher. Its population, lured in large part by Henry Ford's promise of a five-dollar workday, had doubled between 1910 and 1920 and increased another 60 percent between 1920 and 1930, by which time it exceeded a million and a half residents. Italians, Poles, Slavs, Chaldeans, Appalachians, poor southern whites and poorer southern blacks—the Unwashed Masses met the Great Migration in Michigan's southeastern corner.

A great deal has been written about Detroit in the ensuing seventy years, and the thesis of much of it is that, if not worse than everywhere else, Detroit is, at a minimum, worse than most places. Though later commentators have lacked Céline's gift for overstatement, it hasn't been for want of trying, and such efforts may be warranted, as the facts of Detroit's decline cannot be overstated. For more than five decades now, Detroit has found itself on the dwindling edge of an inverted frontier: people have fled it in the hundreds of thousands, the millions, to settle elsewhere. It has a sense of Manifest Destiny that runs in reverse. I once heard a white Detroiter remark, "We're the last of the Mohicans." It was an irony three hundred years in the making.

The city was settled in 1701 by Frenchmen more optimistic than Céline, men who had come down from Montreal in the company of Algonquin Indians to set up a trading post. Today, in the plaza of the Detroit Historical Museum in the city's midtown, three flags stand together: an "ancient" French flag—three yellow fleurs-de-lis, symbol of the French monarchy—that commemorates the city's settling; a

Union Jack, testifying to the British control that began in 1760; and a Stars and Stripes with "1796" etched into the base of its flagpole, the date of the British surrender of Detroit.

The city was incorporated six years later, and the nineteenth century would see Detroit's first mayors; their names—Zachariah Chandler, Levi Cook, Zina Pitcher—read like an index of characters for the collected works of Nathaniel Hawthorne. The sequence of twentieth-century mayors tracks the usual progress of aspirant immigrant groups, with Catholic names like Miriani and Cavanagh eventually taking the city's administration, in the 1950s and 1960s, back to its papist roots.

Before Céline, the most prominent French writer to comment on the city was Alexis de Tocqueville, who visited Detroit twice in 1831 while doing research for *Democracy in America*. His journal entry for July 22 contains this passage: "We arrived at Detroit at 4 o'clock. A fine American village. Many French names on the houses; French bonnets. We went to see Mr. Richard, the priest in charge of the Catholic church in Detroit." Father Gabriel Richard—a Catholic American pioneer, lionized in every Detroit-area parochial school—had arrived back in 1798 to assist at Ste. Anne's Church. From Detroit's earliest days, the place had been crawling with priests; a Jesuit, Father Vaillant, was in the company of Antoine Cadillac at Fort Pontchartrain de Detroit's settlement. Ste. Anne's Church was founded within days. Father Richard took it over a century later, in 1802, and in 1804, with the help of another priest, he began a prep school for boys. He was the first person in Michigan to own a printing press, and he published Detroit's first paper. Entering the village to visit Father Richard, Tocqueville had noted "huts of a sort with a fire in the middle. On one side extreme civilization, on the other the extreme opposite." The city was on the frontier then, with civilization ceasing just beyond its borders.

By the time I was born, civilization surrounded the city and the Wild West lawlessness was contained within. This, at least, was the suburban view. Not everyone agreed. "I'll be damned," Coleman Young once said, explaining his opposition to antigun laws, "if I'm going to let them collect guns in the city of Detroit while we're surrounded by hostile suburbs and the whole rest of the state who have guns, and where you have vigilantes practicing Ku Klux Klan in the wilderness with automatic weapons." This led to a famous "Uncle Coleman Needs *You*" recruitment poster, with the finger-pointing mayor in the posture of Uncle Sam, seeking help to "Defend Detroit Against Armed Suburban Attack." It was still cowboys and Indians, and each side was afraid of having its wagon train surrounded.

Tocqueville notes in his journal that "on leaving Mr. Richard" he felt "embarrassment about which way to set out." My father would have told Tocqueville not to be embarrassed; all he had to remember, really, was that when he got to 8 Mile there—well, it was a bit confusing. Democracy in America was all well and good, but *directions* in America—now there was an idea for a book.

"We took our freedom in 1973," Coleman Young said during a 1989 campaign speech, and though he was referring to his first election, sixteen years before, he could just as easily have meant that 1973 was the year that the city's minority population became its majority population. Blacks accounted for 16 percent of Detroit's citizenry in 1950; 28 percent in 1960; 43 percent in 1970. Trace this arc, and 1973—the year of my birth—becomes the point at which the teeter-totter briefly struck a balance before tilting pronouncedly to one side, as it has ever since.

One can pick any number of points in Detroit's last hundred years and say, *Here*—this is where the city's history took a turn. Though it may not be the historical watershed of Young's 1973 victory, or the 1967 riots, or the 1943 riots, 1972 stands out as the year that Berry Gordy Jr. packed up Motown Records and left Detroit for Hollywood. That event—Motown leaving Motown—helped set the stage for the semantic confusion that has bedeviled Detroit ever since. It was like the wind leaving Chicago, or Los Angeles losing its wings.

If Detroit was no longer Motown, what was it? People were leaving so fast that there wasn't time to ask the question, let alone formulate an answer. Although the city's population had been shrinking, for reasons not exclusively racial, for some time before 1967, the reasons for moving out after the riots—at the time, the worst in American history—were overwhelmingly racial. And Coleman Young's election six years later sealed the deal. "If white flight was a redefining fact of life in Detroit before Young assumed his office," the coauthor of Young's autobiography dryly puts it, "he was a doorman to those with their bags already packed."

The numbers bear this out. In 1950, the city's population peaked at just below 2 million residents; in 1960, it dipped to 1.67 million; in 1970, that number slipped to 1.5 million; in 1980, after Young had served a term and a half in office, the number fell to 1.2 million; and in 1990 the total number of residents stood, on tiptoes, at just over a million. The population of Detroit is now well under that figure, and will never again come within whispering distance of it.

In November 1973, when Coleman Young beat Police Chief John Nichols 52 to 48 percent—when, in his words, he "became the goddamn mayor of Detroit"—he'd received well in excess of two hundred thousand votes. (This came to more than 90 percent of the black vote and about 10 percent of the white.) Thereafter, Young's victory margins widened to the near monarchical—60 percent of the vote in 1977, 66 percent in 1981—though his totals declined steeply. By the time of his fifth victory in 1989, he would receive nearly one hundred thousand fewer votes than he had in 1973, despite receiving a much higher percentage of the total. The distinguishing feature of Young's tenure was that, as the years went on, he found himself in firmer control of less and less. His grip on Detroit tightened and the citizenry slipped between his fingers, with deposits settling north of 8 Mile or west of Telegraph.

It is one of the many ironies of life in Detroit that it was almost always whites who suspected that blacks were undercounted in the city and much more of a majority than was officially reported. This runs counter to the usual urban legend, which holds that blacks are purposely undercounted in the national census. Detroit's whites seemed to accept this story, at least as far as their city was concerned—blacks, in the white mind, were made more culpable for the city's miserable state the more of them there were—and many people in our neighborhood relished the thought of being even more pronouncedly a minority than went down in the books. To this way of thinking, 76 percent, or whatever the official figures said, was severely underselling things. "This city's a quarter white?" the guy at the pizza place would say. His arcade games, like the motorized horse rides outside the Kmart at 8 Mile and Gratiot, wouldn't accept our Canadian coins. Store owners slipped them to unsuspecting customers as change but never took them back. "Detroit's a quarter white—are you kidding? There's me, and you, and who else?"

The white population of Detroit dropped by nearly a million and a half between 1950 and 1990, by which point there were a little more than two hundred thousand whites left in the city—characterized, by the president of the Malcolm X Academy Local School Community Organization, as those "white people who forgot to move out of the city when the rest of them did, or they are too poor to move out of there, or they are city workers or something." That accurately summed it up, at least in our neck of the woods. Her organization supported the Detroit Board of Education's desire to open a school for at-risk black males in a predominantly white neighborhood on Detroit's west side. The response of the city's black power structure to the residents' objections to the Malcolm X Academy, which would open in the fall of 1992, could be fairly distilled as follows: What are you *doing* here?

The residency requirement for city workers had been around since the early twentieth century but went basically unenforced until Coleman Young, who campaigned in 1973 against the overwhelmingly white Detroit police department as an "occupying army," came to power. Once in office, Young worked quickly to integrate the force, in keeping with his campaign pledge. But when a budget crisis early in his first term necessitated layoffs, Young seized on the residency requirement as a way to unload not the most recently hired, almost all of whom were black, but those officers, almost all of whom were white, who were not in compliance with the 1914 law that mandated that city employees live within the city limits.

Most city workers abided by the requirement, living as close as possible to Detroit's borders without living beyond them. 8 Mile Road was the wall, and they lived with their backs against it. To mix historical metaphors, many folks who felt that they were among the last of Detroit's Mohicans also felt that, by living in our corner of the city, they were engaged in something equivalent to Custer's Last Stand.

It wasn't until I read *The Autobiography of Malcolm X* that I began to get a sense of just how signal a role Detroit played in this country's racial history. Among much else to recommend it, the book is an invaluable guide to the early days of Detroit's—which is to say, America's—Black Power movement. I remember being surprised, as a college student who'd left Detroit for a dorm in west Michigan's cornfields, to learn that Malcolm himself was raised just outside Lansing, that he moved to Detroit after being released from prison (that he was, in fact, nicknamed "Detroit Red"), and that in 1931, after Elijah Muhammad met a mulatto door-to-door salesman on the streets of this city, a man with a strange story to tell, the Nation of Islam was founded here. Malcolm X had worked in the auto factories, and in his spare time stood on street corners, recruiting for the Nation of Islam. All of this seemed to give my Detroit experience a history that predated Coleman Young and served to validate my sense that I had indeed been born right smack in the middle of America's racial shitstorm.

Around this time, too, I would discover Ze'ev Chafets's book *Devil's Night*, a survey of the political and racial landscape of late-eighties Detroit. Chafets, who was raised in suburban Detroit before moving to Israel, took his title from the local custom, on the night before Halloween, of attempting to burn the city down. The news the next day would report fire tallies as if they were the winning Daily Three combination: 810 (1984), 479 (1985), 386 (1986). Catholic school friends of mine whose fathers were firemen wore T-shirts under their uniforms that broadcast these totals in front of a background of flames—DEVIL'S NIGHT 1985—already, at the age of twelve, exhibiting the ironic pride in the city's awfulness that was many an adult Detroiter's means of coping. Neighborhood men stood guard in doorways on Devil's Night, in fulfillment of their biological duty. Once a year they loaded guns, gripped baseball bats, and weighed lead pipes in their hands, objects that, the other 364 days of the year, sat in the backs of sock drawers, leaned against basement walls, and awaited the next plumbing project. City officials recommended leaving your lights on. My father leapt off our front porch more than a few times, if only in pursuit of teenagers carrying cartons of eggs. Can't be too careful.

Near the end of the book, in a passage I underlined, Chafets writes: "Under Young, Detroit has become not merely an American city that happens to have a black majority, but a black metropolis, the first major Third World city in the United States. The trappings are all there—showcase projects, black-fisted symbols, an external enemy and the cult of personality." That's what Detroit was, after it had ceased to be Motown. A *Detroit News* editorial cartoon that ran shortly after the publication of the book shows an angry mayor with his press secretary standing beside him, saying: "Look at the bright side—nobody's gonna have the gall to call us a *Fourth* World city."

The cult of personality, of course, centered around Young himself, Detroit's uncontested king; the external enemy was white suburbia and, to a lesser extent, those white city residents like ourselves—"motherfuckers," as Young would have put it—who did not support him; the showcase projects were disastrous civic undertakings like the People Mover, the elevated train system downtown that made a three-mile loop and drew no riders; and the black-fisted symbol was the big black fist at the intersection of Jefferson and Woodward avenues.

After Young himself, The Fist may have been the most disliked entity in Detroit. (Disliked by whites, I mean.) Twenty-four feet long, eight thousand pounds, and set square in the center of Detroit's downtown, The Fist stood, ostensibly, as a tribute to Joe Louis, a native Detroiter. A big man, Louis, though you would never know it from the statue with which Detroit memorialized him: 95 percent of his body was missing. All that remained, the symbolism lost on no one, was his extended right forearm and clenched right fist. Nothing since the political ascent of Coleman Young had so antagonized the ever-diminishing mass of Detroit's whites.

For many white Detroiters, such feelings led to difficulty during the 1989 campaign, when they were forced to choose between Young and Tom Barrow, who happened to be Joe Louis's grandson. My father, who voted for Barrow, voiced a popular sentiment: "I never go downtown anymore anyway," he said. Other Barrow voters—old Italian men in barbershops, particularly—tried to soften the symbolic impact of The Fist by remembering that, at the end of his career, Louis had been beaten badly by Marciano. Others made the decision, bordering on the immoral in their minds, to sit out the election. "It almost seems like a sin," you could hear them saying, "not voting against Coleman Young." "Oh, what difference does it make, really?" someone else would chime in. "You could raise Abraham Lincoln from the dead. Nobody's going to beat Coleman Young."

And yet we stayed in Young's Detroit, in part because we had a means of escape besides the suburbs. The other side of 8 Mile was Macomb County; the other side of the Detroit River was another country.

Though debatably Third World, Detroit has always been the most Canadian of American cities. A few miles from our house was the city of Windsor, Ontario—a place so scrupulously clean, so highly habitable, that it never seemed to qualify as a city. As with many kids in Detroit, I'd grown up watching Canadian television, turning the rabbit ears on top of our set just slightly to the south and east in the morning before school so that I could see the cartoons on Channel 9, the Canadian Broadcasting Corporation. (More confusion: Canada is south of Detroit. Check any atlas.) This was how I eventually learned, multiplying by nine-fifths and adding thirty-two, to convert the day's predicted high from Celsius to Fahrenheit; it's also how I stumbled into certain misspellings, adding an unnecessary *u* to *color*, for instance, or putting the *r* before the *e* in *theater*.

On Saturday nights I'd tighten the tinfoil around those rabbit ears, tilting them this way and that with my arms outspread so that I could watch my favorite program, *Hockey Night in Canada*. The rest of America, I learned later, had to settle for stateside news, weather, and sports. That there were kids in Ohio, Illinois, Indiana, and Kentucky unable to follow the exploits of the Toronto Maple Leafs, the Montreal Canadiens, and the Vancouver Canucks—that kids in these states didn't even know who Guy LaFleur *was*—seemed to me awfully sad. I could sing "O Canada" long before I knew the lyrics to my own country's anthem.

The announcers on *Hockey Night in Canada* provided me with a fourth possible pronunciation of the name of my hometown. Whites in the city said "Di-*troit*," accent on the second syllable; blacks said "*Dee*-troit," accent heavily on the first; and Grosse Pointe girls whose noses sought a certain altitude ironically parroted the French pronunciation—"Day-*twa*"—to highlight how poorly European refinement squared with Rust Belt reality. But the Canadians, whose national sport is curling, were not content to leave Detroit a two-syllable city, and their three-syllable pronunciation was my favorite, particularly when it came from the *Hockey Night* announcers: "De-troy-it are fighting off the Canadiens' power play." "De-troy-it bring the puck out of the zone." "De-troy-it are a hard-checking hockey club." Noun-verb agreement also posed problems.

My mother and I made trips about once a month to a Canadian hockey store for equipment repairs for both my father and myself. To get to the store we took the Detroit-Windsor Tunnel, the underwater mile, completed in 1930, that connects the two countries beneath the Detroit River. That there was always water in the tunnel—that the white tiles along its walls, just inches outside my passenger window, were always leaking—never ceased to cause me alarm, but my mother managed to distract me each time by leaning forward in her seat as we neared the midpoint of the tunnel, trying to be the first of us into Canada, which began at the sweating maple leaf flag on the wall.

For all its obvious similarities to the United States, Canada was still a somewhat baffling place to a kid, a place where people purchased petrol, not gasoline, and bought it by the litre, not the gallon. The bank signs told you that it was zero degrees outside when it felt more like freezing, and money was not worth what it said it was: our dollar was worth more than a dollar over there, I learned, while theirs was worth less than a dollar over here. I entrusted all this to the adults, held my mother's hand, and waited for the man to finish sharpening my hockey skates.

After I got older, and had learned about terms like *liberal guilt* and *reparations payments* and *equal opportunity/affirmative action employer,* Canada seemed to provide a respite from Detroit's racial problems, which are America's racial problems writ large. Could it really be possible, I would think when I found myself on the other side of the Detroit River, that had I been born a mere five miles to the southeast my life would have been indelibly altered? That, rather than having been born with not only the Catholic version of original sin but the white American version of it as well, I would instead wear that special glow that gathers around those living in the land of the Underground Railroad's final, as opposed to penultimate, stop?

Five miles was nothing: drive five miles due west of our house and you were still in Detroit. Another five, and it was Detroit still. Five more: Detroit. My father and I could have driven west along 8 Mile Road in pursuit of those guys with the gun for what would have seemed like forever, and Detroit would have been on our left the whole time. But five miles in the right direction set everything, or at least certain things, right. Visits to Canada—so tantalizingly close you could *see* it—offered a racial escape, a glimpse of life lived without indebtedness and burden.

But there was no escape. Coleman Young's constant presence on our television set and the front page of our newspaper saw to that. "White people," he once said, "find it very hard to live in an environment they don't control." This is perfectly true and, if the demographers are to be believed, increasingly pertinent. Whites, a minority in Detroit for many decades now, may some decades hence become a national minority—not to the same extent, or with same stark dichotomy as in Detroit, but still. The Motor City, as ever, remains ahead of the racial curve—a case study, or cautionary tale.

Or incomparable material, as I began to think of it the night my car was stolen. I'd leave for college a year after that experience with grand theft auto, and the goal of my life from that point forward was to write a novel about the city that I've been trying, with limited success, to leave behind ever since.

In the novel I wanted to shock, after the manner of the foremost literary influence of my youth, Coleman Alexander Young. Like the mayor, I'd say whatever the hell I wanted, consequences be hanged. "I'm smiling all the time," Young once said, sounding his credo. "That doesn't mean a goddamned thing," he added, "except I think people who go around solemn-faced and quoting the Bible are full of shit." Damn right, I thought, and adopted the sentiment as my literary doctrine. But behind the bluster, I knew my book's real burden would be to dramatize the way in which the usual racial dynamic was inverted in Detroit.

There is a theory that goes something like this: blacks can't be racists, no matter how prejudiced their feelings, because they lack the power—the institutional power—to act on those feelings. This was true of the white minority in Detroit: you might have disliked Coleman Young, but you couldn't do a damn thing about it. The fathers up and down our street spent each evening sitting in their favorite armchairs, watching the local news, cursing Young's image on their television screens. Their cursing might have made them feel better—though, in fact, it made them feel worse—but, in any case, it had absolutely no effect. Was this racism, then, or was it something else?

In short, I needed to make clear just what I thought was so funny about my father's shoeshine crack, and I needed to somehow do so without ruining the joke.

No sweat.

6 Mile

IN THE WINTER OF 1995, my parents put a For Sale sign in front of our house. It was our second bungalow in the city, just south of 8 Mile, and it sold within weeks.

This was how the novel I tried to write always ended, in draft after unsuccessful draft: with a family leaving the city behind long after most everyone else had abandoned it. The brother and sister in the book, young adults parentless in the manner of *Peanuts* characters, find a card that their mother and father, departed for Michigan's Upper Peninsula, have left for them on the kitchen table: "The house is yours. Please take as good care of it as everyone else in Detroit does of theirs. Ha-Ha! Love, Mom & Dad." In actuality, my parents were very much a part of the picture, and I came home from my senior year of college to help them and my sister move half a mile outside the city limits on a single-digit February day.

"Put that bag in the basement," my mother said, directing traffic from her new kitchen. It was an oversize black garbage bag, puffed with air, and my father's employment history could be tracked with a fair degree of accuracy by sorting through the T-shirts stuffed inside it. Most of these shirts, for companies with names like General Kinetics, Katech, Booth-Aarons, and Diamond Racing, were ringer Ts—two-toned, with dark stitching around the neck and sleeves—and some dated back to before my birth. The letters were peeling, there were pockets missing or half pulled off, and many had stains on the back from when my father failed to use the creeper and instead slid unassisted under whatever wreck he was repairing, settling on the cement in a pool of oil.

If General Motors gets a cold, the saying goes, Detroit gets pneumonia. My father never worked directly for any of the Big Three, but the succession of car companies that employed him did subcontracting work for GM, Ford, and Chrysler, making our family prone to periodic cases of the sniffles. His working arrangements harkened back to the auto industry's pre-union days: good, steady, demanding work—but you can be replaced. My father viewed the UAW guys, with their cushy, collectively bargained contracts, as soft. Two doors down from our second house was a father who'd worked the line at Chrysler since the age of eighteen, and it pained my old man to contemplate how much his neighbor made, how little he knew, and how little worry went along with it. "I can't imagine how much he's got socked away," my father often said. He had to live by his wits, and his worries were frequent.

Along with his T-shirt collection, my father kept every issue of every car magazine he ever subscribed to or bought off the newsstand, and I carried thousands of such magazines out of my parents' Detroit basement and into the basement of their new home in boxes marked DAD'S MAGS. There were issues, in varying quantities, of *Super Stock, Rodder & Superstock, Rod Action, Rod & Custom, Popular Hot Rodding, Popular Cars, Speed & Supercar, Car Craft, Hot Cars, Hi-Performance Cars, Super Street Cars, Cars Magazine, Drag Racing, Drag Strip*, and *National Dragster* among many other titles, how-to manuals, and spiral notebooks filled with figures, in my father's familiar handwriting, on engine displacement, foot-pounds of torque, and camshaft ratios.

In some cases there were duplicate copies. Unable, say, to wait for his April 1978 issue of *Car Craft* ("Pinto Showdown!") to arrive in our mailbox, he'd drive with me to Custom Speed, an auto parts place on Gratiot just north of 8 Mile, and buy a preview copy a day or two early. Sometimes, instead of actually purchasing it, he'd just stand in the store and read the magazine, along with one or two others, from cover to cover, until I began to complain about my legs hurting and having to use the bathroom. "Just hold on a sec, okay, bub?" he'd say, rubbing my head. More than one store manager, my mother insisted, instituted a "This Is Not a Library: Magazines Must Be Purchased" policy because of her husband's reading habits.

These magazines were the sum total of my father's reading material, and they offer a fair précis of his mental weather. Social context disappears behind these magazine's headlines. The cover of the August 1967 *Drag Strip* trumpets the arrival of a "Supercharged Blue Hell Corvette." The September 1967 *Rod & Custom* carries this headline on its cover, next to the front left fender of a customized '63 Chevy: "The Winner! From Detroit's Autorama." In few other publications in the summer of '67 would the words "Detroit" and "winner" appear side by side.

The March 1973 issue of *Rod Action* carries the usual on its cover—"Tex Smith on Tricking Up Turbo-Hydros," "Low Buck Powertrains"—but on its editorial page contains a veritable call to arms.

> *There has been an increasing, almost alarming, number of*
> *letters addressed to* Rod Action *offices these past several months*
> *concerning automobile legislation in various states. While the*
> *news media has done a presentable job of keeping the average rodder*
> *advised of Federal activity in things related to cars, practically*
> *nothing has been focused on a far more serious threat to street*

rodding; i.e., state vehicle legislation. Such a condition
is extremely dangerous to the health of this sport.

It's not just that my father may well have been reading this editorial, with growing indignation, while my mother was in labor with me. It's that, meanwhile, there's something called Watergate going on. And the Vietnam War. And the campaign for mayor of the City of Detroit, in which a Democratic state senator named Coleman A. Young, trailing in the early polls, is starting to gather steam. But my father was constitutionally incapable of reading an editorial on such topics. Neither war nor politics would have resonated with him like the mounting threats to the sport of street rodding. Years later, the father of a friend of mine, a man who was starting a side business selling insurance, came to our house, sat at our kitchen table, and talked to my father, who had begrudgingly agreed to hear him out about buying a life insurance policy. My father nodded, and smiled, and agreed to think about it, as one does in such situations, postponing his explosion until after he had seen the man to the door and shut it hard behind him. "Bullshit!" he hollered, before storming out back to the garage.

My mother explained, with her more than maternal patience where my father and his cars were concerned, the reason for his anger. Drag racing was classified as a high-risk activity, one that would result in higher life insurance premiums. A man with a family to support, my father would never have engaged in anything he considered dangerous. Did the insurance people know nothing at all of roll bars, parachute packs, the technology that went into today's racing helmets? It wasn't the injustice of these increased premiums (which he wouldn't be paying, as he had no interest in purchasing the insurance) that inflamed him, nor the evidence they gave of society's continuing ostracism, as in a fifties movie, of the greasers who got behind the wheel and gunned it. No: it was the *ignorance* such policies bespoke, an ignorance dangerous to the health of the sport. Every Christmas morning, in his small stocking, flanked by the Italy-size stockings my grandmother had sewn for my sister and me, my father was sure to get two presents: a can of WD-40 and the coming year's National Hot Rod Association rulebook.

The T-shirt and magazine collections had begun in our first Detroit bungalow, near the intersection of 6 Mile Road and Gratiot Avenue. It was the sort of house you saw all of upon entering: look around for a second or two as you stood in the doorway, politely nodding, and you'd taken the entire place in, the whole scope of its seven hundred square feet. Straight ahead was the kitchen. Up and to the right was the bathroom. On either side of the bathroom, at opposite ends of a five-step hallway, were the front and back bedrooms. And that—"We told you it was small," my mother would say, smiling—was about it. Not much to remark on, really, or compliment, unless you cared to take as your conversation piece the white aluminum siding that covered the home's exterior.

A half-mile to our north was Assumption Grotto, the neighborhood Catholic church, where my father had gone for his first few years of grade school and where I would attend kindergarten; a mile to our south were City Airport, Mt. Olivet Cemetery, and De La Salle Collegiate, the storied Christian Brothers high school that was attended, in the early 1960s, by my father and my Uncle Tony and which, during the Depression, had denied Coleman Young admission because of his race. "A Brother in the order asked if I was Hawaiian," Young once said, recalling his admissions interview of decades before. Detroit's first black mayor was light-skinned with freckles, and the product of a Catholic grade school. "I told him, 'No, Brother, I'm Colored.' He tore up the application form right in front of my nose." According to my father, Coleman Young may have been better off. The Christian Brothers, in his affectionate telling, were a bunch of heartless Irish bastards given to dispensing discipline in unorthodox ways, like pushing students down stairwells or having them hold heavy textbooks at arm's length for hours, until the limb became leaden and the spirit was crushed.

I was born a few miles from this bungalow, on the fourth floor of

St. John Hospital, on 7 Mile, in the late winter of 1973. There was an ice storm that March, just after St. Patrick's Day, and so my father drove my mother and me the three miles home from the hospital over slick, dangerous roads. Because he is of that variety of man who believes that we were put on this earth, above all else, to do things *right,* my father no doubt performed this function as responsibly, as meticulously, as he has performed every other function required of him in the thirty-plus years of fatherhood that have followed. Each March my mother tells the story of my difficult birth, and how, after enduring thirty-two hours of labor, an emergency C-section, and six days of uncomfortable bed rest, she had to suffer through a knuckle-whitening ride back into the inner city in a '65 Chevy Carryall truck, a baby boy resting on her sore belly. "They used to just hand the baby to you," my mother said recently. "No car seat. Driving home in an ice storm with no car seat." My mother was born Margaret Mary Saulino, and over the years I've often asked her, when there's been special pleading to be done, to pray on my behalf, believing that no God worth His salt can deny a sincere request made by a girl so named.

The garage behind our house was two-car, accessible from the alley, and home to my father's 1970 Plymouth Barracuda. I would watch him work on it from a high padded stool—he had to lift me onto it— and once his work was completed he would pay me a nickel to hop down, grab a push broom, and sweep the metal shavings out into the alley. Because he often failed to wear safety goggles when grinding, he occasionally had to visit an ophthalmologist at 8 Mile and Gratiot and have the shavings ground out of his eye.

My father worked a good many late hours and frequently on Saturdays—the words "time and a half" had a magical ring out of my mother's mouth—and he returned home in the evening in any of a dozen of his plaid work shirts, his hands stained with oil, his body, which I would bury my head in while hugging him, smelling of hot metal, mineral spirits, and a masculine, earned sort of sweat. The place where my father worked was always referred to by my parents as "the shop." Some men, I understood, worked at "the office," or "the station house." My father worked at the shop. "How was it at the shop today?" my mother would ask when he got home, and I could tell by looking at him how it was: it was tiring.

Until a few weeks before my birth, my mother was working as a secretary at the Uniroyal Tire plant on Jefferson Avenue. Next to the factory was the Belle Isle Bridge (the MacArthur Bridge, officially, though no one called it that), its lovely half-mile span connecting the wooded island in the middle of the Detroit River exclusively to the American mainland. My father had worked at Belle Isle over summers in the early sixties, selling cans of pop and sweeping sidewalks with my Uncle Tony, who had introduced him to my mother, helping to keep clean what the French settlers had originally called Hog Island. Across from the factory, and altogether less picturesque than the bridge— though perhaps more prophetic of the city's future—was one of Detroit's first methadone clinics. After I was born my mother tried to go back to work but cried all day from separation anxiety, and my father told her to quit: they'd make ends meet on one paycheck.

My mother, too, knew how tiring my father's workday was, especially as he was now the sole source of income, and so always had dinner ready for him, along with some strategy or other to downplay the day's bad news. These always failed, for my father possessed what Hemingway would say every writer needed: a built-in, shockproof shit detector. My father could detect sugar-coating a mile off and had an absolute, raging impatience for having the silver lining pointed out when it was the goddamn cloud that concerned him.

The summer I was three and a half I walked off with a friend while my mother was on the telephone. When she hung up we were gone, and though frantic she was unable to search for us: my sister, a year old at the time, was sound asleep in her crib. My mother called the neighbors and then my father at work, who sped home, only to pull up at the same time I did, in the back of a Detroit Police cruiser. The cops had seen my friend Danny and me several blocks over, and, as I'd been taught to do,

I gave the police my name, address, and telephone number. Danny didn't even know his last name. He and his older brother lived a few blocks over with their unmarried mother, a woman whose kids ate the wrappers to candy bars and never had clean clothes, children who always stayed for dinner and seemed to be under no instruction to come home when the streetlights came on, as the rest of us were. They were kids, as my mother said, you felt bad for.

Holding my baby sister, Beth, in her arms, she began to cry when the cops opened the back door of the squad car. My father gave me a hug, gave my mother a look, and went back to work. He wouldn't speak to her for days.

Life, I learned, hangs by the slenderest of threads: this was the lesson of my growing up. Chaos is out there, and only the constant application of common sense—a misnomer, I was to learn: not many had it—could keep disorder at bay. "*Think!*" my father would say, tapping the side of my head, when my actions made it clear to him that I'd needed to and hadn't. Fighting tears and swallowing hard, I'd tell him that next time I would, whereupon his tone would soften and I'd receive a hug. The value of a life accrues slowly, or so said the example he set, not through backslapping and bluster but by the daily meeting of one's responsibilities, however dull they may be. This seriousness, born of worry, was the result of his being the son of a similar father, someone whose childhood in a Catholic orphanage had been harsh and who, as a result, had come to see the two—reality, harshness—as synonymous.

Though he and my mother were wed the summer of 1969 (a few months before Richard Austin, a black candidate, would lose that year's mayoral election by a single percent, signaling Detroit's new demographics), my father was by no means a child of the sixties, nor was the girl he married. My father had not gone to Ann Arbor for college, as one of his sisters-in-law had; he'd stayed home, in Detroit, and was a commuter student. And he hadn't dropped out (or tuned in, or turned on);

he'd flunked out. His lack of application was strictly apolitical. My mother did not attend college at all but worked secretarial jobs and lived at home, paying rent to her parents until she and my father married.

By the time I was to start kindergarten in the late seventies, it was clear that, by living in Detroit, my parents were increasingly living amid the ruins of the Great Society, for which Detroit had been selected a model city. To my aunts and uncles in San Francisco, the sixties may still have meant protest marches, moral certainty, and sing-along music in the Microbus. At 6 Mile and Gratiot it was coming to mean out-of-wedlock births, drug addiction, Devil's Night fires, and (what one could hear at night, when the windows were open) gunshot blasts: everything, that is, that kept pushing those whites who still remained in Detroit closer and closer to its borders. For my aunts and uncles, the signature event of the sixties may have been the March on Washington, or Woodstock, or Monterey Pop. For people like my parents—urban whites without college diplomas trying to hang on in deteriorating city centers—it was probably the publication of the Moynihan Report.

The street my father came home to after work was predominantly Italian. The couple next door to us spoke no English, but their children, Dominic and Maria, did, and based on the smells that came from their house, and the sauce that encircled their smiles, they seemed to eat wonderfully. Down the block was Alinosi's ice cream parlor, owned by friends of my Grandpa Saulino. The Alinosi family had been the makers of premium ice creams and superfine chocolates in the area since 1921—it said so, in lovely script, on the back of their packaging. The *Italian Tribune*—"*La Tribuna del Popolo*," as it said on the masthead— was located at 6 Mile and Gratiot, but moved to Macomb County in 1973.

Across the street lived the Shannons, an old couple whose five children were grown and whose favorite pastime was to make the trip down to Eastern Market each weekend, where Mr. Shannon would buy more produce than he and his wife could possibly eat, most of it from old Italian men who, if asked the price of any item, would point a short, chubby finger and say, "F'you?" Most of this produce was then given away to the neighborhood kids, with a coerciveness we knew well from our own mothers. "If you don't eat it," they'd say, the force of ancestral famine and coffin ships behind them, "we'll just have to throw it away."

The Shannons had a double-wide yard, so their next-door neighbors, a family of rednecks, were actually two lots down. There weren't many such people on the east side of Detroit—people who for all the world appeared to hail from the north of Kentucky—but there were many of them on our street, and they all lived next door to the Shannons, where they hung out of windows, huddled around stalled cars, and slammed doors all the hours there are. I lost my first street fight at the age of five to one of their fat daughters, a girl twice my age and triple my weight. She sat on me, and that was that.

On the patch of grass between the Shannons and the rednecks, the boys of the neighborhood, myself included, played our simple, violent games, the fun of which was not to be matched for the rest of our days. The best game, in which the guy with the football runs for his life until he is gang-tackled by seventeen of his friends, went by several names—Smear the Queer, Kill the Man with the Ball—but we'd condensed it to Kill the Man.

My father was not bothered that I came home dirty and bleeding after such outings—this would help make a man of me—but he did not like a bit what I learned to yell when we jumped onto the guy we'd just gang-tackled. "Nigger pile!" we'd all holler, loud enough for the whole block to hear. The night my father finally caught wind of what was being said he came out of the house and motioned from the front porch for me to come home for a minute. "What did I hear you yelling out there?" he asked when I came in, grass stains on the knees of my pants. I knew I'd done something wrong from his tone. "Nigger pile," I said, my head lowered. "Do you know what that word means?" My father couldn't bring himself to repeat it, so it was simply "that word." I shook my head. "Well, it's a not-very-nice word for a black person," he said. But even the black kids say it, I said. "I don't care what they say," my father said sharply. "You're my son, and you won't say it. Do you understand me?" He took my chin between his index finger and thumb and forced me to look him in the eye. I said that I did and tried to remember that when I went back outside, where everyone was still yelling it while piling onto the guy on the ground, who invariably had the wind knocked out of him.

Ninety-five percent of this story can be chalked up to my father's inherent goodness; there was simply very little malice in the man. His temper was tremendous, but it was mostly directed at inanimate objects—cars that didn't run, faucets that dripped, drainpipes that wouldn't drain—and those members of his immediate family, himself included, whose behavior had been less than bright. "Not very bright, was it?"—this was my father's worst put-down, his five-word rhetorical condemnation for leaving a screen door open or a bicycle unlocked. But malice for people against whom he had no specific grievance was more or less unknown to him.

I remember standing by his side as a small boy, holding his pant leg, while he talked with guys whose cars he was helping to fix, men who spoke openly and often of spooks and coons and how, wasn't it something, that you could take them out of the jungle but you couldn't take the jungle out of them. My father would invariably cut people off before they got too far with such talk, politely changing the subject to something that still invited swearing but was altogether less prickly: gas prices, long-winded priests, those goddamn politicians—anything, really, but jungle bunnies. This was his goodness talking, or not allowing others to talk. But a small part of it, the final 5 percent, was his proficiency at math, which was prodigious. We were outnumbered in the city, and unless he moved us to the suburbs, which he had no plans of doing, we would only become more of a minority in the future. So besides being not nice, this sort of talk was also not smart, which was probably worse.

My father's dream car, about which he dreamt a good deal, always tended to be an older American manufacture—the kind of thing he could pick up for peanuts and play around with. He favored cars of sturdy and powerful design, with an acceleration that planted one squarely in one's seat and a rumble under the hood of such sympathy and warmth that he'd need to remind himself that his car was, in fact, not human. But the anthropomorphic impulse was too strong: like the captain of a ship, my father always referred to his mode of transportation in the third-person feminine. "Oh, she's running real good," he'd say, his hand resting on the hood. Or, "She seems to be missing a little. Could be the plugs."

My father turned twenty-two in the summer of '67 and was on the verge of flunking out of his second of two colleges when, on July 23, a Sunday, he found himself on Woodward Avenue, at the campus of the now defunct Detroit Institute of Technology. As he was leaving the school in the late afternoon, his 1963 Ford Fairlane got a flat. He pulled over to the side of Woodward to fix it, and a couple of black guys—"real friendly," he always says—came along to lend a hand. As the three of them were crouched down, busying themselves with jack stands and lug nuts, one of the guys pointed to smoke a couple miles to the north, in the direction of Twelfth Street. "You best get out of here, buddy," he said. By the time it was over troops would be called in, tanks would patrol the streets (part of what Lyndon Johnson, in a radio address, called "a determined program to maintain law and order"), and fires would burn for days. The final tallies: seven thousand arrested, twelve hundred injured, forty-three dead. Mayor Jerome Cavanagh would compare his city to a "burning Berlin," and in the years to come it would have its metaphorical wall: 8 Mile Road.

When my father told this story—I heard it twice—the riot was granted less importance than the car. It wasn't a seismic event in the country's social history he was talking about; it was a middling car and the trouble it caused him. My father's stories had a tendency to fixate on what others would consider incidentals. From the first moment of the riots, many white Detroiters ceased, in their hearts, to be Detroiters. If I followed the story correctly, my father would remain one, but after that Sunday—even though a flat couldn't be blamed on the manufacturer—he would never again be an enthusiastic Ford man.

His was a shifting automotive faith. The Big Three were churches, their divisions denominations, and from time to time he sampled one of the competing strains in Christendom. General Motors cars were the constant of our life, like Catholicism; Ford was the major Protestant faith; and Chrysler was an oddball Evangelical strain, especially after Iacocca came aboard. He tried foreign makes from time to time, the way an undergraduate might spend a semester dabbling in Eastern mysticism. But GM was home base, and he was quickest to criticize the used Chevys and Pontiacs he had paid good money—that is, next to nothing—for. "There it is," he'd say, pointing to the oil stains that dotted our driveway. "The General Motors mark of excellence."

Like my father's riot story, our eight-millimeter home movies possess an automotive fixation that excludes any sense of social change. If one puts aside the unfortunate fashions and the flickering quality of the film itself, these movies would seem to exist in a certain stratum of white society's eternal present: smiling and waving young mothers, their sinewy-armed husbands, fat babies, and scores of skinny kids, belonging to God knows who, running around in brown-edged tank tops, peeking inside people's coolers at the drag strip on a clear Fourth of July weekend. In many of these movies my sister and I have been plopped in playpens with our cousins, the lot of us wearing outfits passed back and forth between the families. A pair of pajamas featuring "Big Daddy" Don Garlits, driver of the dominant Top Fuel dragster of the era, went through several wearers. My mother, hand on hip, is standing around, talking with our aunt, and my father and uncle, in the next reel, are splattered with mud from head to toe, now racing dune buggies somewhere well outside Detroit, where there are trees and hills and cows in the distance. Someone waves to the camera—people are always waving to the camera—the film goes black for a second, and when it comes back up there I am, a couple years old, wearing my uncle's flame-covered racing helmet, steering his hot rod.

This was that hard-bellied stratum of white America where, to borrow from Heller in *Catch-22*, the men were possessed of a variety of useful, necessary skills that would keep them in a low-income group all their lives. There was nothing these men couldn't build, nothing they couldn't fix, no problem they couldn't solve—and it would never do them a damn bit of good economically. They could fix other people's cars, but such work couldn't be relied on to provide enough money for them to fix their own, let alone trade up to a nicer one. Though largely uneducated, they were skilled enough to go into business for themselves, running towing services, bump shops, and pinstriping places, only to find that being self-employed meant long hours, huge headaches, a lack of health insurance, and—when one's clientele is also working-class—being entirely at the whim of an economy in which very little ever trickles down.

Interactions with blacks were rare, and not to be relished. But they would quickly become, at this rung of the economic ladder, increasingly unavoidable. When a black guy came into Pete's Pinstriping and wanted racing stripes painted on the side of his Buick, he paid half up front and half upon completion. "You're good for the rest, right?" Pete'd ask. The guy would nod. *"Right?"* Pete asked again, upon which he'd get a song and dance about how this guy's uncle, or cousin, or half brother would be coming through real soon with some cash that he'd been counting on, but that he hadn't been able to get his hands on it yet because, you see— "Yeah, yeah, all right," Pete would say, waving him off. When he finished the job a few days later, the guy would look it over, all smiles—and, sure as shit, he'd be twenty bucks short. Never fucking failed. "What's this?" Pete'd ask, looking in his cupped palm at the shortfall, only half listening to the litany of excuses he was being offered. Despite my father's efforts, figuratively speaking, to plug my ears, I more than once heard these Petes, Leos, and Lennys voice sentiments not unlike those spoken by Jason Compson, the cruelest and most bigoted of all the Compsons, in the third section of *The Sound and the Fury*. "I never found a nigger yet," a similarly annoyed Jason says, "that didn't have an airtight alibi for whatever he did." Fifty years after Faulkner wrote that, working-class white Detroiters—many of whom, like the crackers across the street from us, had moved up from the South—were saying much the same.

Among such men, my father, with his Catholic education, retiring demeanor, and genetic predisposition for tolerance, seemed something of a scholar. He wasn't a big man, his voice wasn't the loudest, he never made a spectacle of himself, he wore his automotive knowledge lightly, he kept his cards close to his chest—and all this had the perhaps unsurprising result of making those men who were big and loud and brash treat my father with a good deal of deference. I remember one argument, over what the initials BMW stood for, that grew increasingly heated until it was agreed to turn the question over to my father, the final arbiter of all things automotive. One party claimed (correctly) that it was Bavarian Motor Works; the other, British Motor Works. The deciding vote would be my father's. He smiled evasively. "It's Brazilian Motor Works," he said, and walked out of the room.

My father was always circumspect, sometimes hilariously so. After looking through the Sunday classified ads, he would frequently call about some car he'd seen for sale. He had a conceptual artist's eye for what hunk of junk just might prove useful to him, for the "found object." Spare parts, backup pieces, something to play with: these were among his oft-stated reasons for picking up the odd pile, heap, or rattletrap. "Can I speak to Steve?" he would say, telephone balanced between shoulder and ear, looking down to check the name in the ad. He was, it so happened, speaking to Steve. "Hi, Steve, this is Bob Clark, and I'm calling about your ad in the paper." Sure—what do you need to know, Bob: shoot. My father would then ask a few questions, and nod his head while listening to the answers, with vast understanding. It sounded good, good. Could he come see the car? Absolutely—did he need directions? That he did. Well—where was he coming from? "I'm located in the Toledo area," my father would say, and by the time I'd overheard the third untruth in ten seconds—his first name wasn't Bob and his last name wasn't Clark—I'd start to laugh and be waved impatiently from the kitchen.

Even as a parallel construction—I'm located in the Detroit area—it was still bullshit. He wasn't located in the Detroit area; he lived in *Detroit,* the city itself, a distinction that made a difference. People took pride in this fact, played it up on T-shirts: DETROIT: WHERE THE WEAK ARE KILLED AND EATEN. I'M SO TOUGH I VACATION IN DETROIT. And, with the image of a sniper's crosshairs in the background: COME BACK TO DETROIT: WE MISSED YOU LAST TIME.

White Detroiters, by definition, were those who had not taken part in the flight, and so on the whole were more comfortable with the possibility that they might someday have to exercise the other Darwinian option: fight. My father had no interest in either. He would stay put and mind his own business, showing an abiding faith in the logic familiar to those deathly afraid of dog bites and bee stings: don't bother them and they won't bother you. You keep telling yourself this, believing it less each time, knowing that such a plan can only work until, all of a sudden, it doesn't. This, anyway, was our family's stance toward Detroit's black majority. It wasn't antagonistic, but it was skeptical and inherently static: not much was going to change this point of view.

When I read my way through the black canon in college, my interest always peaked when I came to those passages in which the writer discussed how he had arrived at his stance toward the white world, and how this stance, in turn, shaped his identity. There was such a passage in every book. It was news to me that black folks spent as much time thinking about us as we had about them, that they too needed a strategy. Though tinged with skepticism, this stance was never fixed, as ours had been back in Detroit, and so the writer's identity was fluid—*like jazz,* to use the inevitable analogy, one that, if I had to find fault, I felt was leaned on too heavily in black writing. Regardless of where the writer had started out—Mississippi, Oklahoma, Harlem—there was almost always a progression toward a greater subtlety of worldview, a cogent explanation of the complexity inherent in American identity and the possibilities that this presented for self-creation. Catholic school, for all its benefits, had never been big on self-making.

The mental and emotional experience that I underwent while reading such books mirrored what was before me on the page: my feelings toward blacks, and toward my own whiteness, shifted, became less willfully fixed, as I worked my way through the successive paragraphs, accepting some insights and rejecting others. I hadn't the sophistication of an Ellison or Baldwin, couldn't articulate what I was undergoing with half their craft, but I knew what I felt, and that was that the world was more complicated—somehow bigger—than my upbringing had led me to believe.

But I was still a Detroit kid to the core. Whatever wonders my reading opened up inside me, I was still the product of an environment none too impressed by clever arguments or a clean prose style. Though my father never wore any of those T-shirts that boasted of the wearer's Detroit citizenship, I do remember him once telling me, with a grudging smile, that he'd seen a guy with a shirt bearing a message that was more lament than brag. It seemed to me as worthy a longing as anything in Ellison, and as pithy as any passage in Baldwin: I WISH I'D PICKED THE DAMN COTTON MYSELF.

History couldn't be undone, however. Three houses down from us lived a brother and sister named Lionel and Sondra. They lived in a small aluminum-sided bungalow like ours with their grandmother, a woman who might, years earlier, have been a backup singer under contract to Berry Gordy. Her hair was piled atop her head, sixties girl band–style, and her fingernails grew so long that they curled back in on themselves in a corkscrew. The furniture in her house, to cope with the fact that her home was filled constantly with kids, was covered in plastic—every crinkly, uncomfortable piece of it. All the white kids I knew, with the exception of Danny, lived with both mother and father. But Sondra and Lionel were black, and they lived with the lady with the five-inch fingernails, who lived unattached—and who, in a fit of anger after I'd spilled something on her carpet, had once sent me home, yelling from her front porch that we were white trash. My mother just laughed, and with her hand on my shoulder we went inside. Rarely have words wounded so little.

What did hurt were the punches that this woman's grandson and I traded. Lionel and I never fought out of racial animosity; we were just engaging in the sort of little-boy roughhousing that any decent adult sanctions. Neither my parents nor Lionel's grandmother much minded, but in order to keep us from hurting each other—and from bleeding on her plastic furniture and plush carpet—Lionel's grandmother bought all the boys in the neighborhood a pair of bright red Everlast boxing gloves. The gloves would reduce the risk of broken or bleeding hands and noses and gave our fighting the appearance of sport rather than out-and-out savagery. Boxing matches were then arranged in basements, with victory inevitably claimed by both combatants. I remember the basements better than the bouts: cracked ceramic tiles, cold steel support beams, small pools of standing water in the corners, and washing machines that stood on uneven ground and walked across floors during spin cycles.

It was in such basements that the black kids and the Italian kids and the cracker kids beat the living hell out of one another, all of it done with the easy, he-who-smelt-it-dealt-it camaraderie of young boys. The wisdom of this was reinforced a decade later, when I read a piece of highway graffiti on an overpass above the Lodge Freeway that seemed to have a touch of profundity to it. This was in the early nineties, when Detroit's position as the murder capital of the world had solidified, a time when more people were being murdered in the city in one year than were being killed over the course of several in Northern Ireland or the Middle East due to troubles I only vaguely understood.

But the graffiti I did understand—and so, I think, would Lionel's grandmother. It said: PUT DOWN YO GUNS AND PUT UP YO DUKES.

There is a picture in one of my parents' photo albums of Lionel and me sitting together on our basement steps. It's my sixth birthday party, and we're both wearing pointy hats, with plates of cake and ice cream resting on our laps. Sondra is on the far left, a step below us. It occurs to me, looking now, what I noticed even back then: that they resemble each other only slightly. Sondra is several shades lighter than Lionel, and her face is an oval whereas his is round. Were they, in actuality, half siblings? In high school I would meet a pair of black kids—brothers in the biological sense of the word—who had different last names and about a foot and a half difference in height. There was no judgment in my so noticing: if black kids who were brothers had last names that were unalike, that was all right with me, because it had nothing to do with me. Same went for kids raised by their grandmothers, like Sondra and Lionel. It was none of my concern why they didn't live with their mom and dad—as my dad, the one time I asked him about the situation with Sondra and Lionel, had told me. "That's their business," he said. "It's none of ours."

This is, I think, the perfect answer, declining as it does both the usual conservative condemnation ("They can't even take care of their own kids") and the usual liberal apologetics ("Familial separation was one of the strategies of slavery"). *It's their business.* Lurking in there, too, is the sense that taking care of one's own is enough to ask of any man, and that there is little need for him to look outside this small sphere. My father kept up the mortgage payments, put food on the table, and kept his kids in clothes and Catholic school. The rest of the world was on its own, and insofar as its desires did not conflict with his own needs or that of his young family, he wished it well.

Cars and Catholicism

WERE WE WHITE TRASH? We were Catholics, first of all—ethnic Catholics, on my mother's side—and it never seemed to me, growing up, that Catholics could be white trash. The terms were mutually exclusive, with Catholicism possessed of an imposing grandeur that distanced its practitioners from matters as perfunctory as the screaming, dirty-faced children that white trashdom carried under its crooked arm. To be white trash was to live a life of constriction, of intermittent paychecks bearing greasy thumbprints, while Catholicism was elevating, enlarging. As Catholics, we weren't white trash; we were working class. We worked, while white trash sat on their asses, some mumbled nonsense coming out of their mouths always. Catholics had two parents in the house, while white trash children had mothers, along with enough extended relatives to make your head spin. White trash parents yelled at their kids to absolutely no effect; their entire lives, in fact, were an exercise in pissing into the wind, an endless hokeypokey that, like the cars up on blocks in their driveways, would never get them anywhere. Catholicism, on the other hand, concerned itself with the Last Things—was *teleological,* as the priests taught me—and led its followers through a purposeful progression, from baptism to communion to confession to confirmation to matrimony to extreme unction, with eyes fixed firmly, and forever, on the afterlife.

And yet there was good evidence of our family's being white trash, with the incriminating details existing close enough to our basically responsible, working-class Catholicism that it was difficult at times to distinguish between the competing strains. "Hold *still,*" my mother would say in the morning as she tried before school to smooth down the cowlicks in my hair with a warm wet rag. It was usually still dark when my father left for work and often dark when he got home, so my mother saw to it that he received a formal send-off each morning, dragging my sister and me to the side door, the two of us still sleepy-eyed, to wave farewell. Beth held her Rub-A-Dub Dolly to her chest with one arm as she waved goodbye with the other.

After he'd gone, there was breakfast to be eaten, and school uniforms to put on—clothes that, in the wintertime, my mother warmed in front of the heating vents in the living room, so that I'd be twice burned by the metal on my corduroy pants. My fingertips were singed first as I snapped and zipped myself up, and then my lower belly would be reddened from contact with the pants' top button. My sister wore a plaid skirt and white blouse, like all Catholic schoolgirls, and had no such problems.

What sometimes preceded the waves and the warm clothes was wholly unworthy of the portrait of the well-functioning Catholic family that I've just painted. My father, for reasons known only to God and himself, was not averse to firing up before dawn this or that hot rod of his, and leaving it rumbling long enough in the garage to get a good look at the gauges. This was a length of time sufficient so that every soul within a several-block radius (or so I imagine) sat bolt upright in bed, asking what the hell that was all about. Sometimes he actually took the car out, driving it slowly up and down the street so it could stretch its legs. "I guess your dad took his car out this morning," the mother of a friend of mine, with whom we carpooled, said to me once on the way to school, a displeased smile on her reflection in the rearview mirror. I'm not sure, in fact, which was louder: the gingerly trip down the block out in the open air or the reverb produced by a four-hundred-horse-power '64 Chevelle at full throttle inside a cinder-block garage.

This sort of stunt is, from a good-neighbor perspective, absolutely unforgivable. It also situates itself at white trashdom's essential core, analogous to, and no better than, the high-decibel stunts black people pulled that set our blood to boiling, and that respectable whites—who often seemed to suffer from bouts of hysterical blindness and intermittent hearing loss when it came to black misbehavior—pretended not to notice.

There's a long, debatably noble tradition in this country, on the part of respectable whites and those who aspire to such a station, to assert that white trash are actually worse than the black equivalent. "There's a heap of things worse than a nigger," says Mrs. Turpin, the protagonist of Flannery O'Connor's great short story "Revelation," a character with just such social-climbing aspirations. She debates which she would have chosen, if Jesus had said to her before her birth, "You can either be a nigger or white-trash." "All right," Mrs. Turpin decides, "make me a nigger then—but that don't mean a trashy one." Concerning white trash: "There was nothing you could tell her about people like them that she didn't know already . . . if you gave them everything, in two weeks it would all be broken or filthy."

My mother, no Mrs. Turpin, strove toward very little, and worried about whether we were white trash not at all. Her laughter after the mild slur that Sondra and Lionel's grandmother had lobbed our way wasn't in the least nervous. She knew she was working class. She took in typing from a fat businessman named Mr. Wade, for which she was paid by the word; she clipped coupons out of the newspaper inserts for hours at a stretch and stocked our cupboards full during double-coupon days at Chatham's grocery store; she planned the meals for the week well ahead of time and treated leftovers with the respect due old friends of proven worth, giving them pride of place in our refrigerator. It was a pleasant, stable life, and if in photo albums from the late seventies my sister and I are often to be seen in our muddy backyard in nothing but dirty Fruit of the Looms, one of our father's go-carts in the background behind us—well, that was all right. She knew what her family was, and, certain evidence to the contrary, it wasn't white trash.

She grinned and bore my father's fixation on cars; that the man who was, in most ways, so conservative and cautious, so exacting about getting things right, thought nothing of starting up his dragsters at dawn—that he got this so absolutely *wrong*—was part of his charm. The fact that, on those mornings when the three of us waved goodbye to my father, my sister was dressed in a pair of footie pajamas that bore the red, white, and blue insignia of the National Hot Rod Association— this was no great cause for concern, either. Not very girlie, not what my mother would have picked out maybe, but they did match the T-shirt that I wore to bed. Bought for me by my father at the Mid-America Championship meet at Milan Dragway, it pictured a mean-looking rear-engine dragster, great billows of smoke coming from its back tires.

The poet of this slice of American life in the late seventies was Springsteen, of course, whose early albums—on which he sang about girls, cars, and boys whose ghosts haunt the skeleton frames of burnt-out Chevrolets—sat beside the stereo in our basement, *Born to Run* and *Darkness on the Edge of Town* at the top of the stack. It wasn't just that the lyrics on these albums struck a working-class chord, or that the guy on the cover looked a lot like the men I saw on a daily basis. The resemblance was in the details: the crummy flowered wallpaper Springsteen stands in front of, in his white T-shirt, on the front and back covers of *Darkness*; the dusty, off-white blinds that are closed behind him in these shots, as if there was nothing worth looking at outside anyway; the way his voice cracks in the song "Backstreets" when he sings the line, "Blame it on the truth that ran us down"—his voice breaking so completely on that "down" that it's always a wonder he can get out the next line. But with early Springsteen there's the inescapable sense that the song he's singing is a job, just that, and that he's got to see it through.

The names of the guys in the band (to sneak a peek at the liner notes) were good, too: besides Bruce—vocals, guitar—there was Max on drums and Danny on organ, Garry on bass and Steve on guitar, Roy on piano and Clarence on sax. These were strong urban names, the names of guys you'd trust to fix your brakes or tow your Malibu, nothing like the Jasons and Joshes, Chads and Brads, and Brents and Kents who populated the subdivisions north of 8 Mile Road. Working-class whiteness was all over these albums, so much so that they came to define, indelibly, that whole stratum of American culture. The sociological impact of these albums was not at all diminished by the fact that Clarence, the black saxophone player, was pictured prominently on the back of *Born to Run*. On the contrary, I felt an affinity for him. His last name was Clemons: close enough.

In "Racing in the Street," Springsteen sings, over a melancholy piano:

> I got a '69 Chevy with a 396
> Fuelie heads and a Hurst on the floor

"He gets that wrong," my father once said as we were out driving in my Pontiac, *Darkness on the Edge of Town* in the tape deck. "There was no such thing as fuelie heads on a big block, which is what the 396 was—a big block. Now, with the *small* block Chevy engine, the 327, you could have had fuel-injected cylinder heads. But with the big block, no." "How about a Hurst on the floor?" "Sure, you could have a Hurst gearshift with either the big block or the small block. That's an after-market thing. That doesn't matter." He explained to me, quickly, that he had once gone to Pittsburgh, when the Hurst Corporation was still headquartered there, to interview for a job. "The Chevy wouldn't have come from the factory with a Hurst," he said, finishing the train of thought, "but the Hurst was compatible. Now the big block," he said, getting back to the point, "even though they *called* it a 396, was actually a 402. We had a '70 Nova, back when you were a little guy, that had the big block in it, and that had 396 decals on the side and back. But it was really a 402." "Why'd they call it a 396, then?" "I'm not really sure," he said, "but it was the first new car I ever bought. Twenty-seven hundred bucks."

I knew that, aside from inaccuracies regarding cylinder head capabilities and inflated cubic inch displacements, he had problems, too, with the song's very title, "Racing in the Street," which reinforced the unjust stereotype of car folks as irresponsible sorts who endangered not only their own lives but those of innocent drivers and pedestrians as well. My father let it be known that he *never* raced in the street; he raced far from civilization, out at Milan Dragway, on a quarter-mile strip of asphalt where his elapsed time and his mile-per-hour readings were taken electronically and all appropriate safety considerations were observed. DRAG RACING IS NOT STREET RACING: this was the only bumper sticker my father ever owned, the only principled stance that he sought to publicize through the medium of his car's rear fender. And because he was too modest even to draw this much attention to himself, he simply put the sticker up in our garage.

It wasn't just that Springsteen sang about cars; it was the way that cars were coupled, in song after song, with a pervasive sense of guilt and a desperate need to make amends. Springsteen ends "Racing in the Street" with a wish to "wash these sins off our hands." The song "My Father's House" ends with the narrator looking longingly at his childhood home, which shines "across this dark highway, where our sins lie unatoned." In "Badlands," we're told that "it ain't no sin to be glad you're alive." Catholics sometimes need to be reminded of this.

In a shoe box in my basement I have two letters that my great-uncle, Father Hector Saulino—Father Hec, as we near blasphemously called him—received within weeks of each other in 1988, on the fiftieth anniversary of his ordination into the priesthood. One is on White House letterhead and signed by Ronald Reagan ("Nancy and I join with others to commend you for helping to preserve the traditional and moral principles that made America great"); the other, postmarked Rome, is from Pope John Paul II. After Father Hec's death some years ago, I inherited several articles of his clothing, all of them impeccably cut. His black cashmere trench coat, tailored by Rimanelli's of Detroit, I still wear during the wintertime, particularly on sad occasions in cold weather, when a certain solemnity seems required.

After leaving Sacred Heart Seminary in 1938, Father Hec served as an assistant pastor at the Patronage of St. Joseph—"San Giuseppe," as it was known to the Italian faithful—on Detroit's east side, near Gratiot and Harper Avenue. Five years later, in the late summer of 1943, shortly after the race riot on Belle Isle that would leave thirty-four dead and more than a thousand injured, Father Hec was asked by the Archdiocese of Detroit to start a new parish a few streets outside the city limits in the suburb of Dearborn—"a citadel of racism," according to Coleman Young, and home to Ford's River Rouge plant, the mammoth factory Henry Ford had built over the course of a decade, beginning in 1917, and where Young himself would briefly work the night shift at the plant's pressed steel facility. The parish-to-be was located just blocks from the factory, once the largest industrial complex in the world, in a residential area where many of the Rouge's Maltese and Italian workers—part of a payroll that, at its peak, had numbered some seventy-five thousand—had settled. "A man checks 'is brains and 'is freedom at the door when he goes to work at Ford's," a former Rouge worker, an Englishman, is quoted as saying in *The American Earthquake*, Edmund Wilson's account of the Roaring Twenties and Depression. "Some of those wops with their feet wet and no soles on their shoes are glad to get under a dry roof—but not for me!" The thirty-one-year-old Father Hector Umberto Giuseppe Saulino was asked to gather and tend this flock.

"He started St. Bernadette from scratch," Sister Marcia Saulino, his sister, told the *Detroit Free Press* in 1994, for Father Hec's obituary column. (Of my Grandpa Saulino's four siblings, one was a priest, one a nun, and one a deacon; he himself went on to work at Uniroyal Tire.) "He took the census to find out how many people would be in the parish." The first services at the new parish, the obituary notes, were held in what had been a grocery store. Though certainly more decorous, this information runs counter to the story passed down to me, which held that it had been a neighborhood bar, not a grocery store, that Father had commandeered in the name of Roman Catholicism. The story, in my mother's telling, sounds like the opening line to a joke: a young priest walks into a bar, makes the proprietor an outlandish offer on the spot, assures him that the Archdiocese of Detroit is good for it, and, after the owner accepts, promptly puts up a sign in the bar's window that reads: UNDER NEW MANAGEMENT. Henry Ford's Maltese and Italian workers—twenty-five nationalities were represented in the parish, according to an April 1945 issue of the *Michigan Catholic*— could still get wine in the establishment, but it would now be blessed.

Saulino family gatherings, back when I tugged at belt loops and spent a lot of time looking up, revolved around the figures of Father Hec and Sister Marcia, whose massive authority stood in inverse relation to her slight stature; it increased as she physically contracted, after the manner of Mother Teresa. Their father, Umberto Saulino, had come over from Naples alone in 1904, and then again with his wife, Marianne, in 1905. She would give birth to eight children before dying, while still a young woman, of an undiagnosed form of what my grandfather always referred to as "female cancer," leaving Umberto with five small children (three girls had died as infants) whom he could not possibly care for while going about the business of earning a living.

The oldest and sole surviving girl, Frances, tended as best she could to her younger brothers, who were eventually placed in the St. Francis Home for Boys, a Catholic orphanage. "She was their mother," my own mother always said of her. The St. Francis Home was staffed, in part, by the Sisters of St. Joseph, the congregation Frances would join with Umberto's reluctant permission. Neither my grandfather nor Father Hec ever ceased to call their sister, known to the rest of the world as Sister Marcia Saulino, anything but Frances. I tried to picture Sister, in her oddly named girlhood, wiping snotty noses and smoothing back the hair on the boys' sobbing heads, but could never quite square such maternal imagery with the nice old lady in the habit who said grace before Christmas Eve dinner. Women with maternal tendencies became mothers, not nuns. She'd taught for thirty-four years in Catholic schools, and that I could picture. I'd had nuns just like her, women whose mania for neatness sent them running for the nearest eraser the second a stray mark appeared on their chalkboard.

The priest and nun were people around whom you had to watch what you said; who asked you, pointedly, if you were still going to Mass (in my case, yes); who sat in armchairs and, even much later on, when Parkinson's had set in and their hands shook, were able to down glasses of scotch in between bouts of sleep. At the funeral for Father Hec, his eulogy was delivered by a priest who had attended Sacred Heart Seminary with him some sixty years before and who recalled, with the sort of clarity that the very old often reserve for their youthful indiscretions, a sign that the soon-to-be Father Saulino had taped to his bedroom door: WHERE THERE ARE FOUR CATHOLICS, it read, THERE WILL ALWAYS BE A FIFTH.

Father and Sister—one married to Jesus, the other his earthly emissary—were the only people with whom I was closely acquainted who lived in Grosse Pointe. Sister Marcia, who had been stationed at St. John Hospital in Detroit when I was born there, later moved to Our Lady Star of the Sea parish, nestled in an exclusive spot a quarter-mile from Lake St. Clair, while Father Hec's final parish stop was St. Paul—located, even more exclusively, on Lakeshore Drive. The St. Paul parking lot was filled, each and every Sunday, with the Cadillac Coupe DeVilles, the Mercedes S-class, and the Swedish sports sedans of parishioners worth well into seven figures, men and women clearly afraid of neither camels nor the eyes of needles.

In Grosse Pointe, even the street names were better: Lakeshore Drive, which the priests' residence at St. Paul fronted and over which the sun rose reliably each morning, was Lakeshore Drive only in the Pointes. A couple of miles in either direction—to the south and the Detroit border, to the north and the working-class suburb of St. Clair Shores—and this street reverted back to its pumpkin form, becoming simply Jefferson Avenue. But in Grosse Pointe it was Lakeshore Drive, with all the moneyed, Jazz Age connotations that attached. Every time I drove by St. Paul I was sure to leave a mental note of my great-uncle's post in the glove compartment, along with the registration and proof of insurance, in case I had need to explain my rather shabby presence to a Grosse Pointe police officer.

Near the end of his life, when he was living in retirement at the St. John Senior Community across from Detroit's Balduck Park, we would pick up Father Hec—the only Saulino, aside from my mother, still living south of 8 Mile—and take him out to the suburbs for the holiday get-togethers. His gait was slow, his movements hesitant, his talk could trail off at times, and yet the overall impression was still one of massive purposefulness, here at the hunched, shuffling end of a life dedicated to a single cause. He was always dressed in black, out of a lifetime of habit, and well fortified against the Michigan cold. Ice on the sidewalk posed problems, especially when we dropped him off in the dark after a full day's drinking. My father and I would each take an elbow and an unsteady gloved hand, help him out of the car, and guide him back inside the nursing home.

At such moments I never failed to feel what I've seen referred to as "moral awe": the simultaneously intimidating and inspiring sensation experienced in the presence of figures of tremendous ethical or spiritual authority. This shaking hand had, thousands of times before, steadily held aloft the host during the transubstantiation, that moment in Catholic Mass when the bread and wine are transformed into the body and blood of Jesus Christ. If true (and I couldn't quite decide whether I believed or not), the responsibility these hands had borne had been awesome.

"He's slowing down," I'd say, after shutting his door behind me. "Sure, but his mind's still sharp," my father would reply, getting his keys out of his pocket on the way back to the car. "You can see it. He gets frustrated. He can't quite come up with the words he wants, but his mind's working all the time."

The only fault I could ever find with Father Hec on those holiday trips to the suburbs was that he seemed legitimately impressed by them. "This is a very nice area," he'd say as we made our way inside some relative's subdivision. "They have a lovely home," he'd say on our way back out. And I'd think: But he should *know* better, a man born and raised in Detroit, a man who lived on Lakeshore Drive and whose final room, after a lifetime of reappointments and relocations, was back inside the city limits.

But he wasn't living in the city out of choice, of course. No one lives in a nursing home out of choice, and not many more lived in Detroit of their own volition, especially if they were white. Both were places where undesirables were kept, those people whose usefulness was an open question. This was certainly the stance of many white suburban-ites, in whose minds whites remained in the city for only one of two reasons: because they lacked the wherewithal to live outside it (which carried with it a certain implied stupidity), or because they lived in De-troit deliberately, which was even dumber.

After their moves to the suburbs—and they all moved out, eventu-ally—our relatives were glad that they weren't in Detroit anymore, a stance that caused some friction around the holidays, when their hesi-tation to come back for a Thanksgiving or Christmas dinner at our place brought existing familial tensions to the fore. "Our house is too small," my mother would say sarcastically, repeating what had been said to her over the phone by a sister or sister-in-law. "Well, that's true," my father would say, acknowledging the point even when he knew that it was beside the point. The same house, north of 8 Mile, would have presented no problem. From my mother's perspective, the only thing worse than hosting such get-togethers, with their innumerable preparations, was being denied the opportunity to do so.

My father's father worked for decades at Chrysler and the American Motor Company, which would move its headquarters from Detroit to the suburb of Southfield in the mid-1970s, prompting a pissed-off Coleman Young to order, in his words, "a change in the bidding specifications for city vehicles so that they excluded AMC." Like my Grandpa Saulino, my Grandpa Clemens had been raised in a Catholic orphanage, but he was not "ethnically" Catholic—that is to say, he was not, so far as I know (his lineage is vague), either Italian, or Irish, or Polish. His Catholicism was the result of the Sisters by whom he was raised and perhaps a certain amount of spiritual predisposition, though I doubt this. There was always something slightly coerced about his Catholicism, and I think his piety, such as it was, was directly traceable to his sense of indebtedness to the nuns. A fiercely practical man, he saw education, the importance of which he always stressed, purely as a means to an economic end, not as a window onto the best that has been said and thought. Catholicism, I suspect, he considered likewise: a straight line to an afterlife spent upstairs.

This practicality, as well as his unrepentant bargain-hunting nature, extended even to the Sunday church service that he chose to attend when, while still dating her in the late 1930s, he would visit my grandmother in Toledo, Ohio, where her father ran gas stations. For the first few months of their courtship he attended Mass at her neighborhood church, Good Shepherd, and like many an impatient Catholic he would leave the service immediately after the receiving of Communion. The priest at Good Shepherd noted my grandfather's early departures and after a few months decided to confront him about it. My grandfather decided to take his business elsewhere, and after a bit of poking around settled upon St. Thomas. Nice parish, pretty church, quick service, so he'd heard, and one other enormous benefit: the priest at St. Thomas was *blind*.

The last name Clemens begins with him—it has no previous history—and the literary side of me would like to think that my grandfather had spent long, lonely hours in the orphanage leafing through *The Adventures of Huckleberry Finn* and took the last name that the chronicler of life on the Mississippi had discarded. But my grandfather, as far as I could tell, never read a book in his life; no one in my family did, never having seen the need. There was enough serious content, enough transcendence, in cars and Catholicism; it wasn't necessary for them to concern themselves with ideas buried away in books.

The devout Catholics were able, to some degree, to sidestep Detroit's racial issues with their faith. The city's demographic changes were less lamentable to such folks than were the changes in the Church after the Second Vatican Council. Men like my father, who worshipped at the altar of the internal combustion engine, could console themselves with the thought that, though Detroit may change, or reduce itself to rubble, the city's factories would continue to churn out new Camaros, Barracudas, and Dusters. And both groups, born to earlier generations, could counterbalance, in their mind's eye, Detroit's black present with its much paler past. My problem later on was that I had lost faith in faith and had never been able, try as I might, to muster up much love for cars. Jesus Christ was less interesting to me, as a literary personage, than Quentin Compson. Ideas were my hobby, not hot rods, and books the garage in which I tinkered with them. And because the Detroit I'd been born into was already black and getting blacker, I'd needed to work out a stance, a strategy, fairly early on, and to continue working on it even after we had all left the city. As I'd suspected, "don't bother them and they won't bother you" ceased to work once they began to bother you and yours.

The Lower Sprint

L IKE 7 MILE AND 6 MILE, 8 Mile was so named after its distance from the city center, and referencing these streets as they stood in relation to one's own home was a shorthand way of making clear just how deep into the heart of darkness one still lived. In a pleasing symmetry, the areas around these roads had begun to "go bad" more or less in sync with the calendar. It was time to move out of the 6 Mile area by the late sixties, when my parents had bought our bungalow there; time to move out of the 7 Mile area by the late seventies; and time to move out of the 8 Mile area by the mid-to-late eighties, when the entire city, all 140 square miles of it, was nothing but one big ghetto, and when the citizens of East Detroit, fearful of overspill, began to think about establishing at least a semantic distance from the city it adjoined.

My fifth grade football team, the Denby Bulldogs, practiced at Heilmann Field on State Fair, which was 7½ Mile; the street got its name because it dead-ended a dozen miles to the west, at the Michigan State

Fairgrounds. One block to the east of the field was Burbank, the Detroit public school attended by most of my teammates; one block to the south was St. Jude. In the middle of the field, which was a full city block wide and nearly half a mile long, was one of the city's recreation centers; in its indoor pool I'd learned to swim, and in the hockey rink outside, in the dead of winter, I did ovals under the floodlights, skating into the clouds of breath I blew out before me. Above the frozen rink, abandoned, were basketball hoops missing their nets; the nets wouldn't be replaced until spring, when the ice had melted, the side boards were taken down, and the concrete beneath the rink regained its summertime status as a basketball court. In the corners of the field were the baseball diamonds, where during the spring and early summer I played second base and hit leadoff, to better capitalize on my speed and bunting ability.

No sport is without its racial component, and Heilmann had its shifting seasonal demographics. Swimming and hockey were white sports. Basketball was a black sport, and the friends I made while sweating shirtless over shared jugs of Gatorade were not to be seen in the winter, when the courts were once again flooded and frozen. Baseball, the greatest of American games, was the most integrated: everyone played it. Ninety feet between bases, someone once said, is the greatest achievement of Western man, and though as Little Leaguers we'd have to wait a few years before graduating to such a base length, we agreed. Parents of both races dragged coolers, lawn chairs, and little brothers and sisters to Heilmann Field and settled themselves along the first or third base lines, holding up BLESS YOU BOYS banners, the slogan of the '84 Tigers World Series team that began the season 35–5, still the best start in the history of baseball. I didn't know a kid who didn't play the game. Not to play it and love it was something like a moral failing.

Football, by contrast, was a minority pursuit in a couple of senses: nowhere near everyone played it, and the football team that practiced at Heilmann Field in the fall of 1984 was all black (excepting myself, and a running back who seemed to disappear after picture day), as was its coaching staff. "You know the lower sprint?" one of the coaches asked me at the end of an early-season practice, before we'd played our first game. He was my position coach—I played wide receiver—and a semi-pro player himself. Coach Clyde was tall and skinny, as befits a wideout, and before practice, when he and the other coaches would fool around, punting and passing to one another, I would watch him run with long, loping strides beneath dozens of deep bombs, never seeming to break a sweat. A week or two into the season, when we'd had to pick out our jerseys and equipment, I'd chosen number eighty, the number he wore for his semipro team. Our other wide receiver picked number one, after Anthony Carter, the great wideout for the University of Michigan. Whenever we played pickup games in the street I was always Anthony Carter, as one or another of my friends was always Walter Payton or John Riggins. But to have chosen anything other than eighty under the circumstances would have seemed disloyal. Coach Clyde had selected me as a starter and spent a good deal of time teaching me how to properly run a post pattern. Straight for fifteen yards, then plant *hard* with your outside foot and go like hell, at a forty-five degree angle, for the goalposts. The pass will get there; you let the quarterback worry about that.

"The lower sprint?" I repeated, thinking that this was some new drill he wanted me to demonstrate. Despite our mutual fondness, we sometimes had trouble understanding each other: he talked fast, and I had a lisp and a tendency to stutter. "No, no," he said. "The lower sprint. You know, the 'Our Father.' " "Oh," I said, "the *Lord's Prayer*." The owner of several rosaries, I nodded to indicate that I did indeed know it. Before each game, then, I stood above the reverently bent heads of my three dozen Denby Bulldog teammates, all of them down on one knee, while up above I recited, and had repeated back to me, the words our Savior gave us.

There were three Denby Bulldog teams, sorted by age, and the organization was overseen by Coach Washington, an enormously fat man whose son was the top high school football prospect in the state that year, a running back with blazing speed who had broken Jesse Owens's meet record in the hundred-yard dash at a relay in Ohio the year before and who would sign a letter of intent to attend the University of Michigan the following fall. My playing on this particular football team caused my father no end of concern. In his mind, though he would never admit it, racial pride was most definitely at stake, and his worst fear was that his son would prove to be, as he put it, a "candy-ass." My mother's fears were more run-of-the-mill: broken bones, dislocated fingers, scar-leaving stitches—all of which would happen, in subsequent seasons. But the worst that occurred the first time around were two chipped front teeth. During a blocking drill, my mouthpiece had fallen out just before I clenched my teeth to deliver a big hit; the coaches blew the whistle, play stopped, and I bent over, spitting out bits of tooth.

To prevent precisely this, my mother had stood over the stove several weeks previous, boiling the mouthpiece that I'd been issued, retracting it with a pair of metal tongs, and then having me bite down on it, repeating the process several times until the molded rubber matched perfectly the contours of my teeth and mouth. We'd achieved the ideal fit—and then I let the mouthpiece fall out anyway. The rest of the protective gear was more idiot-proof—helmet with padded chinstrap, hip pads, thigh pads, knee pads, tail pad, the increasingly pertinent cup—and cumbersome enough to calm somewhat my mother's worries.

My father's fears proved more difficult to shake. Between three and three-thirty each afternoon, I would strip out of my Catholic school uniform, put on my shoulder pads and helmet, and mentally prepare myself for practice. "You gotta get *tough*," my father would tell me. Toughness, I came to understand, was a quality of mind as much as a physical attribute, and as I quickly ate a small dinner—nothing difficult to digest—I tried to shift gears, making myself over from a Catholic school student into a junkyard dog. There was never any letting one's guard down with my father, but his usual disciplined approach to life was redoubled while I was a Bulldog. He suggested that I wear ankle weights around the house in the half hour between school and practice, so that my feet would feel lighter when I got to the field. After practice, when the other kids had gone home, we would run wind sprints to-gether across the length of Heilmann Field; and he saw to it that I did not miss a practice, the great secular sin for those engaged in a team sport. Don't want to let your teammates down.

Before one early-season practice, on a ninety-degree late-August afternoon, my mother called my father at work to inform him that I had felt sick at school and was, in fact, running a fever in excess of 102 degrees. "What should I do?" my mother wanted to know, shaking the thermometer down. From his sweltering, windowless workplace, my father said, "Send him," and then searched for some justification. "It'll be good for him to sweat it out." I could have keeled over beneath a beating summer sun and fifteen pounds of pads; better this than reveal myself to be a candy-ass before a bunch of black folks.

And yet none of my teammates made every practice, and not many of them were even consistently on time. A basically reliable core, made up of the more middle-class black kids, the sons and nephews of the coaches themselves, and the team's white wide receiver, soon estab-lished itself. Come late October, we were the ones who'd still be around. Even some of the coaches missed the occasional practice; one of them, a hefty offensive line coach whose car was always at the shop, we gave rides home to on occasion, our little Renault sinking pronouncedly to his side. Black life was on display before me in all its confusion, hope-lessly complicated by factors that, for our family, would have been easily overcome. My father could replace a broken crankshaft; why couldn't Coach? My mother had no problem picking me up from prac-tice each day at five-thirty, while a lot of kids seemed to have parents, somewhere. They walked or rode bikes to practice, singly or in pairs, going down the middle of the street as if sidewalks didn't exist. If they lost a cleat or misplaced the laces for their shoulder pads, they could be out of practice for a week. A broken bike chain could end a season. Life's little details threw them for a disproportionate loop.

This was all just a few blocks away, and about as close to us, spiri-tually, as China. Though my mother was driving me only half a mile to practice, the mind-set there was so foreign that it was as if we'd dug a hole underneath our little corner of Detroit and had continued digging until we'd come out the other side of the earth.

To me, at ten years old, it seemed that my teammates—most of whom lived south of 7 Mile—were from another country. Our second bungalow was five blocks south of 8 Mile; by going to Heilmann Field each weekday afternoon, the black kids and I were meeting in the middle. The new house was bigger than our first, about nine hundred square feet—three bedrooms, one bath—and built on the model of the one next to it, and the one behind it, and the one across the street: row after row of indistinguishable brick bungalows, built just after the Second World War, when people were moving into Detroit, not out of it. In our backyard, growing bigger by the year, was a blackened patch of dirt along the fence line, where my father dumped used motor oil.

Our neighborhood, tucked in the city's far northeastern corner, was by Detroit standards an outright beauty. In the heat of summer, when even the air-conditioned zip codes can seem about to boil, our area always managed to retain a guarded calm. We were bordered on the north by 8 Mile Road, on the south by 7 Mile, on the west by Gratiot Avenue, and on the east by Kelly Road, and it was easy to think of these streets as natural borders, like the Adriatic or the Alps, and of our neighborhood as a self-contained country. The area had been notable, perhaps, less for its positive qualities than for its relative lack of negative ones: no abandoned homes, no broken-down cars, no broken-out windows. Notable, too, was the way the area neatly stood Detroit's demographic on its head. The brick bungalows on our block, and the dozen or so blocks surrounding, were occupied by cops, firemen, autoworkers, bus drivers, and low-level city bureaucrats who were, with few exceptions, white. The city planners, a century back, may have anticipated that ours would indeed be one of Detroit's last bastions of Eurocentrism: the side street one block to our east was named Shakespeare. The neighborhood was a classic, and no one had any desire to open up the canon. That there was an all-black football team practicing just blocks away couldn't be anything but bad news.

My mother soon learned that there was more to fear from my playing on this team than a dislocated finger. "Today, men, we got ourselves a scrimmage," our head coach said about a week before our first regular-season game. This hadn't been announced at the previous day's practice, nor did it appear on the season schedule stuck up on my parents' refrigerator with a magnet from Little Italy Pizzeria. "We're going over to St. Ambrose. Get your game faces on. We're going live," the coach said, using the term that meant this would be no walk-through, but a full-tilt affair.

I was glad to be trading in another dull practice for a full-squad scrimmage, and the fact that we were playing St. Ambrose was reassuringly familiar. Down on Alter Road and Jefferson, on the Detroit–Grosse Pointe border, St. Ambrose was the school that my father's six cousins had attended; I knew people who still went to Mass there. Though it was by this point an all-black school, just saying the name St. Ambrose, the canonized fourth-century Bishop of Milan, felt safe.

There were complications. Kids were late getting to practice, and so held up our departure, particularly if they were starters. Coaches were late. I rode over in Coach Clyde's car, but there was a good deal of discussion among the rest of the players about who would ride with whom. Once this was sorted out and we'd all driven off from Heilmann, some of the coaches were unable to find St. Ambrose's practice field, which was at Alter Road and East Warren, across from Ladder Co. 31, Engine Co. 52, one of the east side's oldest firehouses, where some of my friends' fathers were stationed.

After we'd all arrived at the field it transpired that St. Ambrose, too, had to wait on some of their players and coaches. By the time the scrimmage was over and we'd gotten back to Heilmann—I hadn't caught a pass but threw some key blocks and ran crisp routes—it was well after six o'clock, and my mother had been sitting in the parking lot for half an hour, staring at the empty field where her son was supposed to be.

What the hell was the matter with these people? Who *lived* like this? She let the coaches have it, an outburst that did me no favors on the candy-ass front. "I was frantic," my mother said, stroking my head once I was in the car, safe and sound. Clearly, there was a hole in my family's strategy somewhere. I hadn't bothered anyone, nor had anyone bothered me, and yet here was my mother, visibly bothered. "Frantic," she said again and again as we pulled out of the Heilmann parking lot. "Just frantic."

I attracted my teammates' attention on the first day of practice by wearing a pair of high-top Nike basketball shoes in place of the cleats that I'd yet to purchase. The Nike Corporation had only just begun its conquest of urban America, and my shoes, which many of my teammates also wore, were less a sign of status than was my counterintuitive pronunciation of the brand's name, with a long *e* at the end. (A year later I would study Greek and Roman mythology with my sixth-grade English teacher, Mr. Kent. A few of my older friends had already taken his class, however, so I had some familiarity with the Greek goddess of victory.) Everyone else back then still called their shoes "Nikes," making it sound like "Mike's." I noticed their pronunciations as much as they noticed mine: to a kid, the verb *ask* was transformed into an instrument for chopping down trees.

"Where you stay at?" one of these kids axed, looking me up and down, from high-top sneakers to feathered hair, and smiling. His question was the black Detroit version of "Where do you live?," though hinting at a greater freedom of movement. *Living* somewhere implies strong roots; *staying* somewhere says that the stakes can be pulled up at a second's notice. I named my street and pointed in its direction. "You go to McGregor, then, or Burbank? Never seen you around before." "I go to St. Peter," I said. The school was on 8 Mile, and our nickname was the Keys; I pictured our logo—a pair of crossed keys that unlocked the Kingdom of Heaven—as I said the name. "Oh," my inquisitor said, "he go to *private* school." Lots of laughter, hand-slapping, and a generalized sense of agreement, though what they were all nodding at I had no idea. "Now that's what I'm talking about," someone said.

Despite my black friends on 6 Mile, this was my first real encounter with that headlong rush toward conversational closure, to the inevitable exclamations of "You know that's right!" or "Now that's what I'm talking about!" or "I hear that!" or, more inquisitively, "Y'know what I'm sayin'?"—as if something, anything, had been said, let alone settled. We would start to diagram sentences, too, in Mr. Kent's English class, and I'd search these types of statements for signs of actual content, trying to link the relative pronouns to their nonexistent antecedents. *What's* right? *What* are you talking about? And what's *that?* It was hopeless. No, I wanted to admit, I have no idea what you're talking about. And neither do you.

For a full year, it seemed, we did nothing but diagram sentences. The diagrams helped us visualize what otherwise would have remained murky: the difference between compound and complex sentences, between predicate nominatives and direct objects, between direct objects and indirect objects, between the objective and subjective cases, between active and passive voice. Reading was a separate subject from English, and in that class Mr. Kent spent a great deal of time reading *to* us. We also read, of course, going up and down the neat rows at the pace of a paragraph per student, bumbling our way through "The Lady, or the Tiger?" but my favorite sessions were those when Mr. Kent would hunch forward on a stool at the front of the room, cup a book in both hands, and read "The Cask of Amontillado" or "The Fall of the House of Usher" or "The Lady of Shalott." Sometimes he'd walk around the classroom, declaiming like a troubadour. I still recall a couplet from the Tennyson poem: "The mirror crack'd from side to side / 'The curse is come upon me,' cried / The Lady of Shalott." Some of the girls snickered at that, though I hadn't a clue as to why.

In English, when our diagramming lessons were done and we could be trusted to string consecutive sentences together, Mr. Kent assigned a paper—a persuasive paper, he said, which tried to convince the reader of something. Lacking any strong convictions myself, I chose to parrot the opinion of my father on a topic for which his feelings could not have been firmer: the overwhelming benefits of a manual transmission. I had the litany cold: sticks came cheaper from the factory; they were easier and less expensive to maintain; they got better gas mileage, performed better, and allowed for greater control of the car in dangerous conditions; they kept the driver more alert; the gearbox looked cool.

I started with my topic sentence and let the argument build over several paragraphs until my thesis seemed airtight and my word minimum had been met. I still needed a closing, though, and so decided to address the opposing viewpoint—which, in my father's telling, was that automatics were simply more "convenient." This was all that could be said in favor of automatic transmissions: they were easier. And since people were always looking for the easy out, the whole thing could be explained away as mere laziness.

With this in mind, I closed with a killer pun. Because the papers were to be read to the class, I decided to address my audience directly, employing the second person. "When you turn sixteen," I said in summation, "don't be shiftless."

It was through Mr. Kent's classes that I came to appreciate clarity in thought and language. And so, as the years went by and I still heard nothing meaningful conveyed when black kids had heard enough to offer an "I hear that!," it required a concerted effort to keep quiet.

But I'd inherited from my father the sort of racial common sense that comes of the ability to count; his voice in my head had instructed me to think, and I'd heeded it.

Though the team was supposed to be composed of ten- and eleven-year-olds, a few of my teammates were at least as old as thirteen. In some cases, the coaches and parents had had them lie about their age, for competitive advantage. Phony names abounded, as did nicknames: there was Professor, our bespectacled fullback; Dr. Death, our mean-ass middle linebacker; there was our reportedly fourteen-year-old corner-back, Batman, so named for obscure reasons I can no longer recall; and our split end, who was occasionally called Casper, as in the Friendly Ghost.

The coaches had no patience with this sort of talk, or with much of anything else that came out of our mouths. They walked around Heilmann Field that fall in athletic shorts whatever the weather, their hands on their hips to hitch up their waistbands or down at their crotches to cup their balls. They blew whistles and barked out orders. "Button your chinstrap!" "Stand up!" "Take a knee!" "Break down!" they'd say as we ran in place during calisthenics, a command that meant we were to drop to our chests and throw our arms out wide so that there would be nothing to break our fall, the better to accustom our bodies to absorbing blows. "Laps!" they'd say at the end of practice, and we'd begin the slow trudge around the goalposts, our overweight linemen dragging ass at the back of the pack. "Nigger, get your fat ass going," one of our coaches, a man with quadriceps like tree trunks, would yell to our best defensive lineman, a noseguard who happened to be his nephew. If his nephew ran too slowly, the coach would pick up a football, take aim, and peg him in the back of the helmet. I never saw him miss.

There was very little patience for weakness, and absolutely none for stupidity. And our team had plenty of both: kids who cried when they were hit hard, and who couldn't remember their responsibility on even the simplest plays. Frequently, these were the same kid. "On three, on three," our quarterback would say before we broke huddle with a hand clap, and by the time we got to the line of scrimmage half the offense had already forgotten the count. "What the hell's the matter with you, boy?" the coaches would yell, blowing their whistles and approaching some dimwitted, duck-footed lineman who couldn't, for the life of him, remember a snap count, and who repeatedly got kicked in the ass while down in a three-point stance because of it. "The play was called on three. *Three.* Do you know how many three is? Why'd you jump on one, then? That's illegal procedure, boy. Do you know what that means? That means you moved before the ball was snapped from center. You proceeded illegally. Now hold up three fingers for me, so I can see that you know." There were kids who couldn't remember, on running plays, that the even-numbered holes were to the right of center and the odd-numbered holes to the left. Other kids knew that the holes on the right side were even, but such knowledge did them little good, as they didn't seem to know their right from their left in the first place. One of our linemen consistently wore his cleats on the wrong feet.

I had, by this point in the season, settled into my role on the team, not only as its wide receiver but as its white kid. I'd become something of a mascot for both coaches and players, just as I would over subsequent summers at Heilmann's basketball courts, when I would be affectionately singled out as the bearer of "the disease": the chronic inability, on the part of people of European descent, to leap. I could run better, being one of the faster kids on the football team. Not that this was why Coach Clyde had chosen me as a starting wideout. This was in the days before the coaching of football had been systematized, reduced to forty-yard dash times and repetitions on the bench press. Coach Clyde had had a feeling about me, a gut instinct, and he'd gone with it.

He could in part have been charmed by my novelty, which remained intact throughout the season. There was no learning curve with me, no grace period in this black studies course I was taking before I got the hang of dropping my final *g*'s and saying "which" when I meant "with." I would end the season as white as I began it. The white kids in the suburbs, with their backward hats, baggy pants, and borrowed poses, struck me as too eager for acceptance. They were too dense to realize that indifference can go a long way.

This sounds tougher, plainly stated, than it proved to be in practice; I wasn't a tough guy. The toughest kid in the Denby Bulldogs organization was a linebacker on the team a year ahead of mine, a kid who sported a severe brush cut and whose grandmother lived two doors down from us, in a house of white-painted brick. I shoveled her sidewalk one January for thirty dollars—it was a flat-rate arrangement, regardless of how many inches of snow we got—before calling off the deal. Her grandson was as singular on his team as I was on mine, though his father, a Detroit cop, had altogether less cause for any candy-ass fears on behalf of his son. Scott would be a grade ahead of me at my high school—where, with his rugged build and throwback hairstyle, he'd begin to resemble a middleweight contender from the 1950s, the tough young kid the champ's been said to be ducking.

He was one of a group of similar white kids in Detroit's northeast corner who could do push-ups out of handstands, who regarded street fighting as good clean fun, and whose years in Coleman Young's Detroit had taught them only that there was enormous solace to be found in sarcasm and a good deal of good sense to be found in prejudice. What I often thought of as such kids' lack of common sense—their propensity for saying the wrong thing, at the wrong time, in the wrong place, and for purposely saying it much too loudly—was, in fact, a failure of will on my part. If I'd had their guts, their builds, their almost complete lack of fear, I'd have done the same. Lacking their fearlessness but still needing to make sense of my hometown somehow, I became increasingly bookish, while these kids did push-ups and pull-ups and beat the shit out of the punching bags they'd hung from basement ceilings, all as part of their preparation for what they viewed, perhaps rightly, as the inevitable.

It is nonetheless fitting, perhaps, that my early, playful interactions with black kids—boxing matches in basements, fall football practices—centered around physical contact: violence, supervised and unsupervised. From these early experiences may stem my frequent surprise, later in life, at the belief of many whites that black folks are to be treated with kid gloves—that they are untouchables, basically, about whom there is a great deal that can't be thought or said. In Detroit it was different, with a greater respect given to the black ability to absorb physical and linguistic blows. They hit, and you hit back: it's how the game was played. Coleman Young was quite capable of defending himself.

By the time overcast October arrived I'd learned much that was valuable from the coaches, quite aside from proper blocking technique and how to run a post pattern. "Cold? Put your hands down your pants. Warmest place on your bodies, men, is the family jewels. Remember that. Don't be wearing no gloves to practice. Don't need 'em. Hands get cold, put 'em down your pants." Catholic school was altogether less encouraging about my putting my hands down my pants, but what the coaches said was sound: the family jewels were a furnace.

Have I ever been happier than during those muddy late-fall practices, with drizzle in the air, leaves underfoot, and Halloween fast approaching? Halloween was my favorite night of the year, with all the kids in the neighborhood running from house to house at the first hint of dusk, with no predetermined traffic flow. Some would go up and down the block, some down and up, bumping into one another along the way. At the end of the evening everyone would return home panting, face paint running from sweat, a pillowcase full of candy clutched in his or her fists. It was as if we'd somehow made it back to enjoy the spoils after the safe completion of a dangerous mission, and in a sense we had. The neighborhood's sidewalks had begun the process of returning to their constituent elements years before, and it was easy to imagine that the geographic center of the holiday had moved from the crumbling castles of Transylvania to the crumbling sidewalks of Detroit. On Halloween night animals of the forest lost their legs, kings and queens collapsed, and more than a few animated heroes and heroines took tumbles. There were always skinned knees in the neighborhood the next day.

Of more pressing concern to our parents, who passed out the candy, was the increase each year in the carloads of children—*van*loads—who were being dropped off on our block by outsiders, people who then took up all the curb space to await their kids' return. Worse still was when they followed after their kids, driving slowly along the curb; even driving at a crawl could be dangerous on a dark night on a street crowded with trick-or-treaters. The increased risk that these cars presented, combined with the fact that these were not neighborhood kids climbing out of such cars but kids from other, less desirable sections of the city whose parents "bused" them to better areas in pursuit of holiday candy—well, this pissed people off. It happened more and more each year, and each year a few more porch lights in the neighborhood stayed off all night in protest, causing us to pass over these houses as if by decree from the pharaoh. "Some of these kids are fourteen and fifteen," you'd hear people complain. "They don't wear costumes or say thank you. I don't mind the cute little ones, but enough is enough."

The roads of the neighborhood were always slick with wet leaves in October, causing our front tires to spin as my mother pulled away from stop signs on the way to practice, where some of those fourteen-year-olds who didn't say thank you or wear costumes sat around waiting for warm-ups to start. "It's sweater weather," my mother would say every autumn after the first frost, and the phrase began to seem almost magical, a reminder that, after stripping out of my Catholic school uniform, it would be wise to put on a sweatshirt under my shoulder pads. I could almost understand my father's hatred of air conditioning: this *was* Michigan, after all, and here we were, at the beginning of the eight months of the year when you didn't need air conditioning anyway. After I was forced to endure head-on the heat and humidity of a Detroit summer, my feelings toward these crisp fall days were sharpened and my father's outlook on life began to make a certain sense, granting to our yearly reprieve from the heat the feeling of a well-earned reward. Plus, on the electric bill, he saved a few bucks.

Our home games were played at Edwin Denby High School, the Detroit public school I would have attended were it not for Roman Catholicism, but we met up at Heilmann Field first before driving over. The mothers always bought McDonald's for us before our home games, and we sat in the Heilmann parking lot on those cool mornings eating steaming, heavily salted hash browns out of their bright red sleeves. I sat on a metal parking rail, feeling the cold through my tail pad, and fought off my nervousness by pretending great interest in my fried potato.

Half an hour later, the hash browns just beginning to digest, our quarterback led us onto the field in a straight line ("Look sharp, men!") as we buttoned up our chinstraps, preparing for battle. Our rally cry was done to the accompaniment of hand slaps on our thigh pads, on which we pounded out a dum-dum-DUM, dum-dum-DUM beat. "I said a-boom-chigaboom!" our quarterback would holler, in the same voice he used to call out the play count, and we'd echo back: "I said a-boom-chigaboom!" The second time the *boom* grew louder, and the third time around the levee on the *boom* broke: "I said a-BOOM-chigaboom!" "I said a-BOOM-chigaboom!" "I said a-boom-chickarocka-chickarocka-chigaboom!" "I said a-boom-chickarocka-chickarocka-chigaboom!" A few times through and we'd line up for calisthenics, spacing ourselves on the chalk marks that intersected the field every five yards, and count out our jumping jacks and toe touches in unison. Warm-ups over, we'd run through some offensive plays in slow motion against our defense, with the nonstarters lined up shoulder to shoulder to block our formations and signals from the opposing team's view.

After that it was time to walk to the sidelines for a pregame pep talk from the head coach. "They're coming into your backyard. Your back-*yard*, men. Are you gonna let them take something from you from your own backyard? They coming in here, thinking they're the tough new guys on the block"—here they'd motion to our opponents huddled on the other side of the field—"but that can't be right, can it?" No, we'd all holler: *we* were the tough guys, and we would go out there and prove it. "Son," Coach Clyde sometimes said, pulling me aside, "what you need to do out there is concentrate. And relax. Just relax and concentrate." I hadn't caught a pass in our first three games, and though Coach Clyde hadn't lost faith in me he had clearly lost some patience. But he still smiled and called me "son," something the other kids might have needed but that I didn't. I liked it anyway.

These tough talks and motivational speeches were particularly difficult for me, preoccupied as I was with remembering the words to what I'd taken to calling the Lower Sprint. In my nervousness, I sometimes stumbled over lines I'd said ten thousand times before. While I waited for my teammates to repeat "Give us this day our daily bread" I'd lose the prayer's flow, and be unable come up with "And forgive us our trespasses." My mother suggested that, instead of waiting while my teammates repeated the previous line, I say it along with them, so that "As we forgive those who trespass against us" would come more naturally. The strategy worked.

But before our homecoming game that fall against the East Detroit Shamrocks, into which we carried a 2–0–1 record, my preoccupations with non-football-related matters were compounded. Not only would I be prayer leader; I'd be an escort as well for our team's cheerleaders, little girls who sported pom-poms of blue and gold, our team's colors, and specialized in "The Funky Chicken" and other mideighties urban dance moves that sent their braids airborne. They'd strut their stuff on the sidelines, turning the traditionally demure pastime of cheerleading into another in-your-face form of urban competition. Solo cheers, which my sister, Beth, memorized from the stands, were frequent: "My name is Latoya, and I'm first on the list; I got my reputation because I boogie like this." Next up, not to be outdone, would be Tamika: "My name is Tamika, and I'm second on the list; I got my reputation because I shimmy like this." And so on, each girl strutting her ten-year-old stuff.

The coaches had to pick three players to escort these darlings from the end zone to the fifty-yard line, and I was among the lucky few. Greatly embarrassed—*girls*—I walked with a flower in one hand and a cheerleader's hand in the other, slowly putting one foot in front of the other, conscious of my own locomotion as I'd never been previously. I managed to make it through the ceremony without stumbling.

Split left, 900 drop back, from deep in our playbook, was called early in the second half—"on two, on two," our quarterback said, breaking huddle. We were in our opponent's end of the field, at their forty-yard line, and down two touchdowns. I lined up in the left slot. The play required me to run a post pattern, which I did, planting hard, about fifteen yards out, with my left foot. I made a beeline for the goal-posts, looking back over my right shoulder for the pass, having cleanly beaten my defender. The quarterback got it there, as Coach Clyde had promised.

"Oh!" the announcer said over the PA system. "It hit him in the wrong spot—right in the hands!"

I ran over to the sidelines and took off my helmet, then immediately wanted to put it back on to hide my embarrassment. My mother still recites the announcer's line happily, pleased that he was talking about her little boy, unable to grasp (football never made any sense to her) that I had dropped a sure touchdown. My father can also recite the line, his candy-ass fears still not quite overcome more than two decades later. How could you *not* have caught it? It was right in your hands!

I would catch exactly one pass all season, on a split-end screen a week later that went for three yards against the Grosse Pointe Red Barons, a team without a nonwhite player on its roster.

By Appointment Only

THE POLITICS OF THE AREA could be found, in its most distilled form, at Sal's barbershop. Though a couple miles southeast of our neighborhood, everyone made the trek over to see Sal, whose brush cuts and Princetons were sported by Catholic kids all over the east side. Most of the men who'd filed into the shop were, like the barber himself, vigorously middle-aged, undeniably Italian, and vaguely handsome, in the way of a character actor whose face is familiar but whose name escapes. The younger customers came from the surrounding grade schools—St. Matthew, St. Peter, St. Clare, St. Brendan—and the older boys from the nearby Catholic high schools, all but one of which was single sex.

It seems that it was always the evening before some big holiday that I awaited a trim—the last Wednesday in November, December the twenty-third—and that the inside of the shop, so warm as to be sleep-inducing, was a forest of cashmere overcoats, with big-bodied men trudging in from the cold, blowing warm breath into cupped hands and stamping their feet while swearing away their shivers. The holidays were big-tipping time in the barbershop, when men who'd just gotten down from the chair would put their coats, scarves, and gloves back on before reaching into their pockets and slipping Sal a twenty, or fifty, or hundred, or, best of all, those obviously connected men who would hand him, on the day before Thanksgiving or Christmas Eve's eve, nothing at all, but instead throw an arm around his shoulder, thank him for the shave and trim, and walk out the door with the mutual understanding that, in the very near future, a behind-the-scenes lever would be lowered that would lighten the barber's load significantly. A state representative was among the men who got their hair cut at Sal's, a fact Sal never failed to mention.

Sal's eyebrows drooped down heavily, like icicles from an awning, and his statements tended toward the oracular. "Better them than you-know-who," he said in the mid-1980s, after it was suggested that, due to the steep decline of the American auto industry, the Japanese were taking over Detroit. Comments like these could follow a full minute of silence, and it would take a second to contextualize them. But it was worth the intellectual effort. "You'll learn more in this barbershop than you will from any book"—the man with the scissors was fond of saying this, though it was said less to downplay formal education's importance than to enhance his own. He was a big believer in school—"Sit there, keep your mouth shut, you can't help but learn something"—and Catholic education in particular. This belief he backed up in deed, not only because he'd sent his own sons to Catholic school but because he also bought, however begrudgingly, the fund-raiser items for sale by his younger clients. On more than one occasion did I hand Sal eight bucks for the haircut (a dollar tip), only to have him hand me a good deal more than that for a prize calendar or roll of raffle tickets.

I continued to sit there and keep my mouth shut at St. Peter, even though a block behind our house was the neighborhood's public elementary school, Tracy McGregor. Though we sometimes climbed the school, using strategically placed fences and ledges to make it onto the roof, and though we took daily batting practice at the school during the summer, using the strike zones spray-painted on its side, I'd never set foot inside it and no one I knew went there. Students were bused into the neighborhood until 1988, when the silliness of sending kids from one all-black school to another all-black school farther away finally sunk in and the endless list of things on which our fathers felt money was wasted was reduced by one.

My religious progress at St. Peter can be charted as follows: took first communion in second grade, believing that the wafer and wine were chips and pop; made first confession in fourth grade, admitting to Father DeFina that I was sometimes mean to my little sister; took Joseph as my confirmation name in eighth grade, after that model of selfless fatherhood; and basically behaved as my parents, who were forking over the tuition that my mother's odd jobs and my father's long hours funded, believed I should. The school was all white and, it sometimes seemed, all Italian. Many of my classmates had last names seen on the side of Eastern Market produce trucks, and many of those who didn't had mothers, like mine, with Italian maiden names. A few of the more bewildered-looking parents at after-school functions spoke no English whatsoever, smiled often, and smelled of garlic. Two-thirds of the class lived in the city.

The clearest of my grade school memories revolve around those times that were, to a kid, thrillingly out of the ordinary: the days leading up to a vacation or holiday, or those formal functions that brought us back to school after dark, when the hallways looked strangely unfamiliar. The student projects that lined the walls—our very own handiwork—provided unconvincing proof that these were indeed the same halls we'd walked hours earlier, while still in our uniforms. My favorite two and a half days of the school year were those of Thanksgiving week, days given over to construction paper, safety scissors, and lighthearted lessons, the festivities culminating in an all-school Mass during the half day on Wednesday. The altar would be decorated with pumpkins and gourds, and some of the children in the lower grades would be got up like Indians, wearing ponchos and war paint. Near the end of Mass, at the sign of peace, we'd pretend to be smoking pipes.

The nights of parent-teacher conferences—Thursdays, always—were a special hell. My parents would come home late, my mother smiling in her party dress, my father looking uncomfortable and altogether less pleased as he loosened one of his rarely worn ties. My father never said much of anything but stood watch over these scenes as my mother recited, a bit breathless, my long list of scholastic successes, a litany that had been handed to her, via platter, by my teachers only a half hour before and that proved to her—and this was all anyone could ask, really—that I was doing my best. To my father, whose forearms were folded across his chest, this wasn't really worth complimenting: I'd *better* be doing my best, given the kind of bucks he was shelling out for tuition. The Catholic stuff, the religious instruction that the school provided, that was fine—he could recite the Nicene Creed, too—but if I wasn't going to apply myself to math and science, reading and writing, then I could just as well walk to McGregor, which was visible from our backyard. It was right outside our door, practically, and free.

"What are you talking about?" my mother would ask, looking over at him. "He *is* applying himself. You heard his teachers." "I realize that. I'm just saying that if he doesn't—" "But he *does*. Don't listen to him," my mother would say, turning to me and smiling. As if to compensate, she could have talked all night about the compliments she'd received on her children, and about how this teacher, a nun, knew Sister Marcia, and how that teacher, a layman, attended Sunday services at Father Hec's parish. Wasn't it something, what a small place the world was? My sister and I would smile, excited to have a legitimate reason to stay up late, but my father would eventually put an end to all this back-patting. It was still a school night, after all, and we needed our sleep.

At some level I always preferred my father's pessimism, his sense that things may be all right—for now. Contentment was always precarious, temporary. Neither could I ever really abide being in the presence of an authority figure who had nice things to say about me, even when the compliments were coming secondhand. "Your Paul is doing *wonderfully*," the nuns would sometimes tell my mother as she picked me up from school, and I came to fear such moments the way thuggish kids from single-parent homes fear spelling bees and state exams. Later in life, during discussions with the boss, any turn in the conversation toward "I don't need to tell you how pleased we all are with the work you've done here," and it seemed a certainty that I'd end up on the floor in the fetal position, my fingers stuffed in my ears to drown out the unholy sound of positive reinforcement. Such bucking up might work on the kids in public school, where the culture of self-help seemed to hold sway. But though my mother scolded him for it, my father was right to be so impossible to please. Why send a kid to Catholic school for thirteen years, after all, if not to cultivate, at least a little, the tragic sense of life?

While most of the kids who went to Sal's for haircuts came from Detroit, the men split more or less evenly between city and suburb, with a handful driving a substantial distance, coming in from the subdivision known unofficially as "Mafia Meadows," which was out at 16 Mile Road and Moravian in Macomb County. Most of the men no longer living in the city came from Grosse Pointe, however; this meant, in many cases, that they now lived quite a bit closer to the barbershop, which was located just a couple miles up from the Grosse Pointe border, than they had when they still lived in the city itself. In Grosse Pointe, with its tree-lined streets and well-maintained colonials and Cape Cods, it wasn't too hard to imagine that one was in some college town out East, a place populated by rich kids with winning personalities and progressive social ideals and professors in aged Volvos, listening to National Public Radio.

When I was younger my mother would often drag me to Grosse Pointe garage sales in search of clothes, once worn by rich kids, that her little boy could grow into. I'd reluctantly try on shirts and sweaters in driveways while my mother tugged at fabric and talked, much too loudly, about things like crotch room and putting a stitch in the pants' legs. "Now it says you're asking a dollar," my mother would say, pointing to the tag above the alligator on a faded Izod shirt, "but it's a little worn. And see the stain, right up here by the pocket? Will you take fifty cents?" My embarrassment at her bartering over two quarters was keen, as the whole of Grosse Pointe seemed to me to float above such concerns. The smell of fresh flowers, a scent I believed the rich produced from their armpits and fundaments, permeated the entire suburb.

Though I began at Sal's with a crew cut I switched over, during high school, to the Princeton, a popular hairstyle among the preppy Grosse Pointe boys I both despised and envied. Though the bangs hung over my forehead in the appropriate rightward waterfall, the hairstyle failed to attract the long-limbed girls I invariably saw on the arms of Grosse Pointe boys with identical haircuts. If I'd ever given voice to these frustrations the older men in the barbershop would have sympathized, for they too had grown up in the city and had similar unrequited longings. Grosse Pointe was the citadel, and there were few Detroit kids of whatever generation who hadn't wished to crack it, to enter into the world of pretty girls, private parks, and ivy-covered public schools.

Even those customers who still lived in Detroit—who hadn't yet abandoned the city—had long since abandoned the present tense when discussing it. Detroit was history; the city they were referring to when they said "Detroit" no longer existed. It could be recaptured only through talk, and barbershop conversations were a way to compare notes in a congenial atmosphere. The customers who said the most tended to possess an absolute, unwavering belief in the truth of what their years in the city had taught them, and if those years had taught them anything at all, it was that the city of Detroit was better off before.

On prominent display in Sal's shop, along the back wall, was a By Appointment Only sign, which could be confusing to new customers, as Sal, as a matter of unbending principle, took no appointments. "I got one in the chair and two waiting." He'd say this, picking up the phone, three or four times in the course of any ten-minute span, typically to customers who lived nearby and were trying to time their arrival just so. Some callers would ask an additional question, to which Sal would respond: "Till seven. How long you been coming here?" These two customers-in-waiting could quickly become six, or zero. Customers tended to arrive at the barber's in waves, with three or four character actors showing up within a couple minutes of one another; it took Sal about sixty minutes to get these bit players in and out of the shop.

Each hour, then, started afresh and followed a predictable pattern. The initial fifteen minutes, while the first fellow was in the chair, would consist of a discussion of the day's events or just general banter, the what-you-been-up-to of barbershops the world over. But after the first customer had been powdered by Sal, had put on his hat, paid, and left, those still waiting—men who saw what the neighborhood had looked like on the drive in and, their minds following the first customer as he pulled away, were envisioning what it would look like on the way out—would begin to get angry.

"It breaks my heart," the second customer would say as he settled himself into the chair, "seeing what they've done to my old place."

"At least yours is still standing," the third customer, now in the batter's box, might offer. "My old house? Burnt to the ground."

"My parents' old place is purple," the fourth man, face hidden behind the morning newspaper, would add. And then, as an afterthought: "Who paints a house purple?"

This was the intended audience for that By Appointment Only sign: the sort of people who would paint a house purple. It was rare that things ever progressed to this point, but by the late eighties the neighborhood surrounding the shop had begun to change, and the foot traffic had become more Baptist than Catholic. So, from time to time, a black customer walked in and asked Sal if he knew how to do a *Dee*-troit fade. He sure did, but (turning toward the sign) you needed an appointment to get one, and (motioning to the packed shop) he was booked pretty solid for the rest of the week. Sorry.

There would usually be a moment of smirking silence after the man had left, followed by some earnest self-justification and finally a bit of generalized laughter at the silliness of the entire Detroit enterprise. "Didn't get a lot of that way back when, did you, Sal?" No—*snip, snip*—he sure didn't. Not way back when.

This, then, was the sum total of people's political position: Detroit was once better off—before the riots, before Coleman Young, before affirmative action and a black majority, before The Fist went up, housing prices went down, and people started painting their homes purple. Perhaps *political* is not the right word; it was so all-encompassing as to resemble a system of philosophy. White Detroiters of a generation or two before mine acted as if the city from which they came had become, against their will, a universe lost, and thus the yardstick against which everything else—sterile suburbs, slum cities—would forever be slightingly judged.

My father was not among the men in the barbershop. This was rare, since the place was typically filled with fathers and sons. These were men—breadwinners, heads of households—none too terribly enamored of excuses: yours, mine, theirs. They may have bitched about Coleman Young, but they wouldn't blame his affirmative action program for their inability to rise to the rank of sergeant or to ascend in the city administration. Excuses, whatever truth lay behind them, always sound like bullshit once publicly articulated. The only thing that mattered in life was success—or its poor relation, survival—whatever mollycoddling nonsense our mothers said to the contrary about the importance of doing one's best. My baseball coach, the father of a grade school friend and a Detroit police officer, had a strategy for teaching the game that was as revealing of his philosophy of life as anything else. If, during infield practice, you bobbled one of the ground balls he'd hit your way, he immediately hit another one at you, this time much harder. If you thought that last one was bad, he seemed to be saying, just wait, boy: it gets worse.

It's nearly impossible nowadays to speak of the primacy of the family—by which I mean a mother and father, with children over whom they exert some control—without sounding like a conservative columnist or politician, a humorless man with a severe rightward part in his hair. And yet, when I think of our corner of Detroit, I visualize first its homes, to the front doors of which I mentally tack a family tree, in much the way that genealogies are sometimes slipped into the opening pages of magic realist novels. Mr. and Mrs. So-And-So are always sitting on the top branch (we never called adults by their first names), below which are the children and occasionally, on an awkward outgrowth, a senile aunt or retarded cousin. All the kids were sent to Catholic school. Each August, the mothers would drag us to a nearby department store that stocked Catholic school uniforms and buy us an exact replica, in a slightly larger size, of what we'd worn the year previous—navy blue corduroys and light blue dress shirts for the boys, new white blouses and plaid skirts for the girls. Because there were slight variations between schools—a different plaid pattern in the skirts, for instance—the store would mark the racks accordingly: ST. VERONICA, ST. MATTHEW, ST. PETER, ST. BRENDAN, and so on.

Families were fundamental to the way the area was organized, which is not to say that anyone spent much time getting sentimental over them as a concept. Families were viewed like most other things in this life, which is to say as sometimes dreary and ultimately disappointing, but preferable to a long list of even less desirable alternatives. (Exhibit A being most of the rest of the city, where the out-of-wedlock birth rate was astonishingly close to 100 percent.) Though they cursed aloud while doing so—and, internally, likely cursed the days they'd wed our mothers and fathered us—the men in our neighborhood, whether in hats and gloves during the dead of winter, or sweating and swearing up a storm in the middle of summer, somehow managed to fix broken carburetors, replace drafty windows, and keep basement furnaces going a little bit longer, while their wives bought box after box of whatever was on sale and saw to it that their children didn't waste all their money at McDonald's, like the children south of 7 Mile did, having been born—and this, our mothers knew, was the real root of the problem—

to women who couldn't keep their men. With nothing more than a phone book, a nail file, and a few hours at her disposal, my mother, like all the mothers in the area, could quite effectively have arranged the fate of the planet.

I was driven to Sal's while still in grade school by my mother, who would sometimes wait with me and sometimes, after checking to see when he'd be finished, run a few errands. In front of my mother, the talk in the barbershop was decidedly toned down. There was, after all, a lady present—this was rare—one whose family history was of more than passing interest to them. Where did she grow up? By City Airport, you say? Hey, so did they. She went to St. David's? Hell, them, too. (Well, the fellow in the corner went to St. Joe's, actually, but same difference.) What was that little nun's name who taught at St. David's there? Sister what's-her—? "Sister Marcia Saulino?" my mother would suggest. "That's it! That's the one!" "She was my aunt." "No shi—I mean, no fooling? You hear that, Sal, this little fellow's the nephew—" "Grandnephew." "—the grandnephew of one of my grade school teachers. How about that?"

After hearing such stories, secondhand, my father simply shook his head. This was his first reaction to almost everything, even to news that was unarguably good: immediate, mild disapproval. If, growing up, I had told my father that I'd just won a million dollars, he would have shook his head and proceeded to explain, with massive seriousness, that the taxes on such winnings were sure to be a *bear*. I was never certain why he did this, but I gathered that it had something to do with his disposition, which was geared for disappointment, and which had decided, as a way to ward it off, to do the superstitious headshake, as if the blow had already been absorbed.

He was also, I think, suspicious of the Italian thing—that in the barbershop most of the men were Italian, and as such were prone to talking a bunch of bullshit, talk to which his son, whom for years he had tried to steer clear of such nonsense, was privy. Not that he was prejudiced against Italians. My father had married a Saulino girl, after all, and his best friends from high school had last names like Carnaghi and DiLaura. But my father had serious misgivings about the backslapping and bluster that featured so prominently at Sal's, and that he believed could never be a life's building block. It was as if his son was being presented with another option, an infinitely easier path than the one he'd prescribed, a shortcut that was frequently, infuriatingly successful: that of not giving a shit. Put up a By Appointment Only sign, point to it as necessary, and what happened? Nothing. No repercussions. Blacks left; they just walked away.

Better Than Being a Dumb-Ass

A GOOD EXAMPLE of the kind of kid who lived in the area around Sal's, and toward whom I began to gravitate as a teenager, was Kurt Ketchel. The smartest student at our high school, he had been a classmate of mine for more than a decade, and a friend—if that's the right word—for even longer. We'd gone to grade school together, and during our senior year I gave him lifts to and from school at a rate of ten bucks a week. He had two sisters, both younger, two parents, seemingly absent, and absolutely no talent for intimacy. I never really knew how he felt about anything; he had no intention of telling me, and I wasn't about to ask. Violence hovered around the edges of his personality, and during his darker moods, which were frequent, took on a greater centrality. A good Catholic kid he was not. "When you're growing up, if you know someone crazy-daring and half-admirable, you don't wonder how the beautiful nut got that way," Pauline Kael wrote in her review of *Mean Streets,* speaking of Robert De Niro's Johnny Boy character. "He seems to spring up full-blown and whirling, and you watch the fireworks and feel crummily cautious in your sanity."

Kurt didn't blow up mailboxes, as Johnny Boy does in *Mean Streets*'s title sequence, but existence bored him, and he was always on the lookout for similar ways to set the plates spinning. His favorite pastime was to steal statues of the Virgin Mary out of backyards. In our Catholic corner of Detroit, such statues were everywhere: walk down any side street and you'd see a dozen in old ladies' flower gardens. The statues were light blue and white, and a few feet high. The Blessed Mother stood with her arms outstretched and her head tilted to one side, looking down upon humanity, or at least Mrs. Assisi's daisies, with utmost tenderness.

After hopping the fence, making his theft, and hopping back over, he would place the statue in the middle of a busy street—Mack, Cadieux, East Warren—and wait in the bushes until one of the swerving cars, responding too slowly, crushed it beneath its wheels. The Virgin Mother may have ascended bodily into heaven (as Pope Benedict XIV declared ex cathedra, Pius XII declared infallibly, and the Second Vatican Council confirmed), but for her ceramic likeness there would be no such pomp; she simply lay atop the concrete in shards. In eighth grade, during a violent spring thunderstorm, Kurt had taken the string from one of our classroom's window shades and tied it around the neck of a statue of Jesus, hanging it out to soak in the downpour and hoping for a lightning strike. Such were his feelings toward Him.

Our eighth grade teacher, a layman, read to us each morning from a book called *God Is for Real, Man!*, which sought to make the teachings of Christ accessible by translating them, disastrously, into teenage argot. The book's further problem was that it was published circa 1969 and the argot of that era was Happy Hippie Horseshit, a tongue more foreign to us, in 1986, than French-Canadian or Basque. The book was replete with cool cats, crazy kittens, soulful sisters, and bell-bottomed hipsters muttering absolute, irreligious drivel, you dig? Kurt could never stop laughing, and it was infectious. He was the sort of kid who could get you in trouble by mere proximity.

"Is that welfare cheese?" Kurt asked a classmate of ours during a lunch hour shortly before eighth grade graduation. His target was a Lebanese Catholic kid, Philip, who in earlier years had suffered from the speech impediment in which a great gob of spit seems always to be stored in the speaker's cheeks, making every *s* sound come out *sh*. Thus, when seeking permission to take his seat, Philip asked: "Can I shit down?" He was an easy mark. "Every day this guy brings a cheese sandwich," Kurt said, looking my way. "I bet it's from one of those five-pound blocks of welfare cheese. What do you think?" Philip's feelings were clearly hurt, so I decided to join in. "Looks like welfare cheese to me," I said. "I've never seen him with peanut butter and jelly, or even bologna. Just cheese sandwiches, and always the same bright orange. Mighty suspicious." Philip, the pantywaist, teared up, and later in the day turned us in.

Kurt and I were sent to see the principal, Sister Caroline, with whom I had a history. Back when I was in second grade, her yappy little dog, which she let roam the school's halls, had taken a dump outside our classroom, and I had been the one to step in it. The school's floors were ceramic tile, and my foot had nearly slid out from under me. Sister Caroline instructed me to clean up the mess, not just from the bottom of my shoe but from the floor as well. At home that night I told my mother what had happened. "That *bitch*," my mother said. "It's what happens to women who don't have kids. Their pets become their babies. They go a little crazy. I'll talk to her." My mother did, which made everything worse. By the time my sister, Beth, hit the fourth grade, Sister Caroline was harassing her about the color of her sweater. While it was green, in keeping with the dress code, it was really more of a *hunter* green, and the dress code clearly stated that sweaters must be *kelly* green, to match the plaid pattern in the girls' skirts. "She doesn't have a kelly green sweater," my mother told Sister Caroline, furious. "Well, maybe Santa can bring her one." Santa didn't bring her one, however, and when Sister Caroline called home with news of my bullying my parents couldn't have cared less. They were still stuck on the dog crap from six years before.

In our class picture from that second grade year, the earliest photo of him I can find, Kurt's face is streaked with tears, and his left cheek gouged and blackened by a length of No. 2 lead. He'd wanted to stand next to me in line on the way to getting our picture taken, as had another classmate. A fight broke out between the two of them, which the other kid ended by punching Kurt in the face, a sharpened Dixon Ticonderoga clutched in his fist. Angry and scarred: a fitting first picture of Kurt Ketchel.

The high school we drove to each morning was two streets down from my house, on the non-Detroit side of yet another boulevard separating city from suburb. It was all-boys and Catholic; next door was an all-girls Catholic high school. It seemed every son and daughter of every white cop, fireman, autoworker, and city employee on Detroit's east side put on khaki pants and dress shirt, or tartan skirt and saddle shoes, and went off to one of these schools each morning. Nearly every boy in my high school had a sister next door, and every girl next door was dating one of her brother's friends. There were more near-incestuous unions in our area than there were among the nobility of eighteenth-century Europe, with the difference that in Detroit we weren't trying to safeguard the royal treasures or maintain the blueness of our blood. The city already had its king.

In truth, there were three schools sitting side by side by side, with a coed Lutheran high school next door to the girls' Catholic school. But Lutheranism didn't have the cachet in our corner of Detroit that Catholicism did. It lacked history, weight. It was viewed as having been born about a millennium and a half too late. What was Wittenburg compared to Rome? Where was their Sistine Chapel? Lutherans, damningly, didn't believe in the transubstantiation, and accused Catholics of a cult of Mary. I remember one anti-Lutheran diatribe, delivered by a priest during religion class, that approached something like brilliance.

Five hundred years after the fact, the wound inflicted by the split in the one, holy, catholic, and apostolic Church remained fresh, and he tried to impress upon us the intellectual shoddiness of Protestantism. "The source of the Reformation?" he asked rhetorically, in front of the thirty boys in our junior religion class. "The difficulty," he said, "Luther experienced when trying to move his bowels. When on the pot—put this in your notes, gentlemen—Luther believed he was sitting on the throne of Satan." Constipation, we were left to conclude, led directly to the schism. "Painful feces=tacking of theses?" I jotted in my notebook, or something to that effect.

None of this made any impression on Kurt, for whom Catholic school was simply a way to avoid attending the Detroit Public Schools. To get to his house I had to drive past our high school, taking Kelly Road to 7 Mile, at the corner of which was Calcaterra's Funeral Home. Though the drive was only three miles, it took me through the territories of several parishes—St. Peter, St. Jude, St. Brendan, Queen of Peace. It was also a trip through several socioeconomic strata, one that, roughly speaking, followed a downward slope from bad to worse. Our area, at the top, was working class; Kurt's, in the valley below, was white trash. In between was a mixed bag.

We lived in a corner house, which is why our cars, parked overnight on the side street, were so often broken into. (My father: "The goddamn car insurance is reason enough to get out of Detroit!") Kitty-corner from us was a Polish woman whose sons were several grades ahead of me and who, as a means of earning money for tuition payments, cleaned homes in Grosse Pointe, an idea my mother would adopt. Across the side street from us was an old Polish couple whose son, a Detroit cop living in the suburbs, spent the nights before his shifts at his parents' house, in case anyone should be checking to see if he was in compliance with the city's residency requirement. In the block behind them was a widower, another man with a son who was a Detroit cop with a suburban address, and who slept over for the same reason.

In the block behind us, one house down, was an old Italian couple whose last name was the city in Italy from which St. Francis came. I used to peer over our backyard fence to see if I could spy them talking to birds or carrying on conversations with squirrels, the way the saints sometimes did in the "Parable of Nature" cartoons we watched at school. My best friends, a pair of twin brothers, lived down the block. Their father was a fireman with Devil's Night stories and their mother, also in need of income, would occasionally team-clean houses in Grosse Pointe with my mother. Across from them lived a Mexican woman, Yvonne, a working mother whose daughters, Sophia and Louisa, my mother had babysat three days a week from the time they were born; it was a way to make yet more under-the-table money while at the same time satisfying her insatiable need for bambinos. The family was from southwest Detroit, and everyone in the enormous clan had gone to Holy Redeemer, the Mexican parish near the Ambassador Bridge. Yvonne paid by the hour and made us botanas, and we attended the *quincenerras* of the girls in the family.

The area's common denominator, Catholicism, was a hedge not just against eternal damnation but against social decay. If you followed the rules, as laid out in two testaments and ten commandments and further codified by two millennia of encyclicals and edicts, chances were not only that you wouldn't go to hell, but that your neighborhood wouldn't, either.

It was an area of strivers, and if the striving didn't improve much at least it helped maintain the status quo. Kurt's neighborhood, ten minutes away, was less stable, and the house I waited outside of each morning was a shack—seven hundred square feet, tops. He was sufficiently Appalachian in appearance that the memory of his unkempt blond head, bobbing down the sidewalk after my sixth or seventh honk, puts me in mind of Walker Evans's sharecroppers in *Let Us Now Praise Famous Men*. His neighborhood, with its deep-set houses and old white couples, was one of those hillbilly sections of big cities that, long after white flight, Black Power, and urban sprawl, somehow manage to retain a rural way about them. The men cut their lawns in overalls, sitting atop a riding mower, and referred to their wives, up on the porch, as "mother." These mothers called cantaloupes "muskmelons" and suggested mustard plasters as a remedy for the common cold.

With its mixture of black and white, poor and professional, and its proximity to Grosse Pointe, the area was perfect for stealing hood ornaments, a favorite 1980s pastime. The two most prized ornaments of the era were the Cadillac crystal and the Dodge ram, and each abounded in the area. Like a mermaid on a ship's prow, the ram crested the hood of the rednecks' pickups, and the crystals came courtesy of two otherwise divergent groups—Grosse Pointers and blacks—both of whom suffered a well-documented fondness for the top of the General Motors line. None of this did me any good, however, as I couldn't, for the life of me, detach the hood ornaments from their goddamn hoods. "You gotta *twist* it," friends would whisper in the dark, tearing their hair at my ineptitude. "Twist and pull, twist and *pull.*" I had no head for crime, which would haunt me in later years.

Only once, during high school, did I succeed in acting destructively. If my mother happened to be cleaning a Grosse Pointe house on the weekend, I'd sometimes accompany her to that enchanted place on the other side of the tracks where the daughters were better-looking, the boys played lacrosse, and everyone had attractive overbites. My mother let it be known, usually upon entering the marble foyer, that she wasn't particularly impressed by these people; that, however big their house may be, they lacked responsibility, fortitude, some basic connection to life as it was lived. Money had distanced them from themselves. If they cleaned their own bathrooms (of which they often had four or five) every day for a year they might begin, slowly, to reestablish the connection. But they paid my mother to perform such services instead.

Her tone was similar to the one suburbanites adopted when discussing Detroiters: they were hopeless. Their irresponsibility seemed, at the upper end of the socioeconomic spectrum, to mirror black irresponsibility at the bottom. As I listened to my mother's stories of Grosse Pointe, a picture began to form in my mind of a place populated by wife beaters, pill poppers, absentee parents, promiscuous daughters, wastrel sons, flagrant adulterers, and midafternoon drunks. Those of us in the middle—the white working classes—were the buffer between these two groups and, it went without saying, better than either.

Because she had gone into business for herself, without being attached to an already established cleaning service, my mother had to rely on her considerable resourcefulness and likeability to lure customers. With prospective clients whose last names hinted at an affiliation with the Church of Rome, she traded on her family connections. "Are you Catholic? Oh, really. Do you go to St. Paul? You might know my uncle then, Father Saulino?" It was the best reference in town, and it gave my mother a leg up on the immigrant Polish cleaning women whom Grosse Pointers have long coveted. "People don't want to work anymore," a Grosse Pointe matron laments to Chafets in *Devil's Night.* "You simply cannot get help. Where *are* all the Polish people?" This was my mother's competition, the Bozenas, Wandas, and Jolantas who advertised their ethnicity and "old world" cleaning techniques in the classified ads in the Grosse Pointe papers: "**Polish** girl looking for house to clean." "**Polish** ladies available. Housecleaning, laundry, ironing." "**Polish** lady looking for house to clean, honest & friendly."

Many of the clients my mother managed to land were old women, widows no longer able to reach the cobwebs in the corners of their French colonials and Cape Cods. Before Christmas one year, my mother came home from a day of dusting and scrubbing infuriated by the holiday bonus some old bat had given her. Most folks kept things simple and slipped her a fifty. But this employer handed her a present.

"I can't show you," she said, shaking with anger, as we pressed her to share with us the spoils of a year's worth of floor-scrubbing. But the wrapping was already off, and eventually she held up the prize: a bag of Brach's Bridge Mix. "Nuts," she said. "That rich bitch gave me a bag of mixed nuts for a Christmas bonus. These cost a dollar forty-nine at the drugstore. Can you believe it?"

When my mother mentioned this insult to the woman the next time she cleaned her house—"It would have been so much better to just not give *anything*," my mother kept saying—she was informed that she should count herself lucky: the woman could easily turn her in to the IRS. (She was forgetting her own complicity in the weekly transaction.) As calmly as I could, I asked my mother where the woman lived. When I had enough information to identify the house, I drove to the nearest 7-Eleven, bought a carton of eggs, and made my way to Grosse Pointe.

The high school Kurt and I attended was run by the Marist Fathers, a missionary teaching order headquartered in Boston that modeled itself more or less after the Jesuits, minus the pursuit of world domination. Tuition, at that time, was thirty-five hundred dollars a year; the cost per pupil, to the Marist Fathers, was forty-five hundred, with the thousand-dollar difference to be made up by fund-raisers and donations. If a boy's father died at any point during his four years, tuition was waived. Widowed mothers were not expected to keep up payments on their sons' schooling.

Though there were obvious differences between the student pools at our high school and the Detroit Public high schools—the Marist Fathers could reject applicants, could kick students out on any pretext whatsoever, and could expect a good deal of parental involvement—the fact that the Detroit Public Schools were spending well in excess of this forty-five-hundred-dollar figure, with woeful results, highlighted the fact that money was not the final arbiter of student performance. "They're just *pissing* my tax money away," my father said of the Detroit Public Schools. Because the tax base in Detroit was constantly shrinking, the burden on actual tax-paying citizens was extraordinary, and ever increasing. Young occasionally had to ask the voters of Detroit to approve tax increases to ward off the city's financial ruin, and, despite resistance from white pockets in the city, the voters agreed. During the city's worst fiscal crisis, in the early 1980s, black voters approved the proposed increase by 80 percent. "Goddamn, I was proud," Young said. Some felt otherwise. "They'll pass *any* increase," my father said. "What do they care? They don't pay taxes. I pay taxes to a city administration that can't police the neighborhoods, that can't turn on the streetlights, that can't plow the snow, and that can't teach kids to read. If anyone ever comes asking me for reparations payments," he said, "tell them I've been making 'em to the City of Detroit for the last twenty years."

Though the priests paid the tuition of a boy whose father had died, there was no provision for students who had two parents that were living but apparently out of the picture. As such, Kurt was forced to pay his own way, or at least some part of it. That he was shouldering a load, at seventeen, greater than any of the rest of us was certain. He thus regarded the rest of the world, composed of lesser mortals, as at least a little lazy. His opinions about blacks were par for the white trash course.

He worked, nights and weekends, at Starvin' Steve's pizza, and so, in his sleep-deprived way, never had his homework quite done, or his shirt tucked in, or his hair properly cut. His homework papers, which needed to be typed, were handwritten, half in pencil and half in pen, and hurriedly torn from a spiral notebook, with no attempt to tidy the frayed edges. His explanations were sarcastic and slurred, and spoken to the floor. "Are you being a smart-ass?" he'd be asked by a tough lay teacher. "Better than being a dumb-ass," he'd mumble back, or something to that effect.

Kurt sat in the seat behind me in "Love, Sex, and Marriage," our junior-year religion class. ("Shouldn't it be 'Love, Marriage, and *then* Sex'?" I once asked, just to be a smart-ass.) An essay question on one test asked us, ridiculously, to describe the baby-making process from conception to birth. Several minutes into the period I felt a tap on my shoulder and turned around to see Kurt laughing to himself. He spun his paper toward me so that I could see his beginnings of a response to this question. In dark blue ink he had written, complete with comma, "Upon insertion,". He spun the paper back around, still laughing; not another word, he told me later, was added to this answer. I returned to my response, trying to remember if *fallopian* had two *l*'s and one *p* or two *p*'s and one *l*, knowing full well that he'd written a response—still the greatest prepositional phrase I've ever read—that was simply unimprovable.

We took Advanced Placement courses in English, physics, history, and calculus our senior year. A disproportionate number of the students in each of these classes came from St. Peter. Though there were at least a dozen east side grade schools that fed into our high school, some of them more well-to-do than ours—St. Joan of Arc, St. Clare de Montefalco—it was the former St. Peter students who thronged the Advanced Placement courses, sometimes making up nearly half the roll. On balance, Polish last names outnumbered Italian.

The only black kid in any of these courses took calculus, and he sat in the desk behind me. He was quiet and reserved, but somewhat famous for his father, who showed up to after-school events in flowing robes and a curved walking stick as tall as he was; it looked like a prop from the set of a Cecil B. De Mille production and made him strongly resemble a black Moses. His son had come from St. Juliana, one of the black inner-city grade schools, along with St. Louis the King and Our Lady Queen of Heaven, that sent students to our high school. These would be among the first Catholic schools of which I was aware to close, a process of door-shutting that would spiral out from the city center at unprecedented pace.

Along with two friends, I'd scored near the top on a state mathematics test and was frequently able to solve equations that stumped Moses's son behind me. "How the hell'd you know that?" he'd ask, smiling. These were those rarely discussed moments when the defenses come down and one tips one's hat, however begrudgingly, to the innate talent, not just of another person, but of an entire race. (I myself experienced it, with fair frequency, on the basketball courts at Heilmann.) I liked him for his smile, which managed to suggest both pleasure and a still deeper pleasure kept in check—a disciplined happiness.

I got on well with the black kids, one incident aside. During my sophomore year, as a miler on the track team, I was warming up on the infield grass for a dual meet against Bishop Gallagher when I saw my father in his plaid flannel shirt walk up into the stands. He was, without fail, at every gymnastics meet, tap recital, baseball game, and track meet of mine and my sister's. I knew that he had had to leave work early to make it on time—the dual meets were immediately after school—so I jogged over to the stands to let him know his support was appreciated. My mother was next to him.

"Ain't they at every one of these things?" one of the black sprinters, a senior, said when I returned to the infield. He was on his back, stretching. "So?" I said. "So, you're a daddy's boy." I knew, after sixteen years in Detroit, what both black compliments and black put-downs were worth, and was willing to let it go. But he kept on—which, as *my* daddy's boy, I should have just blocked out. Any son of my father's worth his salt would have known that to do otherwise was stupid. But sometimes I was stupid—I got a lot of taps to the side of the head ("*Think!*") growing up—and so, after yet another "daddy's boy," I decided to speak up. "Yeah, well, at least I know who mine is," I said. A few seconds later, as I hoped they would, fists started to fly.

He was surprisingly untough. "Moolies never fight fair," Sal often said. "It's either five on one, or one on one with a gun." He expressed concern when he heard stories of white kids fighting one another. "Save it for the smokes," he'd counsel. The fists that flew missed their mark, so we moved in close and I took the sprinter down in a headlock. We were separated, immediately, by our teammates, who reminded us that we had a meet to run. Such incidents did nothing to alter my opinions about black people. He wasn't a black jerk; he was just a jerk, albeit in a black way.

Though he never talked about it and I never asked, I suspected that

Kurt got into his fair share of fights with black kids over in that white trash enclave, and that he did far more than his fair share of the losing. He'd often sit down in my car's passenger seat on Monday morning sporting fresh cuts and bruises, along with a look that said: Don't ask.

Every morning, hanging from the ceiling of our school's main hallway, there were four words—one for the freshman, sophomore, junior, and senior classes—that we were to write in our notebooks, along with definition, and be ready to be tested on when the time came. These "Words of the Day" were designed to enlarge our working vocabularies, to complement if not altogether supplant the *shits, fucks, likes,* and *you knows* that constituted the core of our spoken language. One hundred and eighty words per year, seven hundred and twenty for our high school careers: if we remembered a tenth of them, we might be able to converse as Catholic schoolboys should.

"You can run," I remember yelling to a friend I was chasing down the hallway, "but you can't abscond." *Abscond:* to depart secretly and hide. In religion class, I was asked by a priest what it meant to do good works without thinking of eternal reward. "It means that we should do the right thing because it's the right thing to do," I said, "not because we have any ulterior motivation." *Ulterior:* the priest liked that. I developed a reputation, as other boys did in the showers, for the size of my vocabulary.

At the beginning of one of our Advanced Placement English classes senior year I was asked by the teacher, Mr. Conrad Vachon, to define some three dozen words that were written on the board behind him. These were not Words of the Day—he'd taken them out of one of the books we were reading, *Lucky Jim* or *The Immoralist* or *Dubliners.* I got about three-quarters of the words correct, nervous not to have done better, and terribly relieved when I came to a word like *tawny,* which I knew without hesitation. *Tawny:* like girls' thighs in summertime, I remember thinking.

"That's good, Mr. Clemens," Mr. Vachon said when I'd finished, making *good* sound vaguely insulting, like most of what he said. I took no offense. He was one of those charismatic teachers whom eager students long to be insulted by, someone whose wit and sarcasm you want to be deemed worthy of receiving. His voice—and there wasn't a boy in school without a Mr. Vachon impression—was the Wicked Witch of the West crossed with William F. Buckley. He was one of our high school's founding teachers, present at the school's inception in the 1950s, and was said to have studied under Robert Frost at Williams. He was silver-haired, a bachelor in the confirmed sense, and on a couple of occasions showed up to class with a bandaged forehead, leading to much speculation about drinking binges and bar fights. He drove a sports car and coached the track and cross-country teams, of which I was a member. He induced in us distance runners a sort of giddiness. Before his practices, when we all lined up at the urinals to take a last leak before a ten-mile training run, we often repeated aloud our hard-and-fast rule, particularly to the new freshmen runners: two taps. You get two taps, frosh. Any more than that and you cross the line into self-abuse—a mortal sin. *Onanism:* Do you know what that means, frosh? You'd better. It'll be a Word of the Day soon.

In a Catholic high school where even the lay teachers tended to be devout, Mr. Vachon seemed to have absolutely no religious sense at all. He was my first introduction to the religion of art and seemed to relish the famous ending of Hemingway's "A Clean, Well-Lighted Place," with its great atheistic negations: "Our nada who art in nada, nada be thy name. . . . Hail nothing full of nothing, nothing is with thee." He impressed upon us, in light of Jake Barnes's unfortunate war wound, the irony of the title *The Sun Also Rises*. "The sun *also* rises," he said, again and again. "The sun—*also*—rises." He once made us write an opening chapter of a novel in Hemingway style, trying to make us recognize the virtues of simplicity—monosyllabic words, active voice, prepositional phrases, compound as opposed to complex sentences. His Bible was

Strunk and White's *Elements of Style*, and if he caught us walking down the hallway without the book in our back pockets we received a demerit in his course.

"Now a student in the previous class," Mr. Vachon said, motioning to the terms on the chalkboard behind him, "was only able to define about half those words." The previous class was not an Advanced Placement course, but instead a regular senior English class. Words and their definitions, he wanted us to believe, were the key to success in this life, and would separate us, in adulthood, from both our inferiors and our betters, just as surely as they sorted us by skill level in high school. Words might, he hinted, even help us with the girls next door—girls with whom, during the change of classes, we mingled in the parking lot that separated the schools, a spectacle Mr. Vachon referred to as "the meat market."

In his classroom we sat alphabetically in a square—Kurt was opposite me—and before each session Mr. Vachon made us stand up and recite passages of literature, some of which came from books we'd read and some of which, it seemed, were simply among his favorites. We did the opening lines of *The Canterbury Tales* in Middle English: "Whan that Aprill, with his shoures soote/The droghte of March hath perced to the roote"; we did Macbeth's "Tomorrow and tomorrow and tomorrow" speech; we did all four lines of William Carlos Williams's "The Red Wheelbarrow," a poem that still eludes me; and we ended with Thoreau—"I went to the woods because I wished to live deliberately"—our recitation finishing with "and not, when I came to die, discover that I had not lived." A few minutes of class time a day, day in and day out, were lost to these recitations, not a word of which I've forgotten.

"Isn't this brainwashing?" a progressive kid in the seat next to me, Don Cleary, asked after we'd stood up, recited the prescribed passages, and sat back down for the hundredth time. He'd go to college at a sandaled school in the Pacific Northwest that didn't give grades.

"Yes," Mr. Vachon said.

I began, through books, to grow away from what I saw as the anti-intellectualism of my blue-collar surroundings. I understood that, for me, Catholicism faced far stiffer competition than Lutheranism, that literature could fill the basic human need for the not-so-basic, for something transcendent to give shape to ordinary existence. In addition to what we recited before class, I memorized passages from Fitzgerald, from Joyce, from Flannery O'Connor. My mother would ask me what I wanted for dinner, and I'd think: "If personality is an unbroken series of successful gestures, then there was something gorgeous about him." My father would ask me if I'd remembered to fill up the car, and I'd say to myself: "Yes, the newspapers were right: snow was general all over Ireland." Coleman Young would come on TV, and I'd think: "She would of been a good woman, if it had been somebody there to shoot her every minute of her life."

Memorizing passages of literature was nothing new to the kids who'd come out of St. Peter, where part of our grade school training had been yearly poem contests. Such recitations began in the first grade, back when Shel Silverstein was a big favorite. By third grade, I'd progressed to "Casey at the Bat." "Begin," my mother would say when we practiced at home. "Theoutlookwasn'tbrilliantfortheMud-villeninethatday." "Slow *down*, Paul," Sister Helen would say, just as my mother had, when we practiced during class time. "*Enunciate.*" "The . . . outlook . . . wasn't . . . brilliant." Every kid got the same advice, because every kid did the same thing: tried to rush through his poem, slurring his words so as to finish before he'd forgotten it. Speaking a line unclearly was preferable to forgetting it entirely.

Kurt was terrible at these contests, slurring words despite repeated warnings, fidgeting with his sleeves, and staring at the floor. His face was usually smudged. The kids who excelled had a certain spit and polish, along with mothers who took the contests seriously, choreographing hand gestures and suggesting places for emphasis. "And look *up*," they'd say. "Acknowledge your audience." The friend who won in the third grade was the son of a cop and a ludicrously competent mother, and had done something from Kipling.

By eighth grade the winner was a brilliant Italian girl whose parents spoke no English and on whom I had long harbored a mild crush. While the rest of us were still reciting poems with meter and rhyme, she'd progressed to Shakespeare, taking on the role of Brutus—she'd come to bury Caesar, not to praise him. As I sat on a folding chair in our gymnasium on a darkening evening, three thrilling hours after I'd last seen her at final bell, cookies and parents and punch now surrounding us and permission having been granted her to wear a small amount of makeup, as it was a special, scholastic occasion, I fell in love with literature.

In AP History class Kurt sat in the seat behind me, where he continued to display the disdainful, head-on-the-desk superiority of the smart-ass. When he awoke, it was typically to tap me on the shoulder and whisper some bullshit before falling back asleep.

It was in this history class, the spring of senior year, that the only collective venting of working-class white frustrations that I can recall took place. It was near the end of the semester, shortly before we were to take the AP test itself, and our teacher, Mr. Pyle, had taught us all he could. It was now up to us to impress the graders in Princeton, New Jersey, and to secure the 4s and 5s (the test being graded on a 1 to 5 scale) that would earn us college credit. For a week or more, then, AP History had been turned into a current events class, with each student assigned a topic on which to lead a discussion.

My topic—and I'll never forget it, for the word itself remains so little employed—was "how to coexist harmoniously in a 'polyglot' society such as America." The class itself wasn't particularly polyglot, composed almost entirely of clever, quick-tempered, tremendously sarcastic white kids from the city. And it was these sons of firefighter, police officer, and bus driver fathers, the beloved boys of house-cleaning and hair-dressing mothers, whom I was asked to lead through this thick forest.

It didn't work; there were too many trees, and we quickly lost our coordinates. America may have been polyglot, but we were just happy, at long last, to have a platform from which to air our grievances—grievances, by and large, that we expressed in speeches plagiarized from our fathers. Our teacher tried, in desperation, to steer us back on track by mentioning his niece, who was about to marry a black man, but we wouldn't bite. This was the concern of an earlier generation, of Spencer Tracy and Sidney Poitier. We were uninterested in the implications of such a relationship. A black man with a white woman? Go figure.

Discussion quickly turned to Mayor Young—the boss, at several removes, of most of our fathers—and deteriorated from there, bouncing free-associatively from one pet peeve to the next, settling eventually on the affirmative action system the city had set up under Young that so affected our fathers. And then, to cut the specter of Coleman Young down to size, someone mentioned the Chrysler Land Deal.

The sons of a prominent Mafia family parked their jet black Mustang GTs side by side in our school parking lot each morning. Residents of Mafia Meadows, their family had reportedly benefited, in the late 1980s, from what Coleman Young describes in his autobiography, with uncharacteristic understatement, as "an unfortunate overpayment of around $25 million, for which I must take a measure of responsibility." The City of Detroit had purchased some warehouses from the family in order to clear the way for the building of the enormous Chrysler assembly plant on Jefferson Avenue, where Jeep Cherokees would be built. The city agreed to pay for the warehouses and the industrial equipment within whatever price an independent appraiser determined was fair. When the appraiser cited the value at forty million dollars, his "independence" came into question; when the press learned who owned the warehouses, many, including Coleman Young, came to believe that the whole thing "had been a Mafia production." This went over well in Sal's barbershop, where the Chrysler Land Deal was a frequent topic of conversation—Italians, taking Coleman Young for millions.

Our teacher tried to rein us back in, but it was no use. From Coleman Young and his affirmative action policies we were already half a league onward, into the valley of the University of Michigan's admissions policies. The previous October, at the beginning of senior year, I'd received a warm, congratulatory letter, admitting me to the university. Very shortly thereafter, the admissions office in Ann Arbor sent another letter ("Congratulations!") admitting me to the school's honors program—reserved, the letter said, for the top 10 percent of the entering freshman class. Finally, three months after my admittance, I was sent a letter informing me that I had been nominated for a Regents-Alumni scholarship, for being one of "the top graduates of high schools throughout the state of Michigan."

I'd also received a call one evening from a young woman who was phoning, she said, on behalf of the University of Michigan. It was her pleasure to inform me that the admissions office had reviewed my transcript and board scores and had seen fit to award me a one-thousand-dollar scholarship to attend the university the following fall. Like all hippie girls, she spoke in painstakingly cultivated northern California tones, though she was obviously from Bloomfield Hills.

The offer fell far short of the scholarship package that a kid a year ahead of me was said to have received. His award from the previous fall, though he was possessed of far lesser academic credentials, had been a full scholarship to the University of Michigan, or so said the hallway whispers. I told the hippie girl on the phone thank you, but I'd likely be pursuing my higher education elsewhere.

About the abilities of this student—his father was white; his mother wasn't—many of us had firsthand knowledge. During his senior year, he had been enrolled in a course that we were taking as juniors, and though chronologically a year ahead, he was academically in arrears. But this kid, whose academic clock we could clean—he got a full ride. That was the story, and though this was a dozen years before a Supreme Court case made public the University of Michigan's "point system" admissions policy, we all knew the score, even if we didn't yet know the specifics of how that score was kept.

This discussion, through which Kurt had either slept or kept his thoughts to himself, was more than our teacher had bargained for. "I didn't realize how aware you all were of these things," he said.

How could we not be aware? This was Detroit, where such discussions were mother's milk. During the fall of my junior year—making this the 1989 mayoral campaign, Young's fifth and final victory—I'd answered a phone call from a person I took to be a solicitor. When I handed the phone to my father, however, he did not dismiss the caller with his usual, "Thank you, not interested." Instead he stayed on the line, and so I hung around the kitchen, curious as to whose call at dinnertime my father was willing to take. When I heard him give three answers in quick succession—"White," "Independent," "Whoever's running against Coleman Young"—I realized he was talking to a pollster from the incumbent's campaign headquarters. The "whoever" who would receive my father's vote this time around was Tom Barrow, Joe Louis's grandson. The 1989 election was the second go-around between Young and Barrow, in fact, Young having defeated Barrow handily in the 1985 race. Like his grandfather with Schmeling, Barrow hoped for better luck in the rematch.

My father knew that his was nothing more than a protest vote, to be given to any candidate meeting his rather relaxed criteria for holding the office of mayor. So too did the caller, who asked, in her final question: "Is there any way you'd vote for Coleman Young?" To which my father replied: "Only if he were running against Idi Amin," and hung up.

Young beat Barrow again, of course. "On election day," as Chafets puts it in *Devil's Night*, "the voters of America's African-American capital returned their verdict, and it wasn't even close . . . Detroit, the city with the country's highest rate of teenage murder, unemployment and depopulation, twelve thousand abandoned homes, a Third World infant mortality rate and an epidemic drug problem, had spoken: Four More Years."

Even our corner of Detroit was beginning to undergo what the middle-aged ladies, referring to our area's menopause as opposed to their own, always called "the change." My mother witnessed the first neighborhood mugging, which happened in front of our house. "It's terrible to say," my mother said, "but I wouldn't have watched him out the window if he hadn't been black. And then, sure enough, he jumped that lady." The local news showed up, asking for an interview, and the cops on the block urged my mother to avoid this exposure at all costs. "That kid's friends will come back here," they warned, "looking for *you*." It was something we had no trouble believing. The back bumper of every other car in the city bore a sticker for the most popular radio station in Detroit, WJLB. Beneath the station's logo—a flexed black bicep—was its motto: "Detroit's *Strongest* Songs." There was little doubt about the terms of the debate in this city, or who was setting them.

By the fall of 1990, Detroit was national news. "We're talking about Detroit," Diane Sawyer says, introducing a *Prime Time Live* piece that aired the first semester of my senior year, "once a symbol of U.S. competitive vitality, and some say still a symbol, a symbol of the future— the first urban domino to fall. And standing at the center of it all, a controversial mayor, facing charges that a lot of the blame lies at his feet."

The words "Detroit's Agony" scroll across the screen. Then, over an oft-repeated scene of abandoned homes and burnt-out city blocks, rises the voice of reporter Judd Rose. "This," he says, "is a racist story." That is the opinion of Mayor Coleman Young, who believes that the following report is an attack on him and on the city he governs—and so is, by extension, antiblack.

"Every city has arson fires," Rose says during a nighttime scene, houses burning behind him, "but only here is there one angry night like Devil's Night." Other cities have "trick-or-treating and window-soaping," while "Detroit is engulfed in an orgy of arson. It's a holiday tradition, a mean-spirited Mardi Gras."

Rose is in Young's office. "Are you proud of Detroit?" he asks the mayor. "Certainly I'm proud of Detroit," Young says. "I wouldn't be here if I wasn't." Beneath his Coke-bottle bifocals, Young is jowly and mustachioed—editorial cartoonists tended to emphasize the walrus resemblance—and below his double chin his tie is enormously knotted. His mayoral desk is large enough to create a chasm between him and Rose.

"Is it a safe place to live, a good place to live, a good place to raise a family?" Rose asks. Young answers halfheartedly in the affirmative— "It's as safe as any other"—and then gets visibly angry. "So don't *bring* me that crap about Detroit's . . ." He doesn't finish the thought, but motions with his hand as if to push that negative crap away. "We're no different," he says. "We have the same problems as any city in America."

Rose stands in front of an empty lot, the skyline of Detroit in the distance behind him. The building that dominates the shot is the Renaissance Center, the downtown skyscraper that was to signal the city's rebirth when ground was broken on it in 1973. A couple blocks from our house, at the 8 Mile and Kelly border crossing, was a sign that said: WELCOME TO DETROIT, RENAISSANCE CITY. FOUNDED 1701. Rose grants that other cities have even *worse* problems than Detroit. "America's cities are on a dark and dangerous road," Rose admits. "But you come here and you get the feeling that this, this is what the end of the road looks like."

Back to the mayoral office. "In my time in Detroit," Rose says to Young, "I have driven past mile after mile of decayed, rotting neighborhoods that look like war zones."

"Those were there when I became mayor," Young says.

"There are also people that say that any white mayor who had developed the downtown area and let the neighborhoods collapse would have been kicked out of office a long time ago."

"Well, that's [bleep]. The neighborhoods collapsed," Young says, pointing his finger at Rose, "because half the goddamn population left!"

Newspaper headlines of Young administration scandals float across the screen, including information about William Hart, Young's chief of police, who was then being investigated for stealing police funds.

"Look, man," Young says, "I have been hounded for ten goddamn years with allegations, rumors, and not one concrete charge. Now, after ten years, you get tired of that [bleep]."

"But your police chief?" Rose pleads.

"I wouldn't give a [bleep] who it is!"

"A federal grand jury," Rose's voice-over says, "is investigating charges that Young had a secret business that sold Kruggerands, the gold coins that symbolized South African apartheid." On screen is a shot of Young standing behind Nelson Mandela at a speech and applauding. "We tried to bring it up," Rose's voice-over concludes, "but the mayor cut us short."

Young, glasses off, leans across the mayoral desk. "You came in here to do a chop job, obviously."

"No, I didn't."

"Oh, [bleep]. Okay, I'm through now." Young waves the interview off.

Immediately after Young concluded the interview—not before closing with a final "Who the [bleep] do you think you are?"—I began to write the article that would appear in our school paper. "Well, *Prime Time Live* has spoken," I began. "Mayor Coleman A. Young has spoken (sworn?). Every person who lives in Detroit, around Detroit, has heard of Detroit, or can spell Detroit has spoken. Now I will." I first listed my credentials—"I was born in Detroit and have lived within the city all of my life"—and then, over the next six paragraphs, proceeded to say nothing whatsoever. In the last paragraph, I took Young to task for dismissing Detroit's troubles by saying that all big cities have these problems. "If the mayor doesn't do something to turn things around," I wrote, "he won't have to worry about Detroit being a big city for much longer."

What would Coleman Young have thought? I entertained the

happy notion—believing, with Kurt, that it was better to be a smart-ass—that he would have said what he'd said to Rose on national television that night:

Who the *fuck* do you think you are?

By the spring of senior year our thoughts were actually less about high school than about college, less about Detroit than about East Lansing and Ann Arbor. Of all of us, Kurt talked about college the least. If he had plans, no one knew what they were.

In my case, applying to the University of Michigan had been perfunctory, part of what any moderately bright kid from metropolitan Detroit did by default. Infinitely more important, to my mind, was my parents' permission to apply to one or two "prestigious" schools. I'd set my sights a couple hundred miles past Ann Arbor, to the big city to our south and west. I saw its name on highway signs along the westbound side of the Ford Freeway, past downtown, on the way out to Metropolitan Airport: ANN ARBOR 28. CHICAGO 262.

During my junior year of high school I had taken the PSAT and placed in a smart-kid percentile. The predictable result was that my family's mailbox was stuffed, every day for months on end, with application packets from many of the best colleges and universities in the country. Brown, Duke, Chicago, Northwestern, Bowdoin: all wrote to congratulate me on the promise I seemed to hold as a student and scholar, and to wish me the best as I embarked upon the important process of choosing a college. The sense of possibility those packets represented, particularly to a kid who'd never, for any length of time, left his corner of Detroit—"Greetings from beneath the pines of Maine!" the letter from Bowdoin began—was considerable.

The first piece of mail that I received from the University of Chicago, in the spring of my junior year, contains some scribbles at the bottom in my mother's handwriting. She'd followed up this letter with a phone call, clearly trying to get the lay of the economic land. In her cursive: "Tuition, 14,500. Rm & Bd, 5400. College Honors Scholarship

(40) btw half & full tuition. Top 5% of class, etc. Separate form over & above application." My mother went ahead and made an appointment for me with an admissions counselor at Chicago.

The summer before my senior year, then, I drove along I-94 through Ann Arbor, Jackson, Battle Creek, Kalamazoo, and Gary, until, four hours later, accompanied by my father, we arrived on Chicago's South Side. Coming from Detroit's east side, Chicago's South Side seemed familiar; its deterioration had history, depth. As with my home-town, it was a place where there was something serious at stake; its seediness said as much, and said, too, that much had been lost. I imme-diately longed to call Hyde Park home. "Chicago isn't the only place," my father said. "There are other schools." He sounded like a concerned father lecturing his love-struck daughter about an unsuitable boy-friend.

"If you want to go to college," my father had told me a few years before, as we were driving up Gratiot Avenue toward Custom Speed, "you're going to have to get a scholarship. Otherwise, community col-lege is the best I can do for you." He was already contemplating a return to school, one that would cause him to quit work and would preclude his continuing to make tuition payments for me.

I took this in stride, barely having started high school by this point. And though it was a college prep high school I'd begun to attend, nei-ther of my parents had graduated from college—my mother hadn't even attended—and the word itself held little magic for me. Neither did it matter a whit what qualifier went before it: state, private, Ivy League, community. My father took an occasional class at Wayne County Com-munity College while I was growing up—usually something on elec-tronics, at the campus by City Airport—and I saw no problem with following in his footsteps.

My attending a community college was brought up in the context of a larger conversation we were having about work—about its being a bitch, and a bear, and something for which one must be sure to be fairly compensated, because it'll take up most of your life, not just the work but the worrying about it. "Don't take anything less than thirty," my father said, citing a figure—I took him to mean thirty thousand—that struck me as outlandish. It was about what our house was worth. "It's just not possible to live on less," he said. I didn't know if he was suggesting that I get a good-paying job straight after high school or if, instead, I should be keeping that figure in mind for several years down the road, after I'd finished with the rest of my schooling.

I had a fear that it was the first. My father had a tendency, when discouraged, to throw the baby out with the bathwater—or, in his case, to throw the car out with the carburetor. There were times in the garage when, if he couldn't fix whatever part it was he was working on, he'd curse the whole goddamn machine, declaring it a shit-heap unworthy of his trouble. Perhaps he was thinking along the same lines: If I can't send the kid to a good school, well, then the hell with it.

Two miles north of Custom Speed on Gratiot was the epicenter, on Friday and Saturday nights, of adolescent cruising on the east side. It was between 10 Mile and 12 Mile that the Macomb County kids hung out windows, blasted stereos, and tried and failed to get laid. Shop students with wispy mustaches, bad complexions, and bitchin' Camaros, they were suburbanites with fewer prospects than I had, kids whose futures were circumscribed in a way not unlike that of my father's. Twenty-five years before, my father had been one of these kids, though his strip of Gratiot had been farther south, in the heart of the city. Detroit's car culture had since moved to Macomb County, and it was Gratiot Avenue, more than any other thoroughfare, that had conveyed that culture northward.

It was a culture that made more sense in the city, where life came in three dimensions and one's days cast a shadow. The car culture in Macomb County felt flat—flimsily suburban. When my father and I drove out to car shows at 16 Mile Road, the sight of the forty-something couples huffing and puffing in their "Heartbeat of America" jackets made me homesick for the city. The same Chevy logo that had looked natural next to the 396 decals on my father's Nova in the garage at 6 Mile and Gratiot looked just like any other corporate emblem when worn on the back of satin jackets by middle-aged suburbanites.

My father had been offered a job fixing broken-down Detroit city buses stored in a lot in a warehouse district by City Airport, in a tableau that resembled the abandoned airplane sites that dot the desert landscape. "What do I know about buses?" "More than anyone else," my mother said, confident in her husband's overwhelming mechanical competence. He never gave himself enough credit, to her way of thinking. His modesty, coupled with his obvious expertise, produced an oddly immodest effect—a sort of self-deprecating cockiness. When, bent over the hood of someone's stalled car, he launched into a bout of earnestly bumbling modesty—boy, it beat the hell out of him what the problem was here; honestly, he wouldn't want to have to say—you wanted to tell him to cut the shit.

He declined the bus repair offer and continued to work at a shop in the suburbs, making the opposite commute of most metro Detroiters by driving out to Macomb County each morning and back south of 8 Mile each evening. The shop was started by a friend of his who had hired my father and a handful of other guys who'd been nuts about cars from the time they were kids and in no need of a college education to teach them what was what. As the business expanded, however, the owner had hired one or two younger guys with engineering degrees from the General Motors Institute in Flint. "They don't know their posterior protrusions from an earthly depression," my father said of these credentialed young fellows.

And yet, while mocking their college educations, he was making plans to return to college to study computers, in hopes of securing work a little more white collar. He had those thirty-year-old credits from the Detroit Institute of Technology, along with his occasional electronics course work from Wayne County Community College. Thirteen years of Catholic school tuition payments would be the extent of his outlay for my education; such an investment should make of me a scholarship boy, after which he would be free—freer, at any rate—to complete the education he should have finished long ago.

For the time being, however, we were still blue collar, and I continued to help him set up his table each January at the State Fair Swap Meet at the Michigan State Fairgrounds, between 7 and 8 Mile at Woodward Avenue. While the strobe lights drew auto executives, television crews, and the local black-tie crowd down to Cobo Hall for the yearly unveiling of sparkling new models at the Auto Show—another January ritual in automotive Detroit—my father and I carted cylinder heads and rocker arms, camshafts and lifters out of our garage, loaded them in the back of the truck, and then carried them into one of the Fairgrounds' enormous unheated hangars, our breath so visible before us that it looked as if we were blowing steam off the top of a cup of coffee.

Inside the hangar, manning hundreds of similar tables, were urban men—factory workers, construction workers, tool-belted climbers of utility poles—who handled hot drinks in cold weather with a reverence that others reserved for the Eucharistic wine, men whose ability to tolerate scalding hot beverages seemed to be matched only by their ability, while standing out of doors in frigid weather, to tolerate full bladders. I was impressed by the wads of bills these men had in their pockets, not yet understanding that those rolls of tens and twenties bespoke nothing but their possessor's pennilessness.

"Go help your dad," my mother often said when my father had been at work too long on whatever family car was giving him trouble. "It's Sunday, and he's been out in the garage since Mass. It's supposed to be his day off." I'd trudge out the side door, and as I neared the garage I'd hear the sounds of a Tigers game on WJR, the local superstation. I would stand by silently and watch my father stare for a while at whatever was broken, tilting his head this way and that to get a read on it. "Mom told me to come out," I'd explain, to break the ice. He'd nod and ask me to hand him something.

It was ridiculous, of course, to think that I could help my father; what my mother meant was that I should keep him company and perhaps learn something in the process. What I learned early on was that, no matter what might be broken, it was often just a matter of swearing at it right. "God*damnit*," he'd say, as he lost his grip and his hand slipped off a socket wrench. "Come on, you *bitch*," he'd say, trying to break loose a lug nut from a rusty rim. Or, during a delicate bit of surgery, his head under the hood: "Oh, you *bastard*—Paul, hand me those pliers, will ya?—aw, this piece of shit. Hold that light up, will ya? Because I've just . . . about . . . got—oh, *hell*. I almost had it there. If I could have just hooked that *mother* of a valve spring—" We'd sigh, in unison, and take a step back for perspective, hands on hips. "Oh, well," he'd say. The Tigers game was long over by this point; the day had come and gone. "I give up for the night. This goddamn thing. Go inside, it's all right. Tell Mom I'll be in in a sec." But he never did give up, and I never went back inside, and before going to bed whatever had needed to be fixed was fixed; the sun would not have risen otherwise. Though I never did much of anything on such occasions aside from holding the droplight for him as he peered under the hood, I always finished exhausted. "Did he help?" my mom would ask when we got back inside, turning on the oven to reheat his dinner. "He sure did," my dad would say. I'd shrug.

Cars, I sometimes thought, would kill him—not in a crash, but from the insistent, wearying demands of their upkeep. There was always something wrong with one of the "By Owner" wagons or hatchbacks he'd seen sitting in a vacant lot on 8 Mile and had bought for my mother as a grocery-getter. From years of racing he knew how to make a car perform; but he also knew how to make a car *last*, how to minimize wear and tear, and he tried to impart this knowledge to his family. If you just listened to him, everything would be fine.

At work he tested racing engines on a dynamometer, stressing them to check water temp, fuel temp, water flow, and oil flow while also measuring more important things like torque, on the basis of which horsepower could be calculated. Like a British Invasion guitarist with a famously loud amp, my father was slowly going deaf from running engines on the dyno. After the races, where he sometimes worked in the pit crew, he'd tear the engines down and check them over. The road-racing team that he built engines for, sponsored by General Motors, had two drivers; his favorite was the guy who got the most out of the car while doing the engine the least damage.

My mother was not among his favorite drivers. She never had a middle gear, figuratively or literally. "We have plenty of time," she'd say on Sunday mornings before Mass. And then, five seconds later: "We'd better get going—we're going to be late!" Life was a constant hurry-up, and she hated to wait. She accelerated toward red lights—stop signs, too. She revved the engine and gunned it from standing starts. Worst of all, in cars with manual transmissions, she "rode the clutch," meaning that she didn't fully remove her left foot from the pedal after shifting gears. There was, my father insisted, no better way to burn those things out. I received this warning when I began to drive, along with its unspoken, half-pleading subtext: If you ride the clutch you'll burn out the clutch; then I'll have to *replace* the clutch, either after work or on the weekend—so could you please, for the love of Christ, when you're done shifting, just remove your foot from the goddamn clutch? In the old days, my father said, there was an Indy car driver who, if he didn't like the engine he'd been provided, would "clutch it"—that is, depress the clutch at full throttle, blowing the engine. My mother's sin was venial rather than mortal, but in the same vein.

His hot rods were a vacation from such headaches. He worked on them because he enjoyed working on them, in the way that making a dessert can still please a woman who otherwise resents the demands of cooking. The State Fair swap meet, populated by men similarly dispositioned—cars were frequently both their work and their hobby—was the meeting of what seemed to me, at ten and twelve and fourteen and sixteen, a secret society, one dedicated to the lofty goals of increased horsepower and better low-end torque. The swap meet lasted two days—we'd put a tarp on our table overnight—but the second day was always a disappointment, with our best stuff already sold and other people's picked over, too. Day two was dominated by the creeping thought of how much we *hadn't* sold and would have to cart back home. "Well, how'd you do?" my mother would ask when we got back. "Hmm? Oh, a few hundred," he'd say. "Did you at least get rid of some stuff?" "Some," he'd say, declining to mention the things he'd picked up over those two days, keeping the number of parts in his possession, like the amount of matter in the universe, a constant. Whatever pieces my father might have sold at swap meets over the years, the floor of the garage never got any less crowded, and the wooden rafters up above continued to bow beneath the weight of my father's automotive ambitions.

For me, I knew, he had academic ambitions. "I'll get a scholarship, Pop," I promised.

Why I wanted to go to the University of Chicago so badly I wasn't sure; this was before I'd come to associate the school with the Great Books, and with a Jewish-American intellectual tradition I'd come to admire. I think I liked the directness of the name: Chicago. Where do you go to school? Chicago. You could say you went to school at Michigan, but Michigan was a state, with an upper and lower peninsula, and it didn't seem to me that you could be schooled by something as large as a Midwestern state. A city, on the other hand, could serve as a classroom, as London had for Boswell. By attending Chicago, I was looking to trade up.

It was a warm summer day when my father and I took a walking tour of the Chicago campus, and the place was sparsely populated, except for our tour group of parents and their sons and daughters—my prospective classmates. "You'll probably change your major a couple of times," our guide said, in response to a question about the university's general education requirements. She herself had switched from philosophy to chemistry, or vice versa, after taking an introductory course in the new subject and falling for it. "Professors consider it a failure if they can't get you to change your major at least a few times," she said. While others in our group smiled at this testament to our guide's intellectual curiosity, I could see my father making mental calculations about the lost credit hours, the cost per credit hour—Christ Almighty.

Aside from campus landmarks and academic concerns, our guide also spoke of opportunities for extracurricular involvement and discussed different ways of volunteering in the surrounding community—which, from the looks of it, needed the help. "Never underestimate the power of liberal guilt," she said. Everyone laughed.

It was the first time I'd heard the term. More guilt? Who needed it? I sure didn't. I still had Catholic guilt in spades. In later years, I'd come to think of liberal guilt as a luxury item—something you needed money to afford, and to feel.

When it came time to meet with the admissions counselor at Chicago I walked into his office alone while my father waited outside. There was a file on the counselor's desk: my PSAT scores, presumably, along with some personal information—name, address, and so on. I was surprised, slightly, to see that he was black, and he was somewhat more surprised that I was white. The address in my file said "Detroit."

About our conversation I remember next to nothing. I recall his being friendly and remarkably free of cant, particularly for someone working in higher education. He looked me in the eye and told it to me straight. "You'll more than likely get in, depending how you do this coming year, of course"—smile—"but I can't say that the odds are too good you'll get a scholarship. You're very bright, but we get a lot of very bright kids. There's financial aid, of course. Most families find a way."

I told him that I could possibly be first or second in my graduating class and asked if there were any scholarships for valedictorians or salutatorians. He laughed at this. Many of the university's students were valedictorians or salutatorians; and did I have any idea how low the ACT scores were of some of the valedictorians of Chicago inner-city high schools? "Fourteens and fifteens," he told me. "We can't give scholarships to kids like that. We can't even accept them. Not even close." I found this refreshing; a white counselor, I suspected, would have engaged in much hand-wringing over "underserved student populations" and whatnot. ("Underserved!" my father would have hollered in the hallway. "Do you have any idea how much tax money I've paid into the Detroit Public School system! I've been serving those bastards for decades!") The counselor told me of Vietnamese students whose parents purchased Laundromats, where members of the extended family worked sixteen-hour days to put the child on whom familial hopes were riding through the prestigious American school. "It can be done," he said.

My acceptance letter arrived the following spring, and my financial aid statement shortly thereafter. At the top of the page are my mother's scribbled notes, condensing the somewhat baffling statement to its basics. "Total, 23,400. Parent, 8605. Paul's assets, 145. Work—summer, 1000. Work—school year, 1800. Student loan (we are eligible), 1800, or max of 2600, lowering our contribution by the diff of 800. School grant, 10050." Though this doesn't quite tally, the picture was clear enough, and plenty bleak: my parental contribution was more than half of my mother's yearly salary. My father's imminent return to school meant that my mother, who'd taken a full-time secretarial job, would be the family's sole source of income for the foreseeable future. There would be precious little money coming in; but the aid package had been based on the previous tax year, when my father was fully employed and, relatively speaking, did rather well.

My personal worth, $145—"Paul's assets"—was, I had heard, more or less the value of any human body, broken down to its constituent elements. Was this how they'd arrived at that figure? "This acceptance letter seems a lot like a rejection letter," I said. "Hey, at least you got in," said my father, who seemed surprised, and not a little proud. He'd since heard that this Chicago was supposed to be a pretty good school.

As we prepared for commencement at the end of senior year, practicing our slow, straight procession and orderly filing into rows, the priests consistently pulled me out of such exercises, along with our valedictorian and Student Council president, who would be seated onstage during commencement itself and thus not marching in with the rest of the graduating class. I thought, at first, that this was to spare me the pain of walking—I'd developed a stress fracture in my left hip during the spring track season—but it soon became evident that the priests had other designs.

Our valedictorian was a grade school friend, and though part of our common training had been those yearly poem contests, he was terrified of public speaking and so was asked by the priests to deliver the shorter address at commencement, typically reserved for the class salutatorian. I was asked to deliver the longer, valedictory address. "If you speak half as well as you write," our principal, Father Louis, said to me in his office, "you should be fine."

I suspected something was up but didn't know for certain until after commencement, when I opened the report card I'd been handed along with my going-away gifts. Below my final semester's marks was my cumulative class rank: 3. "Congratulations! Salutatorian, Class of 1991!" it said at the bottom of the report card.

Bullshit. I'd known from the beginning whose place I was taking on stage, who it was who should have had his photo, as salutatorian, in the May 1991 issue of the *Michigan Catholic* with Archbishop Maida on the cover. No other kid's parents—no other kid, period—would have tolerated this demotion. Everyone else would have stormed the priests' house and demanded an explanation. When, on graduation night, I found myself at a party and heard the host explain to his father—to lend an air of respectability to what would turn into a rather disreputable get-together—that both the valedictorian and salutatorian were present, I felt like a fraud, advanced on the basis not of who I was but who I wasn't.

There were rumors: that Kurt had been asked by the priests not to attend commencement, that he'd been kicked out of school at the last minute, that he'd taken an incomplete in a course and so wasn't graduating. Though possible, each of these explanations struck me as overworked; they missed the essence of Kurt's character, which was that he just didn't care. Like the men in Sal's barbershop, he'd chosen, at whatever cost—minuscule, incalculable—to not give a shit. It was his strategy, and he was sticking to it.

I never saw him again.

Not in Detroit Anymore

M Y ONLY CRITERION for choosing a college, after my experiences with Michigan and Chicago, was that I not go to a school with a direction in its name: no Western Michigan, Eastern Michigan, Central Michigan, or Northern Michigan for me. I briefly considered attending the University of Detroit, the Jesuit school, which offered me a full scholarship—I'd already earned eight credits at U of D as part of my high school calculus course—but the thought of four more years in Detroit, and four more years of Catholic school, was killing. I eventually accepted a full scholarship, covering tuition, fees, room and board, and books, to a directionless school, where for four years I felt likewise. It was a state university on Michigan's west side, a school populated by kids from the outskirts of Flint and Kalamazoo and Saginaw, semihicks with bad haircuts who'd grown up in the no-man's-land between the outer suburbs and the country and who, for some reason, seemed to fancy themselves city kids, despite the cow shit on their shoes.

The first time I filled up at the service station across from campus I tried to pay the cashier before I'd pumped any gas. "What's this?" she asked, looking at the twenty that I'd put on the counter. "It's for number four," I said, specifying the pump. "No. Why are you paying? You haven't gotten any gas yet, have you?" I told her that where I came from, 180 miles to the southeast, every gas station had a sign demanding that customers PAY FIRST. "Well, sweetie," she said, "you're not in Detroit anymore."

That was clear. My roommate, Shane—named, he said, after the Alan Ladd character—had received the same scholarship I had. He came from a small town in the southwest corner of Michigan, ten minutes from the Indiana border, a proximity that caused him to set his watch to Central time, a habit he maintained even when he was on campus, a couple hours north of the state line. Half of the year— though I could never remember whether it was after we'd sprung forward or fallen back—Michigan and Indiana time were in sync. The other six months Michigan was an hour ahead, so I had to add sixty minutes to whatever time he'd quoted me. I learned early on in our first semester not to ask.

The first night in our dorm, Shane began to set out pictures from back home, perhaps a dozen in all. I chalked this abundance up to small-town sentiment—the sort of thing you heard about in John Cougar songs. I hadn't put out any pictures of loved ones, but was happy to use his as a conversation starter. The problem was that the circle of people pictured was small, as Shane himself was in each and every one. In many of the pictures there was no one but Shane—shooting a basket, hitting a serve, smiling at graduation. He would join the crew team first semester, so soon there were pictures of Shane in his singlet, part of the lightweight four. To make weight, he was out of bed each morning before dawn, to run, row, and lift weights. He was an achiever—he had come out of a hick high school and, money aside, could have gone to any university in America—and he had a work ethic, so I'd let him handle such humdrum details as renting our room's minifridge and signing us up for cable. Because no cable providers would come south of 8 Mile, we'd never had it.

I hadn't heard of Shane's hometown before getting his name, address, and telephone number on a postcard the summer before. His area code was 616. At the time, Michigan had three area codes—313 for the east side of the state, 517 for the central part of the state, and 616 for the west side. Phoning across area codes was like jumping across continents to me, and his hometown may as well have been Outer Mongolia. I pictured it as a place populated by non-Catholic people who attended church services in aluminum-sided buildings—the First Assembly of God, the United Church of Christ—visible from the interstate. Neither of us called the other, and I couldn't begin to sound out his last name, which was rendered unpronounceable not through an excess of vowels, like the names I was accustomed to, but through a collision of consonants bunched at the back of the alphabet.

Whereas I was unfamiliar with his hometown, Shane was all too familiar with mine. He was less than thrilled, he said, when he saw that his soon-to-be roommate came from Detroit. Looking back at the brochure for our university's convocation that year, which carried both of our names and hometowns at the top of the list of the day's honored students, I see "Detroit" and think, Okay, who's the affirmative action kid?—only to look above those seven letters and see my own name. During our first week on campus, at a get-to-know-you meeting in the dorm, everyone on our floor introduced himself and said something about where he was from. "Detroit," the guy before me said, a black kid from the east side—Finney High School—who'd come over the nearly two hundred miles on a football scholarship. "And just let me say that I've never seen so many white people in my life." "I'm also from Detroit," I said, when my turn came next, "and just let me say that neither have I."

The RA on the floor of our freshman dorm was a junior with the musical name Dontrelle Dell. That his name rhymed was fitting: he was a rap fan, his fondness for the music being such that it was not just his life's head-bobbing soundtrack but its organizing principle. He was often to be seen wearing T-shirts for N.W.A.—Niggaz with Attitude—and Public Enemy, whose albums *Fear of a Black Planet* and *It Takes a Nation of Millions to Hold Us Back* I could frequently hear blaring through our dormitory walls, his room being next to ours. When I met him on my first day, while my dad was helping me carry in boxes and my mom was organizing my dress shirts by color in the closet, I was a bit taken aback. I had picked this school, the campus of which brought the word *bucolic* to mind, in part to get away from this sort of thing. I was eighteen, a city kid who had never seen a deer and wanted to. Niggaz with Attitude was not a part of this deal. When I waved to him on campus in those first few weeks, he returned my greeting with a fist held aloft.

My racial education in Detroit, college soon taught me, had been incomplete, and tragically skewed. I learned that, due to institutionalized racism, African Americans—or blacks, as we'd called them south of 8 Mile, at a savings of six syllables—had to be twice as good as whites to get anywhere. In Detroit, where the institutions were black-controlled, the widely held white belief had been that blacks didn't have to be half as good. (Well, I remember thinking, *someone's* off by a factor of four.) College, too, marked the first time that I'd heard the word *white* used as a sort of sheepish, shrugging pejorative: "Now, I'm just a white guy, but it seems to me . . ." The priests had taught me, or had tried to teach me, to speak articulately, to talk like a man. And yet here were men of considerable education purposely stammering and stuttering, pretending to be less articulate than they were in order to achieve a feigned harmlessness.

But it took me a while to get used to all those things I was no longer supposed to notice. Shane, possessed of what I'd come to think of as rural reserve, had much less trouble not noticing—or, rather, he was able to notice without caring. I began to call him "Mr. Detachment"—nothing touched him. This was altogether different from Kurt's indifference back home, which came with an almost unsustainable intensity. Shane's detachment was surrounded by perfect calm. As with most good kids, he'd learned early on the wisdom of a little bit and no more. He'd observe, and think, and then let the thoughts and observations go. Strong emotions he left to others, while he went about the business of getting his life properly situated.

As students in the school's honors program, Shane and I had overlapping freshman-year schedules. I was struck, in one of these courses—a yearlong team-taught survey of Renaissance European literature—by the reaction of the white professors to the class's sole black student, a guy from Saginaw who sat in the back row and said very little. Perhaps because of this, anything he did say was greeted by the professors as if he'd just succeeded in squaring the circle. This was an eye-opener for me, and served as my introduction to the world of liberal guilt, which I'd heard about during my campus tour at Chicago. "What's that all about?" I asked Shane after one class. "It's standard," he said. "The teachers at my high school were always that way with the black kids. Weren't they like that at yours?" I said, with some pride, that they were not. The priests would never have stooped to that sort of thing.

Neither, it seems likely, would they have smiled upon the course reading list, which featured book after book critical of the Church of Rome. A few of them—Chaucer, for instance—I'd been exposed to during high school, but whereas the critique of the Church was in the background of our high school discussions it was often the focus of my college reading. Things reached their apex second semester when, after plowing through More's *Utopia* and Erasmus's *Colloquies,* we devoted an entire unit to readings from *The Protestant Reformation,* a collection of writings by assorted Swiss and German Anabaptists, by Martin Luther ("His books are to be eradicated from the memory of man": the Edict of Worms), and by John Calvin, whose ideas concerning predestination drove me to begin one paper by saying that, as a depressed eighteen-year-old, I'd yet to resign myself to the fact that this life was unfair; the last thing I wanted to hear was that the afterlife was rigged, too.

But these were Catholic Detroit thoughts, and, though the center of my universe, the city's northeastern corner couldn't have been less helpful in preparing me for encounters with the larger world. And that's how the world outside Detroit now appeared: larger. Visits home, from which I returned to campus with care packages of Little Italy pizza, were an exercise in perspective, the city appearing a little smaller in my rearview mirror each time I left it. Midnight Mass at St. Jude, during Christmas vacation my freshman year, felt, for the first time, precious—as if there might not be an endless succession of them. Everything I saw in the old neighborhood seemed to possess a built-in obsolescence I'd never before noticed.

This was in part because the portion of the city that was ours kept getting smaller. The southern perimeter of our neighborhood, previously at 7 Mile, had moved north to State Fair; the western perimeter, at Gratiot, had moved east to Hayes. "We live in the ghetto," my mother's occasional housecleaning partner, Mrs. Kolarski, told me on one of these trips back. Because her husband was a fireman a few years from retirement, he wouldn't risk losing his pension by moving out of the city. This was the opposite approach of those cops who lived five miles away in Warren and slept at their fathers' houses the night before their shifts. The Kolarskis were willing to ride it out in the city for a few more years and then, after retirement, relocate—not to southern Macomb County but to somewhere in the vicinity of Newfoundland. This was a common theme among people who subscribed to this school of thought: not moving away until you had enough money to move *way* away, somewhere well beyond the ring of inner suburbs that, in ten years, would look like the city one had fled a decade before. To such people, the only thought worse than living in a ghetto at age fifty was that of having to move again at age seventy. "It used to be ten blocks away. Then six. Now it's three. Pretty soon it'll be here, on this block, and we'll have bars on the windows. I tell Jim—let's go. But he won't do it. After all these years, he's not going to take the chance."

While the livable space inside the city shrank, the suburbs that surrounded the already enormous city continued to expand. To the south, they stretched nearly to Toledo; to the southwest, they touched Ann Arbor; to the north, they just missed making it to Flint; to the northwest, Lansing loomed. (The only reason the suburbs didn't sprawl to the east was because they were blocked by Lake St. Clair and, beyond that, Canada.) Highways were built that, instead of moving people between the city and its suburbs, moved people from suburb to suburb, bypassing the city entirely. One of these, the Walter P. Reuther freeway—named after the former UAW president—became, in the early 1990s, the metro area's main east–west thoroughfare. It was a few miles to our north, meandering between 10 Mile and 11 Mile, and rendered the stoplights and forty-five-mile-per-hour speed limit along 8 Mile, the former east–west thoroughfare, relics of a former age. "Detroit has had its day," a prominent antagonist of Coleman Young—the Oakland County prosecutor—tells Chafets in *Devil's Night*, a copy of which was back in my dorm room. "I don't give a damn about Detroit. It has no direct bearing on the quality of my life. If I never crossed 8 Mile again I wouldn't be bereft of anything."

As I crossed 8 Mile, going the other direction, and drove back to campus through the Macomb, Oakland, and Livingston County suburbs to which half of Detroit's goddamn population had fled—subdivisions behind cornfields, horse farms alongside highways—it was clear that my upbringing belonged to a different epoch. Black cities still made sense, as did white suburbs—there was an obvious symbiosis between the two—but urban whites, with all of our working-class bric-a-brac? As the black cop had wondered: What were we doing still hanging around the joint? Metropolitan Detroit was now four million people, with less than a quarter of that in the city itself. To most people, "Detroit" now meant everything but.

I was struck by the strangeness of things actually sent to me from the city. Our return address, in the upper-left-hand corner of letters in my campus mailbox, struck me as odd. Even stranger was seeing my father's signature on the birthday or Christmas card inside. I was used to seeing numbers in his handwriting, his notebook calculations, but not his script. My mother always wrote a longish message on such cards, then "Love," then "Mom," and she would finally add the ampersand, so that all my father had to do was sign "Dad." Three hours from Detroit, and those three letters—"D-a-d"—looked lost, completely out of context.

Fast approaching his fiftieth year in the city, my father was now working full-time as a draftsman for the Detroit Public Lighting Department, in a building down the block from City Airport. Public Lighting, where the kindhearted father of my high school locker partner had worked for decades, had the distinction of being the city department Detroit residents complained about most to the ombudsman: the streetlights, in some areas, were simply never on. The lights in our area were intermittently illuminated, and they could be checked, since ours was a corner house, by simply looking out the kitchen window. One windy night years before, my father had called Public Lighting to complain about the lights being off. "Sir," he was told, "it's very windy out." "Windy?" he replied. "What the hell do you have in them— *candles?*" He was now a department employee.

He couldn't *not* work; and though the plan had been to go to school exclusively, he'd decided to work and study simultaneously, hoping against hope to beat his son to a college diploma. "How's school going?" my sister asked in one of the chatty cards she sent to me freshman year. "School's fine for me. Dad starts tomorrow."

Dontrelle, it turned out, was from Flint, and so liked talking with me about Detroit, the even bigger, blacker city one hour to the south. He'd appreciated my comment, at the introductory meeting for our floor (which, as RA, he'd organized), about my never having seen so many white people. That, he thought, was funny. He was thin, almost frail, and had not the least interest in intimidating anyone, despite the clenched fist and strident music. He possessed that strain of enthusiasm common to college students who believe that the four years spent on campus will be the most important of your life and that the most important thing about those four important years is getting involved. Never much of a joiner, I begrudgingly accepted Dontrelle's invitation at the beginning of the winter semester to attend one of the school's Martin Luther King holiday events, during which he would be reading a portion of the "I Have a Dream" speech.

Dr. King struck me as a little too accommodating for Dontrelle, who seemed more the Malcolm X type, but he said several times that he wanted me at the memorial. My days in Detroit have often served to legitimize me, during the initial stages of friendships with blacks, as a white person whose opinion might—*might*—matter. "Where you from?" "Detroit." "Which suburb?" "No suburb—Detroit." "*Really.*" Where things went from there was another matter, but I felt a connection with Dontrelle. Shane attended as well, so I was the sole representative neither of my people nor of the first floor of Copeland Hall.

There weren't many attendees at the event of either race. We sat in a small circle and, after some preliminaries, Dontrelle stood in the middle, clearing his throat, a little unsure, as everyone is at first, what he should do with his hands. It dawned on me almost immediately that he wasn't going to be reading a portion of the speech, as he'd said; he was going to be doing all of it. And he wasn't reading the speech; he was *reciting* it, and doing so without the slightest stumble.

One doesn't get the full impact of the speech from the snippets one usually hears, and as Dontrelle got into the spirit, sweeping his listeners along with him, his hands now doing more or less what Dr. King's had done, the sheer forward momentum of those words was enough to knock me back. Shane, whom I could see peripherally, was crying.

"Did *you* cry?" he asked me afterward, back in our room.

"No."

This was not to be mistaken for a lack of emotion on my part. Like my father, I was beginning to admire, not the finished product, but the hard work that went into things. The part of the deal where people applaud and pat you on the back is nice, but not nearly so important as the enormous preparation that makes such a moment possible. Instead of being touched by the speech's sentiments, noble as they were, I was more impressed by the thought that Dontrelle had studied that speech, word by word, line by line, until, as one of my English teachers always put it, he had it by heart. Hour upon hour of dull, dreary work had occurred in that room next to mine, completely unbeknownst to me, at the end of which—my father's philosophy of life—there was a little something to show for it.

Never have the congratulations I've given to someone after a public performance been so sincere. "You were great," I told him, shaking his hand.

Some years ago, in one of my alumni newsletters, I came across a death notice that caused me to gasp: Dontrelle Dell had been killed, it said, in a car accident along a two-lane country road. Years later, digging through boxes to write this book, I found an old Christmas card ("Have a beary merry Christmas!") with a teddy bear in a Santa hat on the front. Inside, Dontrelle had written: "Thanks for helping to make our floor the best. Your personality is the greatest. Your RA, Dontrelle Dell." At the top is the yellowing tape I'd used to stick it up on my dorm room wall, next to the Christmas cards sent up from Detroit.

Hatred and Despair

O N T H E 2 9 T H O F J U L Y, in 1943, my father died," James
Baldwin writes at the beginning of "Notes of a Native
Son." "On the same day, a few hours later, his last child was born. Over
a month before this, while all our energies were concentrated in waiting for these events, there had been, in Detroit, one of the bloodiest
race riots of the century." This was what I liked: Detroit, a race riot, a
birth, and a death, all in the first paragraph. As reading went, it seemed
applicable. That my own father would be conceived in Detroit a year after those '43 riots, and had nearly been swept up in the city's 1967 en-
core, merely served to strengthen my belief that Baldwin's essay about
blackness was also, however indirectly, about me.

I had a lot of time for such reading, and for the sort of thinking—
profoundly, adolescently self-centered—that it engendered. Thanks to
a handsome four-year scholarship, I didn't need to work during the
school year. The university gave me a check at the beginning of each semester for room and board, which I was free to spend as I wished. Since

such expenses were calculated at campus rates, and off-campus living was much cheaper, I was able, after my first year, by living a few blocks from campus, to bank a substantial portion of these checks. When, as a freshman, I saw others in my dorm receive their midterm grades in the campus mail but did not myself, I suspected an oversight and feared that I was somehow to blame. But no: midterm progress reports, I learned, were sent only to freshmen—and, because of my AP credits from high school, I had sophomore standing. By my senior year I had only a handful of required classes left to take.

I worked out my thoughts and mentally wrote my papers during long runs on the trails and ravines around campus. The stress fracture in my left hip suffered during track season my senior year of high school had more or less healed by that fall, but it was still helpful to run on soft dirt instead of the concrete that had contributed to the fracture in the first place. Unlike in Detroit, there were no bus stops to run by, no exhaust fumes to inhale, and none of the urban distractions—including, on a few occasions, a Detroit police helicopter that had shone its searchlight on me at night—to intrude on the mental solitude that was my main reason for running. Occasionally, deep in the trails, I'd see a pack of deer. One Saturday night that first October, with all my friends away for the weekend, I ran fourteen miles in the dark during a fall thunderstorm. Though I could sometimes hear rifle shots in the distance, I was never fired at by hunters out poaching on college property, about whom one sometimes heard stories. I averaged between sixty and seventy miles a week, logging my daily totals in a journal at the front of which I'd written a quote from Alan Sillitoe's *The Loneliness of the Long-Distance Runner*. I'd read the book during high school and had loved the simplicity and truth of the protagonist's statement—his credo—"I'm a long-distance runner, crossing country all on my own no matter how bad it feels." It was like Catholicism—redemption through physical suffering.

I was often approached by dogs during my runs and carried rocks in my hands to ward off the worst of them. During the last stretch of one winter run I'd been followed by a friendly black Lab from a house at the foot of an icy hill about a mile from campus. Before crossing the busy two-lane highway that bordered campus, I stopped and packed a snowball about the size and weight of a baseball, and threw it as if I were trying to hit the cutoff man from deep in the outfield. I was happy to have had the dog's company—I'd never had one growing up—but didn't want him crossing with me. I'd thrown the snowball back toward his house ("Go get it!") and crossed the highway while he ran off in the other direction.

Seconds later I heard the thud. When I turned around I saw him on his side in the middle of the road, cars swerving around him. I ran into the traffic, scooped him up—he was still breathing, with blood dripping from the side of his jaws—and left him on the side of the road with a friend who had stopped to help. I ran back to campus and hailed an acquaintance in a pickup. We put the dog in the back and drove to its owner's house, at the bottom of the hill.

The dog was in shock. After the owner had taken it down from the bed of the pickup, the dog suddenly came to and began to run wildly around their yard, encircling the family's horses, all the while letting loose a high-pitched bark as if its tail were being continuously stepped on. The owner went into his house, returning with a rifle. "Don't shoot it!" I said. "I nearly got killed saving him!" It seemed like something out of one of Hemingway's Michigan stories, set not far from where I was: a man killing the animal he loves because it's what he must do.

Moments later the man's wife and kids came running out, begging him not to shoot. He put the rifle down and, after several minutes and much swearing, managed to catch the dog, which he put in his pickup and drove hurriedly to the vet. It was icy, but the truck managed to make it up the hill. A couple of weeks later, the dog was back running alongside me.

I did most of my reading on the fourth floor of the school's library, the womblike warmth of which contrasted with the cold outside, lasting from October to April and through which I once ran seven miles on a day when the windchill was fifty-five degrees below zero. The library's warmth encouraged the sort of muddled, half-asleep thoughts that bookish college students collect like beer cans, and that resemble nothing so much as fumbling intellectual foreplay.

Because I'd gone to an all-boys high school, I wasn't used to seeing girls in an academic context. As they sat down at the tables around me, taking off first their hats and gloves, then their scarves and coats, and finally rubbing some warmth into their small hands before opening their backpacks, I understood the parochial school suspicion of coeducation. Concentration was difficult. And when these girls, after another half hour in the library's heat, lazily slipped out of their sweaters and began to sprawl out on the tables in front of them, putting their heads down for a spell of rest that could easily turn into an hour's light sleep, I often found it impossible to resume my reading. The backs of the T-shirts they wore under those discarded sweaters—CLASS OF '91 RULES!—revealed which small-town Michigan high school they hailed from, the letters in the name of their hometown curving forward along with their delicate spines: Edwardsburg and Vicksburg, Webberville and Greenville, Zeeland and Holland. Everyone, it seemed, was from a Burg, a Land, or a Ville.

I persevered with my reading. Just as I did when I ran repeats on the hills around campus, I forced myself through books despite the pain. "One more chapter," I'd say, urging myself through not only all eleven hundred pages of *Don Quixote* but each footnote in the back of the book as well, where I kept a finger to mark my place. On the verge of sleep, I'd vow to finish *The House of Mirth,* not only to see what happened between Lawrence and Lily but to be able to check another book off the required reading list. Edith Wharton: done.

Why I was in such a rush—what the mental to-do lists were for— I have no idea. At times it felt, in its very lack of specificity, something like mortal fear. Whereas the great benefit of adolescence is the assumption that it will last forever, I was burdened with the foreknowledge that it would all quite quickly be over—before you know it, as older people, who knew it, always put it. I carried with me, at all times, a sense of an ending. During dinner conversation in Joyce's "The Dead," talk turns to the monks of Mount Melleray, men who "never spoke, got up at two in the morning and slept in their coffins." One of the dinner guests, Mr. Browne, who is not Catholic but "of the other persuasion," professes not to understand this last part. "The coffin," the hostess explains, putting a stop to this religious talk, "is to remind them of their last end."

It's tempting to blame Catholicism for my acute awareness of the coffin—all that time on kneelers, staring up at a crucifix—but the truth was that, in some sense, this was not a religious but an aesthetic choice, one that Catholicism simply put forward. Autumn was always my favorite time of year. I liked my happiness not blissful but bittersweet. Perhaps the fact that I was capable of only temporary contentment paralleled the fact that I was my father's son, and so saw pleasure as something impermanent, unable to compete with the pressing responsibilities of the coming day, and the day after, and the day after that, on each of which there was sure to be plenty to take care of. Life was a slippery slope, and the least bit of slacking off gave failure a foothold. Better not to make the slightest slip in the first place. Better to read some more in my book and then, before it got too dark, take to the trails.

When I tired of my assigned reading but wasn't yet ready to brave the cold and leave the library girls behind, I'd walk over to the stack of periodicals and skim through the magazines, the names of which were new to me: *The New Yorker,* the *New Republic, The Atlantic Monthly*, the *New York Review of Books.* The only paper we'd subscribed to at home was the *Detroit News,* the more conservative of the two Detroit dailies; and the only magazines that came to our house were *Car Craft* and *National Dragster* and similarly sophisticated fare. The most prized object to appear regularly at our doorstep was the weekly television guide, an insert in the Sunday paper.

Reading, I soon learned, led to more reading. This article referred to that book, and that book referred to this writer, and that writer, it was said, was influenced by writers X, Y, and Z—though the influence of Z, according to one of the critics cited, was decidedly for the worse. Sometimes the publications that I'd started to read would review the same book and disagree completely on its merits. I was surprised to learn that I could read a review, agree with the writer's argument, then turn to an article in another periodical, which took an opposing view of the book (or political platform, or piece of social policy), and agree with that, too. "Whenever I feel bad," says the narrator of Walker Percy's novel *The Moviegoer*, "I go to the library and read controversial periodicals. Though I do not know whether I am a liberal or a conservative, I am nevertheless enlivened by the hatred which the one bears the other."

In Catholic school, anything between bound covers was accorded the status of scripture. It seemed to me now that it was altogether more respectful of writing to try to pick it apart to see how it worked. I began to write in the margins of books and magazines, blending the acts of reading and writing.

This was truest with the black writers I read, Ralph Ellison and James Baldwin in particular. I fell for Baldwin—the term is apt—when I read his "Autobiographical Notes" at the beginning of *Notes of a Native Son*. After discussing the ambivalence with which he approached Shakespeare, Bach, and Rembrandt, he admits to having hated and feared white people all his life. He immediately follows that admission with another: this did not mean that he loved black people. "On the contrary," he writes, "I despised them, possibly because they failed to produce Rembrandt." Part of me, as I read on, was beginning to dislike the whites among whom I'd been raised because they had failed to produce, among much else, a Baldwin.

Where Baldwin was all exposed nerves, his writing an attempt to overcome what seemed an ineradicable sadness, Ellison was more relaxed; his essays, which made terrific points, took their time in getting there, and his great novel meandered unbelievably before reaching a finale never bettered in American fiction. Ellison so clearly possessed the strength, moral stature, and meticulous intelligence that tolerant whites always spoke of blacks possessing, but that I'd somehow over-looked during my days in Detroit, that I felt a bit blindsided.

The last line spoken by Ellison's Invisible Man—"Who knows but that, on the lower frequencies, I speak for you?"—made me blush. *Me?* I felt like a shy girl who'd just been asked to dance: You mean *me*? Yes, Ellison admitted in his essays: he was directly addressing his white read-ership with that last line. After finishing his novel and essays, I was more apt to let Ellison speak for me than any white person I knew.

Above all, I was struck by how important the concept of America was to these writers. I'd never really thought of myself as American. Catholic, yes; someone from the east side of Detroit, certainly. But not an American. I didn't even consider myself a "Michigander," the absurd term applied to people from our state that conjured up an image of ten million Midwestern birds always said to be leaving for better-paying jobs in the Sun Belt, as if this were our migratory pattern. But Baldwin and Ellison repeated, again and again, that I had more in common with them than either of us might care to admit. And the link could not be broken; moving to the suburbs, putting distance between oneself and black people, would do nothing to break this bond.

Still, it was Joyce, the Catholic apostate—to whom neither Ellison nor Baldwin, nor anyone else, could hold a candle—who obsessed me, who dramatized, with ferocious linguistic brilliance, those battles "fought and won behind your forehead." For a junior-year class with *Invisible Man* on the syllabus I wrote a paper tracing the influence of Joyce on Ellison, building upon the scene in Ellison's book in which the narrator remembers a black college professor who, with quotes from Joyce on the blackboard behind him, says of Stephen Dedalus's famous boast that he would go forth to forge the conscience of his race: "Stephen's problem, like ours, was not actually one of creating the un-created conscience of his race, but of creating the *uncreated features of his face*. Our task is that of making ourselves individuals. The con-science of a race is the gift of its individuals who see, evaluate, record. . . . We create the race by creating ourselves and then to our great astonishment we will have created something far more important: We will have created a culture." I quoted, too, from an interview in which Ellison equated the position of Negro writers with that of the Irish, who'd taken the language of their oppressors and perfected it.

My professor told me the paper was probably publishable; I didn't pursue it. My roommate, Shane, who edited the campus paper, asked me to contribute articles, invitations I declined. Like a Catholic schoolgirl, I was saving myself. I wasn't going to write about anything else, I told myself, until I'd first succeeded in writing about Detroit.

Sitting on the top floor of the library, reading through those periodicals, I'd run across an article by a black writer speaking of his displeasure with recent books about race in America, criticizing them for their lack of artistic subtlety and the narrow range of reaction they allowed. It's either the clenched fist of racial solidarity, he wrote, or the hung head of social understanding. I thought: That's beautifully put, and no less true for the neatness of the formulation. Coming from a corner of Detroit where disagreement with blacks was seen as something of a patriotic duty—one to be demonstrated, in a losing cause, every four years at the polls—it was a relief to discover black writers who were saying things—things about race—with which I agreed.

With Baldwin's essay "The Black Boy Looks at the White Boy" I agreed totally. A consideration of Norman Mailer's infamous "The White Negro," Baldwin's essay had tactfully hinted that the Mailer piece was pretty bad. I read it and concluded it was bottomlessly so. Baldwin quotes some of his jazz musician friends, with whom Mailer had hung out to research his piece. "The only trouble with that cat," one of them says to Baldwin, "is that he's white." My response to "The White Negro" was similar, deviating only slightly at the end. That cat's only problem, I remember thinking, setting the essay aside, is that he's Jewish. No Catholic could have written it. Catholics weren't impressed enough by humanity in general to be this bowled over by blacks in particular.

I wondered at the tendency—visible in the Mailer piece, and particularly apparent in the hippie kids on campus—to abase oneself before blackness. These people seemed to me not unlike the old ladies on kneelers in church, asking forgiveness of a higher power when simple fortitude would have served them better. Despite my admiration for a handful of black writers, I felt nothing of the sort; my reading of Ellison and Baldwin was an intellectual exercise, not a moral one. I didn't want to be them, or receive their blessing, or lower myself before their greater sense of my own insecurities. I wanted neither to clench my fist nor hang my head. I wanted to learn from them—as Baldwin had learned from Dickens and the King James Bible, as Ellison had learned from Hemingway and Eliot, Melville and Joyce.

I was sick of feeling guilty. As both a Catholic and a white American, I'd been born with original sin—the difference being, in the latter case, that there was no baptism to wash it away. In each case, the historical crime was wrapped into the very fiber of my being, making any further instances of guilt redundant. Enough already. I was born, I told myself, one hundred and ten years after the signing of the Emancipation Proclamation, nine years after the signing of the Civil Rights Act, and the very year of Coleman Young's election, which is to say that I was part of the first generation that not only entered a country where blacks were not enslaved or denied their civil liberties, but was also part of that small fraction that entered a city where blacks were in the majority and in power. My parents, for reasons I could never completely comprehend, hadn't taken part in the flight, and though my father may not have liked Coleman Young he paid taxes to the Young administration, which was more than could be said of many of the mayor's most ardent supporters. Guilty I may have been, but I'd have eaten my hat if someone could have explained to me how this was specifically so. The guilt, such as it was, was astral.

It was impossible, of course, to be a good Catholic and a racist; at the same time it seemed difficult to be a Catholic and a good social progressive, and not just because of the many things that were accepted parts of the progressive worldview that the Catholic Church staunchly opposed. The difference ran on deeper currents, approaching the irreconcilable. Where the progressive view of life was predicated, to some extent, on society's perfectibility, the Catholic Church sought perfection from the individual members of its flock, while taking a frankly realistic view of human failings. Has there ever been an institution that has lasted as long as the Catholic Church, and has had such influence, in which the sense of how limited we are has loomed so large? There were saints who had overcome human weakness, of course—but they were *saints*. For the rest of us, the Church provided a head-spinning set of rules, prohibitions, and recommendations—and at the end, should such strictures prove insufficient, there was still purgatory.

And there was always an exception to each rigid rule. Over Easter vacation my junior year of high school I flew to France, along with a dozen classmates and the two priests who were chaperoning us. My parents were concerned about the trip's expense, which Father Hec— happy to support a Catholic schoolboy's desire to see Notre Dame— offered, in part, to defray. My mother was sweet-talked into covering the rest of the cost by one of the priests, a suave Frenchman who assured her, during a parent-teacher conference, that a trip to Europe would be just the thing for a young man of my talents. (One of the nuns at school, who spent her summers at Lourdes, was always asking for strapping young volunteers to help carry crippled pilgrims to the healing waters, but this trip to France sounded more fun.) We flew out of Detroit on Good Friday, when Catholics the world over fast and fill churches from noon to three, marking the time when Christ had hung from his cross and praying on bended knee for the salvation his suffering made possible. As with all Fridays during Lent, meat was forbidden; but to eat meat on Good Friday wasn't just forbidden—it was obscene.

When the meal carts began to work their way down the aisle, we could smell it in the air, and we started to whisper among ourselves: *steak*. The stewardess informed us that filet mignon was one of our meal choices. We looked at each other and smiled. As the best student in the bunch—the most verbal, anyway—I was nominated to walk up the aisle and ask the priests what we should do.

Our French teacher, Father Racine, seemed surprised I'd asked—surprised and pleased. He was a great mix of the pious and the worldly himself, the crucifix around his neck nestled in the chest hair exposed by his unbuttoned black shirt. "You're growing boys, you're traveling, you need your strength," he said, waving away my question with a smile. This unexpected dispensation emboldened us, and since ours was an international flight we started, shortly after requesting the fillet, to buy drinks from the stewardesses. The priests, drinking themselves up ahead of us, didn't seem to much care what went on in the plane behind them.

For all its bluster about premarital sexual abstinence, natural birth control, and the hair-palmed perils of beating off, there was within the Church a strong, indirect acceptance of life as it is—an acknowledgment, in the sheer amplitude of what it told us *not* to do, that we are all traveling, and need our strength, and so probably can't help but leap headlong into whatever has been forbidden. That's what confession was for.

Baldwin ends "Notes of a Native Son," which he'd begun with his father's death and the '43 Detroit riots, on a similar note of conciliation. After describing his father's funeral, where he reflects on the racism that had poisoned that man's life and was beginning to infect his own, Baldwin speaks of the need for "acceptance, totally without rancor, of life as it is, and men as they are." This poses a problem, for if one accepts life as it is and men as they are, then "it goes without saying that injustice is a commonplace." Baldwin asserts, however, that "one must never, in one's own life, accept these injustices as commonplace but must fight them with all one's strength." He finishes: "This fight begins, however, in the heart and it now had been laid to my charge to keep my own heart free of hatred and despair."

The Church, too, accepted people as they were, knowing that sin could never be anything but commonplace; yet it insisted that one fight the tendency with all one's strength. As for freeing one's heart of hatred and despair, Church teaching and Baldwin agreed. Despair, according to Catholicism, was the unforgivable sin, as was its logical end, suicide, both being evidence of a loss of faith in God's grace. Hatred, according to enlightened folks everywhere, was a disease, one especially widespread in Detroit. I'd do my best to avoid both.

My time away from the city had made clear that my Detroit upbringing was unique—singular, almost—and sullied if it produced nothing more than the same lazy prejudices available to everyone else. I couldn't stand those suburbanites who characterized the city, and the blacks who populated it, as hopeless. Such a stance was racism, pure and simple. As for me—someone who had seen the crime, corruption, and lack of common sense that was everywhere in the city, and who had noted the complexions of those acting nonsensically, corruptly, and criminally—I thought the city and many of its inhabitants hopeless. Such a stance was not racism; it was an accurate apprehension based on the available evidence, and neither could I tolerate those misty-eyed suburbanites whose kindheartedness prevented them from acknowledging, or even noticing, the obvious.

What was never quite clear to me, no matter how much I read, was whether or not I could expect the same sort of understanding, the same acknowledgment of life's extenuating circumstances, from blacks that I received from the Catholic Church. The Church was family; blacks were strangers, and no amount of reading, no number of basketball court friendships, no backlog of Detroit experience would ever change this. If, like all white people, I was a racist, I could pin the blame in part on an upbringing few whites shared. Whether or not this distinction would mean anything to blacks themselves was another matter, and I had a hunch that, unlike the priests, they would pay altogether less attention to the fact that I was traveling and needed my strength.

City Workers or Something

THE FIRST PIECE of creative writing I tried my hand at, the summer after freshman year of college—the summer East Detroit became Eastpointe—was a strictly factual account of my morning drive along the Ford Freeway, heading downtown from Detroit's east side. The graffiti along the westbound lanes of I-94 featured prominently, as did the highway advertising—limited, by and large, to billboards for fast food chains and Baptist ministers, middle-aged men in sweater vests whose signs carried vastly unsubstantiated claims regarding salvation. A few miles farther along, where the Ford Freeway rises to meet the Chrysler Freeway, there was an enormous garbage incinerator, positioned so that its thick stream of smoke would be carried by the prevailing winds into the airspace of our Canadian neighbors, with whom we shared the world's longest-standing peaceful border. It was ten minutes to seven when I drove past the incinerator each morning, half asleep behind the wheel.

I tried, too, to write a scene set in an east side barbershop. I had a first line: "Though the sign on the wall behind him said By Appointment Only, the barber took no appointments." I didn't know how these scenes connected, but figured I'd find the narrative thread eventually.

My summers home were a reality check, a way to test the relevance of what I'd spent the past eight months reading in that invitingly warm library on the other side of the state. I got back to Detroit, after freshman year, on April 28. The next day, four Los Angeles police officers were acquitted in the beating of a black motorist. For the next few days, along with the rest of the country, my family watched the riots on television, and we were stricken by the repeated image of a white truck driver being pulled from his rig by a group of black men and hit in the side of the head with a brick. We'd seen the video of the police brutality over and over, and had felt less and less with each viewing, eventually feeling more frustration with the news broadcasts that seemed to take a masochistic pleasure in wearing the tape thin than with the officers whose actions the tape had captured and who had nonetheless—incredibly—been acquitted.

The video of the truck driver was another matter. We hadn't been desensitized to it, as we had been with the first video during the long buildup to the officers' trial. And though it was the wielding of their batons that sickened in the first instance, it wasn't the brick to the head that was most bothersome about the second video. The violence, however vulgar, could be countenanced. It was the taunt that followed, the two-handed point by the man who'd thrown the brick as the truck driver fell to the ground unconscious—that "Gotcha!"—that did it. Oh, that sick-ass sonuvabitch. Did you see that bastard? How he pointed like that? I'd thought, with my bookish interests, that I'd left behind the opinions of white Detroit. Watching this video the day after returning from my first year of college, I thought: Maybe not. Freeing one's heart of hatred and despair, clearly, would be no mean feat.

Everyone in our family worked in the city—my dad worked for the city—and there was much talk, among whites who'd witnessed the '67 riots, that another was possible. Los Angeles had just surpassed the records Detroit had set twenty-five years before, and could now lay claim to the title of Worst Riot in American History. Would Detroit sit silently by? Watts had gone up in '65, after all, and Detroit had bettered it two years later. It could happen again. A good deal of advice was dispensed about locking car doors on the drive downtown, a drive that my mother and I made each weekday. "Good morning," my mother had said to a black coworker the day after the verdict that precipitated the riots was delivered. "What's so good about it?" the woman snapped back. When I dropped my mother off downtown at the Detroit Medical Center, where she was a secretary, I recalled Camus's line about Algeria: "I believe in justice, but I will defend my mother before justice."

When we found ourselves a car short that summer, I'd have to drop my father off before work at the Public Lighting Department building next to City Airport. To get there I'd turn off Gratiot onto French Road, which dead-ends almost immediately at a set of railroad tracks just beyond a steel processing plant. French picks up again on the other side of a small airfield about a quarter of a mile wide, and then runs straight for a mile or so until it dead-ends again at 6 Mile, where Mt. Olivet Cemetery begins. For that mile between the airfield and 6 Mile, French Road is wide and free of traffic, and runs parallel to the airport's landing strips; much of the illegal racing in the city—the sort of racing in the street that Springsteen sang about and that my father frowned upon—occurred here. Huge bets were said to be placed on the outcomes of races, and occasionally, when a bet went south or a car lost control, the eleven o'clock news dutifully reported the loss of life.

Our family had flown in and out of City Airport on a few occasions, taking advantage of the twenty-nine-dollar flights to Chicago occasionally offered by a discount airline. Because the runways were short, takeoffs and landings could be terrifying. "Any landing's a good landing," the pilots said, a bit shaken, each time we touched back down in Detroit. The city had plans to expand the airport, but there were those who opposed expansion, including the Polish mayor of Warren—

the largest suburb in Macomb County, the third-largest *city* in Michigan—who cited flight patterns and noise pollution. "I can't believe that the mayor of Warren is so stupid," Coleman Young said. "He's opposed in the latter decade of the twentieth century to having airplanes fly overhead." The airport never did expand, however, and the last major carrier left the airport shortly after my wife and I flew out of City near the end of the nineties on our honeymoon.

"Biggest crowd I ever saw in my life," my father once said as the two of us drove past City Airport, "was when Kennedy flew in there during the 1960 presidential campaign. I was in eighth grade. Someone got impaled on a post from the crowd pressing in to see him. See the lights around the football field?" he asked, turning his attention to the other side of the street, looking at what was once De La Salle Collegiate. "On top of them, and on top of the school itself, were landing lights for the planes coming in. Are they still there, on top of the stadium lights?" He leaned forward in the passenger seat. "Oh, hell, I can't see."

The running track around the football field was overgrown with grass, but the stadium lights, the stands, and the scoreboard—bearing the words BROTHER GEORGE SYNAN ATHLETIC FIELD—still stood. The school building had been sold by the Christian Brothers at the beginning of the previous decade and was now in the hands of holy men of a different persuasion. Barbed wire surrounded the building.

Like Coleman Young, I, too, had escaped the Christian Brothers' discipline. The old school had closed its doors by the time I came of age, and the school's new suburban campus, out in Warren, was just far enough of a drive as to be inconvenient. "I used to run to that track," my father said, pointing to the grassy quarter-mile oval as we pulled away, "run a couple miles around it, and then run back home. Used to do that a few times a week when I was feeling good." None of this was said with much sentiment. It was a fact, one that could be checked in the running logs in my parents' basement, the mileage totals recorded in the same spiral notebooks that he used for his horsepower calculations.

Growing up, we identified people with the church they lived nearest. So-and-so's family lived next door to St. Raymond. What's-his-futz lived over by St. Jude. You know, that *girl,* from Guardian Angels. This was how people talked, as if street names and points on the compass were unnecessary. Everything could be oriented by one's proximity to a particular parish. But the people who spoke this language had long since left the city, leaving behind the schools and churches (over a third of which were closed in the late 1980s, a scale unprecedented in American Catholicism), and the result was an uncomfortable layering of civilizations, an unspoken, aesthetic argument between Detroit's white ethnic past and its nonwhite present. The peeling sign that sat in front of my father's old high school may have said DOVE ACADEMY, but the concrete scrollwork still said DE LA SALLE COLLEGIATE. Which was it? I still call the place where my cousins went to school St. Matthew, but it was closed by the archdiocese a while back. On the side of the building that faces Outer Drive, at the top, are block letters still identifying the structure as the BISHOP DONNELLY ACTIVITIES BUILDING. In the ground below is another sign, identifying it as the MAYA ANGELOU ELEMENTARY SCHOOL.

In grade school I had learned, from some lemon-scented nun, that one out of every five people on the planet was Chinese; since four out of five Detroiters were black, it seemed to me mathematically impossible for there to be any white people in Detroit. I recalled this fourth-grade lapse in logic during these drives. Every few blocks or so we'd pass a bungalow with a fenced-off yard and flower pots on the front porch, a place that I suspected of belonging to an old white woman—a widow, I imagined, whose husband had passed away thirty years before and whose children hadn't yet found the money to move her to the suburbs. Aside from a few downwardly mobile Desdemonas imported from the near suburbs, that seemed to be about it: half a dozen holdovers from the time when the city had mayors with last names like Miriani and one's offspring bought a house around the corner instead of out in Oakland County. Every time we passed one of these homes, I wondered who cut the grass.

This drive, part of our daily commute, was a pilgrimage that suburban Detroiters sometimes made—doors locked, windows up—to those special places that held pieces of their past. What people professed to be after from such trips tended toward the vague—they just wanted to have a look at the old place—and they were invariably disappointed afterward, as it was impossible not to be when the ostensible reason for the trip was so fundamentally dishonest. (It was to have one's worst fears confirmed that such trips were undertaken.) Older couples drove down from the suburbs on Sunday mornings after Mass, the message of Christian charity still fresh in their ears and pleasant, anticipatory butterflies in their stomachs. As they crossed below 8 Mile, the contentment that comes of wearing one's Sunday best began slowly to fade; smiles tightened and then disappeared altogether. By the time the car had stopped in front of the house where their children were conceived, the sound of the priest's voice had vanished, and the message of Christian love had begun to seem almost offensively simpleminded—insipid, even. How, they asked themselves, do you extend charity to *this*? You mean to tell me that these are the people who shall inherit the earth? They've already inherited Detroit, and look what they've done to it. *Look.*

There was an empty plot of land where our first bungalow near 6 Mile had been. I don't remember who discovered its absence, but it had burnt down, or otherwise disappeared, within a decade of our having sold it.

The supply of abandoned homes in the city, with its preponderance of single-family structures and its rate of depopulation, was nearly endless, with stockpiles enough to last years. "To a unique degree," Coleman Young said, seeking to explain the Devil's Night fires, "Detroit had buildings to burn." It also had buildings to demolish, and it's possible that our house, rather than being a Devil's Night fatality, had instead fallen into the hands of drug dealers and been knocked down during Young's "Crack Down on Crack" campaign. Regardless: it took forty or fifty years for people of my grandparents' generation to see pieces of their past begin to vanish. For people of my parents' generation it was twenty or thirty. It took less than a decade before I began to lose the first tangible links to what became, once such links were severed, a bygone era in my life. A sense of life's impermanence was imprinted on my psyche, along with the knowledge that nothing ever really returns. When things—neighborhoods, landmarks, businesses—go, they're *gone*.

It was clear that our corner of Detroit was beginning to change beyond recognition already. Clearer still was the knowledge that it would be up to me to do the literary preservation work.

"X" hats were everywhere that summer, in anticipation of the release of the major motion picture. That same summer, in sync with the zeitgeist, the Detroit Board of Education decided to open an African-centered academy—its third, after Marcus Garvey and Paul Robeson—in a predominantly white neighborhood on the city's west side, to be named after Malcolm X. This decision went over like a lead balloon, and the angry reaction of whites in that section of the city made news all summer.

That the school board would seek to open a Malcolm X Academy didn't surprise me—I'd assumed there was one already—neither did the media's portrayal of white residents' resistance as simply racist. Analogies to Little Rock were frequent. Hostile whites, black parents seeking the best for their kids, black students who just wanted to learn—it was the same story line, or presented as such. Little attention was paid to the fact that almost everything about this situation was different—that blacks, far from being powerless, controlled the city, including its school board; that the building the academy would occupy had already housed a school, closed by the Board of Education seven years before, and that the remaining neighborhood public school, predominantly white, was severely overcrowded as a result. And although in a concession to the overcrowding issue the school board had indeed opened a few slots at the academy to neighborhood kids, the unwillingness of white parents to send their kids to the academy was probably something more than the usual working-class racism, because it wasn't just the three R's being taught in the school but an Afrocentric curriculum, the driving impulse of which, aside from the usual mumbo jumbo about melanin and libations, may have been best illustrated at a Board of Education meeting when white residents who had questions about the curriculum were sneered at as "white devils."

When the Archdiocese of Detroit proposed opening a similar academy for at-risk black males, to be run by the Jesuits, a member of the school board said: "My concern is whether we as a people should allow white men—whether they are priests or pimps—to be the educational guardians over our black boys." During a radio interview, this same individual, angered by the resistance of white residents to the Malcolm X Academy, raised the possibility of leveling the neighborhood by armed force. This was a public statement, made by a city official. It was easy to feel that at least a little of Little Rock's moral authority had been lost, while registering simultaneous relief that the academy had been designated for some other section of Detroit populated by white people who had forgotten to move out or were city workers or something.

I'd assumed that there was already a Malcolm X Academy in the city because a year and a half before, during our senior year of high school, a friend of mine had written a front-page article for the school paper about the initial vote of the Detroit Board of Education in favor of opening such an academy for at-risk black males, to be named after Malcolm X. Infuriatingly fair-minded, the article noted that race-and/or sex-segregated public schools were open to legal challenge (the American Civil Liberties Union and the National Organization for Women would eventually force the Malcolm X Academy to accept female students), as were Catholic schools, like ours, with a tax-exempt status.

Catholic schools had to be able to justify the sex segregation, which our principal, Father Louis, did as follows: "The purpose historically [of single-sex schools] is to alleviate some of the pressures." We thought that was what girls were for, but his point was more persuasive. The principal of the girls' school next door, Sister Shirley, was given the same opportunity to justify her single-sex institution: "There are no male counterparts in a girls' school, so the girls must take all the leadership roles. Statistics show that women who head companies probably got their education in an all-female environment." The article, which concludes by saying that "schools separated by sex, religion and race are difficult issues," was accompanied by a picture of two of our classmates, one white and one black, with a caption stating that they "couldn't be friends in a race-segregated school."

Back on campus the next fall, the professor of my minority literature class had us attend a lecture by the originator of Kwanzaa, one of the very experts in Afrocentric education who had advised the Detroit School Board on the curriculum for its African-centered academies. I thought to make mention of this lecture during a visit home, to get a rise out of my father, but I didn't think it would work. He wouldn't have cared, for strictly economic reasons. I could anticipate his line of thinking: The kid has a scholarship, thank Christ, so at least over there I'm not *paying* for this crap.

It was against this backdrop that I worked during my summers home. Baldwin and Ellison—I kept the latter's *Going to the Territory* on my lap when called down to the City-County Building for jury duty—seemed infinitely remote, even though their subject matter was much closer to me in Detroit than it was on the fourth floor of the college library. It was one of the paradoxes of bookishness: though drawn to certain writers because of the skill with which they handle their material, you eventually come to care more about the skill than the material, and the book itself comes to mean more than that to which it points beyond its covers. Rather than directing your gaze outward, the book's very quality causes you to burrow in deeper, as external considerations recede.

I cut grass my first and second summers home for a college located in the Cass Corridor. The campus grounds crew was predominantly black, with a handful of white guys of the bearded, big-bellied Vietnam vet variety. My favorite crew member, a black guy of considerable charm, once walked into work well after seven o'clock, not at all concerned to be punching in late, swinging the door open wide enough to make an *entrance*—the undisputed champ, nonchalantly climbing into the ring.

"Well, well," one of the white guys at my table said, "if it isn't the black Jesus."

"Is there any other kind?" my hero asked, a line that went straight into the next scene I began to sketch.

Each morning, the supervisors handed out the keys to the trucks to the full-timers, along with verbal instructions regarding the day's assignment; then the summer help, like me, would be paired with a senior groundskeeper who, being a good union employee, would sit back and watch the college kid do much of the work. At the end of my first day, when I'd been sent out alone with a push mower to take care of a patch of grass inaccessible by riding mower, I ran up to the steward, quickly explaining why I'd failed to finish the job. "You think that grass ain't gonna be here tomorrow?" he asked, smiling.

After receiving our assignment, shortly after seven, my partner and I would head off to breakfast. Our favorite diner, located a few streets south of Tiger Stadium, was owned and operated by Macedonians, or Armenians, or Albanians: some variety of hirsute, shuffling people who accumulate their fortunes through coins left on countertops, and thereby build their empires across the sea. They never seemed more than one remove from their mercantile roots. I could always picture them standing in a town square somewhere in southeastern Europe, bartering for the pots and pans they'd need to set up shop in America. The waitresses in the place—all of whom looked to be sisters, or at least cousins—were coarsely beautiful, with full, rounded features and fabulous noses. When I went up to settle the bill and the girl behind the counter closed the register with her hip, I fell smack in love.

My partner tried to be considerate regarding the radio as we drove around the city, but by and large we listened to black stations while he was behind the wheel. When he got out of the truck for some reason, leaving it running with me inside, I'd switch the station, changing it back upon his approach. Though the truck was an automatic he drove with two feet, using his right foot for the accelerator and his left for the brake. Was this a black thing? According to my father, there were drivers who could handle a stick shift's three pedals with a single foot, whereas my partner employed both feet for an automatic.

Occasionally I'd work alone, driving around in an old green truck—it was a stick, with three on the tree—with a two-thousand-gallon drum loaded in the back. I could spend the better part of a morning filling the drum with water, with the afternoon dedicated to driving around to the planters that dotted the campus. I'd stop, hop out, grab the hose, and water the flowers as heavily as I could without drowning them in the process. The soil was often cracked from dryness.

The truck was wide, and the drum in back filled the rearview mirror. I had to rely on the side mirrors to see behind me, but the width of the truck was such that I couldn't see anything in them that wasn't a considerable distance off my back bumper. One afternoon I parked along the I-94 service drive, climbed down from the truck, and watered a planter full of dying marigolds. When I got back into the truck there was no one behind me, so I put it in reverse and backed up. "Stop!" a man yelled, running along the sidewalk toward the back of the truck. "Stop!" When I got out of the truck the owner of a tiny Ford Festiva, the front fender of which was totaled, explained, at unbelievable decibel levels, exactly how he was going to go about collecting damages.

I drove back to the shop and told the steward what had happened. I was afraid that the damages would be taken from my paycheck and that I'd end up *owing* the shop money, having to work the rest of the summer as a way of settling the debt. "He parked on your back bumper?" the steward asked. "The bumper of a truck that big? The hell with him!" He went over and told the shop's repairman, a white guy, what had happened. "What the hell was the guy thinking?" the repair-man asked. "Don't worry, kid," he said to me. "It was his fault, the ass-hole. And we're insured."

My partner made an enviable supplementary income moonlighting. Many times he'd take the truck and, on company time, go cut the lawns of homeowners who'd contracted him to do so. This made perfect sense, given the poor wage groundskeepers were paid, and I admired his entrepreneurial spirit.

Other workers with whom I was paired left campus for no better reason than to buy lottery tickets or beer, or to drive back home and watch television. One older, southern fellow—he was "a Georgia black," and proud of it—actually did all three: he stopped at a liquor store, bought ten dollars' worth of scratch-off lottery tickets (all losers) and a forty-ounce malt liquor, and then drove both of us back to his house at I-94 and Chalmers. There were bars on the front and side windows, and I was fairly certain I was about to be killed. All he did, however, was tune his TV to one of Detroit's UHF channels, and for the next several hours we sat together in silence, watching the morning lineup of sit-coms: Jeannie, Gilligan, the Hillbillies. He had us back to the shop in time for lunch.

There were a couple of Indian graduate students on the crew, sum-mer help like me. They were both studying computer engineering; both were effeminate and often taunted. "Hey, want some of my cheese-burger?" a black crew member once asked the weaker of the two over lunch. Without missing a beat another black worker came in: "Naw, man, you know they worship the cow and shit. Could be eating their cousin." It was with one of these students, Trilochan, that I once drove to a photo shop on Woodward Avenue. I'd cut out a picture from a run-ning magazine of the great John Ngugi, the Kenyan distance runner who'd won the World Cross Country Championship five consecutive times. I wanted this picture blown up, the idea being that I'd tack it to the wall of my off-campus apartment to inspire me to hit the trails when I went back to school in the fall. Trilochan snickered. "Why do you want that picture bigger?" he asked, making a bad face. "This," I said slowly, "is John Ngugi, the greatest distance runner the planet has ever seen. He can run ten thousand meters in—" "He's a black." "He's not an American black," I said, unsure if the drawing of such distinctions was an act of open-mindedness or its opposite. I pressed ahead anyway. "He's Kenyan. An East African. Most American blacks are West Africans." "He's a black," Trilochan said again, ending our little talk.

There was a basketball hoop in the grounds department parking lot, and in the fifteen minutes before the end of work, when everyone had brought the mowers back but it wasn't yet time to punch out, we played games of pickup basketball. I could hold my own on the court, which helped my standing with my coworkers, but my stock rose immeasurably one afternoon just before the Fourth of July. There was a discussion of the upcoming fireworks display downtown in Hart Plaza, and the relative merits of attending the celebration (which draws a million people a year) in person as opposed to watching it on TV. "You wouldn't catch me down there for anything," a fat white worker, a Warren resident, piped up. "People get shot down there." This was met with silence, for its logic was easy enough to follow. There had, in fact, been several racial incidents in years past.

These were tense times, and not only because of the L.A. riots and the Malcolm X Academy. Something—you could sense it—was set to go off in the city. A few months later, in November, two white cops, nicknamed Starsky and Hutch in the neighborhood they patrolled, would kill a black man during a struggle after a traffic stop. The deceased had his fist closed, and the cops fought to get him to open it—for fear, they claimed, that he was carrying a weapon. According to the prosecution, death resulted from repeated blows to the head, courtesy of the officers' flashlights. The defense cited the cause of death as cardiac arrest, resulting from the drugs in the deceased's system at the time of the struggle. In a nationally televised interview before the trials began, Coleman Young made his views known, calling the death a "murder." A Detroit jury agreed; at the end of my second summer home, the cops were convicted of second-degree murder and sent to prison in Texas. My sister's soccer coach of a year before the murder occurred was the daughter of the officer who'd received the lighter of the two sentences.

As the "people get shot down there" comment continued to hang in the air, I felt it contingent upon me—a white Detroiter, and so a bridge between the two camps—to lighten the mood. "Oh, go back to the suburbs," I said to the white guy, getting a big laugh out of those within earshot. My partner particularly appreciated the line, as it reminded him that I too was a Detroiter.

"Where you stay at?" he asked me. When I told him that I stayed on the east side, not far from where he lived, our friendship became a fact, and the white kid, not for the first time, became something of a mascot. He began taking me to the weight room where he and a few other black guys on the crew worked out on their lunch hour. "You've got a good build," he said, slapping my pectorals, "but we need to bring out that chest a bit."

The next summer, as he and I were driving along I-94 to the east side so that he could cut somebody's grass while still on the clock, a radio news report informed us of Coleman Young's decision not to run for reelection in the fall. It was the summer of 1993, and Young had been Mayor of Detroit for as long as I'd been alive: twenty years. "What do you think of that?" I asked. "Oh, you know, he's had a good run. It's time."

Outside the truck, at the end of Young's good run, Detroit's rate of decline was like the sun's daily progress across the sky: you couldn't actually see it, on a second-by-second basis—you'd go blind from the staring—but you knew it was happening, if only because it kept getting darker. It dawned on me that, though it was a right I'd yet to exercise, I was now of voting age, and that his retirement meant, among much else, that I'd never get a chance to cast a ballot against the mayor.

For Sale by Owner

AFTER CATHOLIC SCHOOL, nothing academic would ever be difficult again. I eased my way through my junior and senior years of college, taking my required classes, continuing with the required reading list that I'd made up for myself. The list was preparation for graduate school, which my English professors were pushing me toward. "You'll need a Ph.D. in English if you want to cut my grass," my father said. Why, with my talent for them, I hadn't gone into math or science was beyond him.

"The neighborhood's changing," people kept saying over summers home, and no one ever bothered to delineate how because everyone knew how—the only way anything ever changes in working-class areas: for the worse. It was time, you heard again and again, to get out, and this meant out of the city itself. From 6 Mile you could still move to 7 Mile; after 7 Mile there was still 8 Mile; but once your neighborhood abutted 8 Mile Road and that neighborhood itself began to go, the suburbs beckoned. We began saying goodbye to more and more people. It was hard not to feel left behind. There was a bumper sticker, as ever, that said it best: DETROIT—WILL THE LAST ONE TO LEAVE PLEASE TURN OUT THE LIGHTS?

We stuck around a little while longer, and my third and fourth summers home—over which I continued with that reading list—I worked at a machine shop on Trumbull Avenue, a mile north of Tiger Stadium. My father had worked at the shop, where performance camshafts were ground, in the early 1970s, back when the business was thriving. He would sometimes take me down to the shop, the proud father of the little boy in the blue baseball hat with the "STP" decal on the front. The boss's German shepherds slept inside the building, and I'd pull their tails and use them as pillows while my dad talked business with the big men with booming voices who shared their thoughts about the new Edelbrock intake and the aesthetic as opposed to performance benefits of dual exhaust, which provided minimal boost on a four cylinder but was a bit more advantageous on a V-6 or V-8. Back then, the business was located in what could rightfully have been deemed a bad neighborhood. By the mid-1990s, I was working behind bulletproof glass.

But it was still in the same building, with the same boss, who was descended from a long line of Galician Jews and brilliant in the skewed way lunatics often are. A big believer in conspiracies he couldn't begin to articulate, an intellectual who couldn't be bothered to read a book, a one-track mind that was always untracked, a drug-addled health nut—a Noam Chomsky fan, in short—he spent a good deal of each day defending the former Soviet Union, about whose policies he believed himself an expert, and answering those few customers who still called the shop and politely asked how he was doing by invoking the specter that was, at any rate, still haunting him: "Struggling!" he'd yell into the receiver, half a dozen times a day. Not "fine," not "not bad—yourself?" It was always the same answer, delivered with the same laugh, one that came down, just barely, on the sane side of hilarity.

Things hadn't always been such a struggle. At one point during more prosperous days another of my father's former bosses, a man who owned a place in the suburbs, had offered the Communist machine shop owner a million dollars for the building on Trumbull Avenue, along with the machinery and stock. He declined the offer. Years later, as business dwindled, he considered seeking a share of the Federal Empowerment Zone grant money that Coleman Young's successor, a bespectacled lawyer not much given to public cursing, had received from the Clinton administration. The grant to individual businesses was reported to be two hundred thousand dollars a throw, but it was earmarked for *new* business development; the machine shop owner had been in the area for three decades as the neighborhood imploded around him. He toyed with the idea of closing the shop and opening under a new name—he'd done this before, after declaring bankruptcy—but no dice.

He lived in the house behind his business, having only to walk through his backyard, where dog shit grew instead of grass, and cross the alley to enter his shop's rear door. In the early 1970s, an eighty-page company brochure had described his operation as "the fastest-growing camshaft maker in the industry," with the popularity of its cams "evidenced at every drag strip throughout the nation by the growing list of satisfied users. . . . A favorite in the winners' circle!"

Seventy pages follow, listing the camshafts on offer and providing a description of each: "Really hot street/strip cam. Requires at least a 4-bbl carb; headers recommended." "Street/strip terror. Revs to 6800 rpm." "For ultimate street engine. Low duration provides low end torque." "Wildest cam considered streetable." My father wrote the descriptions and my mother typed up the brochure, which ends with a photo gallery featuring the cars of satisfied users at the drag strip. Checkered flags, the logo of the cars' sponsor, Gratiot Auto Supply, are painted on their sides.

I could, in a pinch, change the oil on a car, dumping the old oil in the far corner of our backyard, but that was about the extent of my automotive know-how. I made deliveries for the shop. "Oh, you must be Bob's boy!" other machine shop owners would say (to use the name my father gave himself) when I walked into their offices, carrying performance cam-shafts and assorted components in boxes under my arms. I'd nod, acknowledging that I was indeed Bob's boy, while they talked at length about the parts I was delivering. They were under the mistaken impression that I had the same appreciation for valve springs and steel retainers that my father possessed, an enthusiasm that many of these men, overseeing what were now family operations, had managed to pass on to their own sons. "It's just a summer job for me," I wanted to tell them, "not a way of life." But my disclaimers were quickly dismissed. "Oh," they'd say, "I'm sure you picked up plenty, hanging out in the garage with your old man." Aside from his expertise, they thought that I'd also inherited my father's modesty. "No, really," I wanted to say. "I don't know shit."

Some of the shops where I delivered or picked up parts were still in the city, situated in similarly down-at-the-heel buildings on Chene, Mt. Elliott, and West Grand Boulevard, their street addresses spray-painted on solid metal doors. But the majority were out in the suburbs, with the preponderance in Macomb County industrial parks, where the roads curved every which way and branched off in half a dozen directions before ending in identical-looking cul-de-sacs. I was provided the use of an old Chrysler station wagon without working windshield wipers—during rainstorms, I drove with the driver's side window down, using my left arm to wipe water from my line of sight—and with brakes that locked up if any pressure above a light tap was applied, sending the car into a dangerous skid. My predecessor had been the owner's own mother, an elderly Jewish woman who continued to drive around Detroit and make deliveries well into her nineties. She lived at 6 Mile and Livernois, near the University of Detroit, and remembered me from my boyhood trips to the shop, right down to my baseball hat. She despaired of her son—no wife, no kids, a business going bust—but never ceased to help him while her health held out.

If I'd been at the shop a few years before, I'd have made deliveries in one of the fleet of company cars—four in all—that the owner had purchased for a total of fifteen thousand dollars, cars imported from Eastern Europe and so fantastically cheap that reverse was said to be an option. None of them was still functioning when I started work at the shop. The only employee who remained from the 1970s was the head of the shipping department. After I was done with deliveries, or on days when there were none to make, I'd help him stamp the cams that were being shipped that day—this involved driving a steel punch into the end of the cam with a heavy hammer—and fill out the invoice slips before boxing the cams and stacking them up, pyramid-style, on a cart, which we'd push to the shop's back door. Everything had to be ready to go by four o'clock, when the UPS truck came by, honking up a storm in the back alley, after which the shipping manager would relax and enjoy a joint, his workday done.

By the mid-1990s the business was unable to generate the crime-preventing antibodies that prosperous enterprises use to repel law-breakers and bar undesirables, so a revolving cast of characters hung around the shop in its final days: drunks and drug addicts, the diseased and the deformed, violent criminals and harmless kooks. Some of these folks actually managed to make it onto the payroll, particularly the neighborhood kids who, like me, were hired as gophers and (unlike me) spent their workdays dealing drugs out of the shop's back door. Though this sort of permissiveness angered the guy in shipping, who claimed to care more than the boss about whether or not the business stayed afloat, the boss himself was in no position to throw stones where drugs were concerned. Before stumbling into work around eleven o'clock or so, he'd often snort a line or two.

A drunken cabbie who sometimes helped us make deliveries had the distinction of not only being a permanent fixture at the shop, where he drank wine out of Styrofoam coffee cups, but of living with its owner in that house behind the alley. He was legally handicapped, suffering from a mental disorder—nothing too severe—that made him eligible for aid checks from the government, which his roommate, the shop's owner, skimmed before passing along. This was done both to cover the cabbie's room and board and to prevent him from spending the entirety on booze. The cab company also withheld a portion of his pay, as a means of recovering the money it had lost on cabs he'd destroyed while driving under the influence.

Such stories were either true or they weren't. One either believed them or one didn't, and it wasn't altogether clear which was more gullible, to believe or not to believe. They certainly sounded like bullshit, but take a look around the place. Take a look around the *city,* and at the people who stepped in off its streets and crowded the shop: a burn victim who rode around on a ten-speed with bent rims and bore a serious grudge against one person this day, another the next; a Native American in sunglasses and cowboy boots who always seemed to have something cooking; a mathematician with massive Popeye forearms who claimed to have been molested by the Jesuits at the University of Detroit and who sent me letters describing, in single-spaced detail, the airborne diseases that could prove problematic on military submarines. Nothing in this city could be ruled out. According to my father, the owner of the shop— a card-carrying Communist, whose scattered copies of the *Nation* and the *Worker's World* enabled me to continue my periodical reading over the summer—had once run a successful business. Impossible, but there it was.

There was more: stories that the boss, who claimed to be broke, had stashed seven hundred and fifty thousand dollars in a safe-deposit box in the Renaissance Center, along with stories that, for failure to keep up the nominal yearly fee for the box's rental, its contents had been seized. True? Not true? Sixty years before, just a few miles away, a door-to-door silk salesman had spun a story about an evil scientist who'd been banished to a desert island and, as revenge, had created a devilish, bleached-out race of people, forced to live like savages in the caves of Europe. Laugh if you like: such laughter, in this city, would always be at your own risk.

The shop had an occasional receptionist, a pretty Italian girl in short shorts whose father, one street back, controlled the area's drug trade. Its only other consistent employee was an old automotive hand who'd come to Detroit way back when and who could still operate, with immigrant ease, any of the grinders on the floor of the shop, supplying the additional grinds needed for competition-only cams. He didn't speak much, but something about his tired presence brought the names of World War I battle sites to mind. Watching this slightly stooped figure work the grinders, a mass of white hair drowsing atop his head, I recalled schoolbook photographs of deeply dug trenches and muddied Flanders fields, and tried in vain to remember the death toll at Belleau Wood.

By my second summer at the shop his health was bad, and his attendance was no longer all that consistent. He'd begun to live in the boss's house along with the cabbie, and he limped into the shop with a heavy gauze wrap around his right foot, which was gangrenous. I learned from the boss that the machinist was a diabetic, that his circulation was bad, and that things didn't look good. I'd sometimes watch him hobble across Trumbull Avenue to the football field, where he'd spend his lunch hour sitting in the sun with his foot propped up. Later, no longer able to walk under his own power, he'd lean his crutches next to him as he sat in the sun. Near the end of that summer, the boss walked into the shop, unhurriedly making his usual late-morning arrival, and asked me to drive him to Receiving Hospital. The machinist, he said, was dying.

The hospital was full of the friends and family of others who were sick and near death. They flipped the pages of old magazines and stared at the television in the upper corner of the waiting room, wondering what else was on. The boss talked, nervously and loudly, his speech punctuated with hyena laughs. It was a mindless, miserable chatter, and more or less nonstop. I wanted to tell him to shut it—a hugely inappropriate response under the circumstances, but something I'd said to him on past occasions. It was something that everyone said to him, sooner or later. He took no offense.

There were two white Detroit cops in the waiting room, and I gathered that they'd brought in an injured suspect. The boss had gotten up to pace, but stopped near one of the cops, a young officer with a blond brush cut and a Polish last name visible above his badge. The boss, whose eyesight wasn't the best, had to squint at close range to make out the name. "What are you looking at?" the cop asked. At first I thought he was kidding—there's always a delay of a second or two before belligerence registers with me, a moment when my good nature gets the better of me and I give someone the benefit of the doubt before concluding that the guy is just an asshole. The boss was oblivious. "Karpinski! Oh, I thought it said Kowalski. That's the name of my accountant, you see. I thought maybe you were a relation." "What are you looking at?" the cop asked again. "See, I thought your last name—" "I heard you the first time." "—was Kowalski, which is the name—" The cop thrust out his broad chest, to give the boss a better look. "My badge number is there above my name, if you want to get that, too. I'll take the badge off if you'd like, and the two of us can step outside."

I'd gotten up by this point, walking toward the two guys with batons in their belts and handguns in their holsters. Aside from the cop and his partner, the boss and I were the only whites in the waiting room, and this little law enforcement display was a show of strength, one safely freed from any racial overtones. I wanted to say to the cop: Look, I understand you're frustrated. I understand that you'll never rise through the ranks. That you make twenty-six grand a year and that your annual increases will be garbage. That you hate the people of the city you patrol and hate yourself for patrolling it. That you hate yourself for living here—or for having to provide a phony address if you don't. That your life is in danger during every shift and that any attempt to enforce the law, let alone defend yourself, opens you up to charges of police brutality upon a black populace. And so it's easier to pick on my friend here. But that's not his fault. His friend's dying and he's sad as hell. So give him a break. In other words—fuck off.

"Can you believe that?" the boss said when we both sat back down. He sounded like the nerdy kid on the playground, brushing the gravel off his back, furious at himself for having been knocked down yet again by the class bully. He was going on sixty and sounded six, so full was he of impotent rage. For the first time since I'd known him, he sounded as if he were actually struggling.

I'd come home several months before this second camshaft summer, during the winter of my senior year, to help my parents and sister with their move out of Detroit. It was February, frigid, and I asked the steward overseeing the operation—my mother—about the number of boxes marked DAD'S MAGS that I was expected to carry up one set of basement steps and down another.

"These are all *Car Craft*?" I asked, surveying the dozens of boxes stacked around the old basement, where I knew each crack in the tile. "Yes, they are." "Jesus." "Move them, mister." By the time I'd finished hauling the boxes, I was ready to write a scathing letter to the editor of *Rod Action*.

Before any house in Detroit is sold it has to undergo a city inspection, which mandates assorted improvements to the property as a condition of its sale. "They made us put a bar across the back door," my father said, recalling the inspection. "You know, the one off your sister's bedroom that didn't lead anywhere? They didn't want that door to open at all. Fine. They made me ground the outlets in the bathroom, and do some tuck-pointing—minor stuff—between the bricks around the front steps. What else? I paid a guy to replace four or five squares of sidewalk, which wasn't bad, since there were about forty squares, total, along the front and side of the house. And in the garage—can you believe it?—they had me disconnect the gas line and cap the heater that was up in the rafters." My father had spent hundreds of winter nights working in that garage, an impossibility without the heater, but the city inspection was famous for such nitpicky pointlessness. "The first thing the new owner did, I'm sure, was to take off the cap and reconnect the gas," he said.

My parents had paid twenty-nine thousand dollars for the house in

1979 and sold it, sixteen years later, for forty-five thousand. I said that a 50-percent appreciation seemed pretty good. "What difference does the percentage make?" my father said. "When you go to the store to buy something, do you pay for it with a percentage? No, you pay for it with dollars, and the house went up a thousand dollars a year for sixteen years—less, if you factor in inflation. This place went up peanuts. If you really want to figure it right, factor in the city taxes we paid over the years, and you're looking at a net loss."

The For Sale by Owner sign still stood in front of my parents' new house, and that was because neither the sellers nor my parents could get it out of the frozen ground. I had to rock the sign back and forth for several minutes in mittened hands before I could pull the thing up. I put it in the back of my parents' new garage—which, I discovered upon opening the door, was structurally unsound. It leaned pronouncedly to the west, preventing the garage door, when I came to shut it, from closing completely; there was a two-foot gap at the bottom. My father, who'd always asserted that garages were more important than houses, had bought a house with a garage that was tipping over. Times were changing. My mother, the morning after moving in, saw a rabbit in the backyard. "It's like we live in the country now," she said, standing in the living room of her new house half a mile outside the city limits.

It occurred to me, as I pulled up that sign, that this was how my novel had to end. Except instead of pulling up a For Sale sign, my narrator would be planting one.

Of course we carried things with us out of the city that couldn't be packed in boxes, that transcended the merely material and went to the core of our identities as belated former Detroiters: a sense that life is, in the main, a movement from bad to worse; a belief that Detroit was a toilet and its suburbs were more so—that there was nowhere to live, but that you've got to live somewhere; and the self-congratulatory feeling that, whoever might have destroyed Detroit—the whites who'd fled it or the blacks who'd inherited what the whites had fled—it wasn't us.

We had, on the whole, done our best. We hadn't left the city in 1955, or 1965, or 1975, or 1985, but 1995—long after all but the smallest percentage of whites, and an ever-increasing percentage of blacks, had done the same. It was hard to shake a feeling of anticlimax; it trailed us out of the city.

Also following us out of the city was my sister's boyfriend, who'd presented a further complication to a close-minded relative or two around the holidays. In fact, her boyfriend's race—he was half black—was bound up with our having remained in Detroit: "That's what happens when you stick around the city too long. And such a nice girl, too." A couple years earlier, when they'd begun going out, my mother had said to me, in her serious tone, "Your dad just thinks, sooner or later, it'll be a problem." "For *whom?*" I asked, the open-minded English major highlighting the breadth of his worldview by stressing his proper use of the objective case. "He's a helluva nice guy, Ma." My mother didn't disagree; she agreed completely, in fact. He may not have been the best catch—my sister, it was clear, would be the breadwinner—but there wasn't much bad that could be said about him.

Like most big brothers, I'd spent a good deal of time growing up torn between the desire to put a protective arm around my baby sister and the urge, barely repressible at times, to smack her snotty little face. Long after leaving behind Sister Marie's second grade class, my sister retained something of the look of the Catholic school angel who's been told how darling she is just one too many times. During fights as kids, she'd often make me laugh myself into a state of utter defenselessness; as I curled up on the floor, convulsed with laughter, the pint-size menace with the bad bangs—our mother was growing them out—delivered body blows at will.

I was our mother's favorite, and my sister was the cute one: this was the sibling deal we'd struck. "Mom loves me more," I'd say. "Well, I'm cuter," my sister would reply. Sometimes my sister would go first; but regardless of who began it, the argument never went past this point. It was a draw, a wash. In this way, things were kept *even*, something that was of paramount importance to our mother. The middle child in a family of five, born a mere ten months after the arrival of the only boy, she'd always felt slighted, and was determined with her own children to keep everything fair and square. What is done for one must be done for the other. "Here's three dollars," she'd say, handing me the bills on the sly. "What for?" "I just gave your sister five dollars to go to the movies." "So?" "So, yesterday I gave you two bucks for Mr. C's pizza. This way it evens out." "Ma, really, I don't give a shit." "Just *take it*," she'd say, pushing the bills back into my palm.

Single-sex Catholic high schools had stunted our social growth to such an extent that neither of us had any real means of gauging the seriousness of our initial college relationships. What for more seasoned late adolescents would have seemed nothing more than a Saturday night's distraction took on, for us, the character of something preordained: to our great good fortune, we'd each met someone special straight out of the gate.

I'd moved beyond this premature monogamy by the time I completed my undergraduate degree, and so at the tail end of that post-baccalaureate summer, before leaving to begin graduate school, I traveled with a new girlfriend through the Northeast. By the time we made it down to Boston after spending a week together in Maine, where she'd taken a three-day kayaking trip in the Atlantic, I and my belongings—a newly bought mountain bike, along with a backpack full of books and dirty clothes—were deposited downtown, near Boston Common. Though we'd spent weeks plotting the trip beforehand, this stop was not part of our itinerary. For a hippie chick she had a temper, and she continued on alone to Cape Cod while I pushed my bike along the sidewalk, plotting my next move.

The priests. The thought came to me as I walked past my second or third church, searching the signs outside them, as I do reflexively, for service times and pastor names. The Marist Fathers, the men who ran my high school, had their headquarters in downtown Boston, not far from where I was standing. I went to a pay phone and called information. The order's main residence was just blocks away. I called ahead first.

A secretary put me through to the priest heading the order, a man who had been a religion teacher of mine at our high school. In his capacity as dean of discipline, he'd had several run-ins with my friend Kurt—a sadly wasted intelligence, according to the priest—but he had always thought well of me. He offered me a room for the night in the priests' residence, a several-story brownstone, and cleared his evening schedule to take me to dinner. My stumbling opening remarks, to remind him who I was, he had politely cut short. He remembered, he said, and was happy to hear from me.

"Your hair isn't dress code, Mr. Clemens," he said, looking me over as I walked into the priests' residence with my bike and backpack. Part of his job had been enforcing the school dress code, which did not allow for hair to touch one's collar. "Neither is his," I said, pointing to a painting of Jesus on the wall.

Over dinner I tried to explain how I'd arrived at his doorstep in a mild predicament, but he didn't press me for the means by which I had come to be this far from Detroit with no way, as yet, of getting back. As mine were in some sense girl troubles, it would have felt strange telling them to a priest. He suggested that after dinner I go to Cambridge, where I would find good bookstores, bars, and other things that might divert me. He had a subway map back at the residence. He would also give me the key to the front door, as everyone would likely be asleep when I got back. The room where I would be sleeping was on the third floor, and he'd see to it that there was a towel and wash cloth placed at the foot of the bed. Did I have money for the night? I told him I did.

I got back to the residence in the wee hours only a little drunk, worked the lock with difficulty, and tiptoed up to my room. There were some ancient priests snoring in the brownstone—how many I didn't know—and a nun or two to tend to them. That I was the only layperson in the house was certain, and something I could sense. I felt coarse, much as I had when I was ten years old and my fourth grade teacher, Sister Edna, walked over to our pew and asked my mother and me to carry up the offertory gifts at a Saturday-afternoon Mass, the family scheduled to have done so having backed out at the last minute. After my mother accepted she remembered, to her horror, that I wasn't dressed for the occasion. In the rush to make it to Mass on time she'd failed to notice that I was still wearing my play clothes—in this case, a black-and-white jersey T-shirt that one of my older cousins had bought for me at an AC/DC concert. The shirt was emblazoned with the title of the group's classic album *Highway to Hell*.

Catholicism, at its best, should retain an element of creepiness, and that creepiness came over me as I climbed the two flights to my room. I felt as if I might faint, and this light-headedness had nothing to do with the alcohol in my system. It was a sudden drop in blood pressure, brought about by proximity to crucifixes and incense and men of the cloth.

As a child I'd passed out several times at Mass. My parents and teachers sent me for tests to check for inner ear imbalances and blood problems (it turned out to be a mild anemia), but my real problem may have been an inability to take anything less than seriously, including Catholic ritual. The stations of the cross scared the hell out of me. Transubstantiation made my head spin. Lines from prayers constantly bounced around my brain as a child, and did so again as I held on to the handrail going up the steps. Of all that is seen and unseen. Born of the Virgin Mary, and became man. Suffered, died, and was buried. On the third day he rose again, in fulfillment of the scriptures. He has spoken through the prophets. He has spoken through the prophets. He has spoken through the prophets.

Once in my room I began to undress and prepare for bed. I decided against brushing my teeth, the search for a toothbrush, somewhere in my backpack, seeming not worth the bother. This hygienic lapse was typical of me on trips. When I was about to settle in, I heard a voice. "Paul," it said. My name had been whispered, the way one imagines hauntings beginning. To respond, it seemed, would have been to let my susceptibility to mysticism get the better of me. "Paul?" it said again. "Yes?" I ventured tentatively. "I just wanted to make sure you got in all right." There was, I realized, an intercom somewhere in the room—for elderly priests, in case of emergency—and Father was speaking to me through it. "Yes, I did. I got in fine." I was being overprecise, as I often am when drunk or frightened. "Did you wait up for me?" "No, I fell asleep, but I thought I heard you come in." "For a second I thought you were God." "No," he said, laughing, "just a priest. Good night."

In the morning we walked together to an airline ticket counter, on the first floor of a nearby downtown hotel, and I got a terribly expensive one-way ticket to Detroit, purchased with the credit card of a man who'd taken a vow of poverty. I would reimburse him, I assured him again and again, as soon as I got back. I told him that I had enough money to get a cab to the airport, but he said it was no problem for him to take me out to Logan.

Before we'd left the brownstone, he thought it wise to pack up his car, so that when we got back we could go straight to the airport without having to go inside and get my stuff. His car was parked on the street, right across from the residence. "We'll put it all in the trunk," he said. Though the backpack posed no problem, the bike didn't fit in the trunk, no matter which way we turned the handlebars, or whether or not I took off the bike's front wheel. "Let's put the bike in the backseat," he said. "Do you think that's a good idea?" I asked, as politely as possible. "If it fits," he said. It did, and he shut and locked his car's rear passenger door. I looked at my bike, still concerned. It was clearly visible from the sidewalk. "It's a pretty safe neighborhood," he said, and though he didn't give me the "you're not in Detroit anymore" speech— it was his hometown, too—he did hint that my concerns may have been exaggerated by my days in Detroit, where the downtown was deserted. This, on the other hand, was vibrant downtown Boston. People everywhere.

I'm not sure which one of us, on our return, was the first to see the glass on the sidewalk. Moving our eyes upward, we saw the rear passenger door swung open, and the window above it knocked out. My first instinct, upon seeing the glass—force of habit—was to grab the Easton by my bed and go after the bastards. But Boston was not Detroit, and Father was not my father.

He went inside, got a bucket and broom, and began to clean up the mess. I insisted on helping, tossing bits of glass into the bucket, and we took turns trading embarrassed apologies while crouched down on the sidewalk. "I'm sorry about your car," I said, feeling utterly helpless. "I'm sorry about your bike." "When I send you the check for the plane ticket, I'll be sure to include money for this." "Insurance will cover this. Did you have your bike insured?" "No." "Then there's no need to reimburse me for the ticket. You're out enough money already, and it's my fault the bike got stolen."

I rode to Logan Airport with broken glass on the floor in front of me and a breeze coming in from the open window behind. During the half-hour ride we discussed books—he knew I was about to go to graduate school at the University of Miami, where the English Department specialty was Joyce—and I was reminded of the dead priest in "The Sisters," the opening story in *Dubliners,* which I'd first read back in Mr. Vachon's AP English class. The story is narrated by a young boy with whom the priest had been close. "He had explained to me the meaning of the different ceremonies of the Mass and of the different vestments worn by the priest," the boy says. "Sometimes he had amused himself by putting difficult questions to me, asking me what one should do in certain circumstances or whether such and such sins were mortal or venial or only imperfections. His questions showed me how complex and mysterious were certain institutions of the Church." This was reminiscent of how the man driving me to the airport—who'd once defined the word *morality* on the chalkboard by using *moral* in his definition, a circularity to which I'd taken exception—had acted while my high school religion teacher. The boy continues: "The duties of the priest towards the Eucharist and towards the secrecy of the confessional seemed so grave to me that I wondered how anybody had ever found in himself the courage to undertake them."

And this is the story's secret. The priest, we learn, had broken a chalice near the end of his life. "They say it was the boy's fault," an old woman says in the narrator's presence, the implication being that it had happened during Mass and that the altar boy had somehow been remiss. "Of course, they say it was all right, that it contained nothing," she says, meaning no wine—no blood of Christ—had been spilled. Nonetheless, the priest, out of guilt-induced insanity, ends his days "sitting up by himself in the dark in his confession-box, wide-awake and laughing-like softly to himself."

I wondered: If a broken chalice could cause this much trouble, what about a broken window on a midsize American sedan? Father would suffer no crisis of faith over the incident (he'd take a position in Rome shortly thereafter), but the bike and broken window seemed like symbols—overly literary symbols, perhaps—for a break I had been contemplating anyway. After twenty-two years I was leaving Detroit, a city that for me had strong associations with—well, everything—not least broken-out car windows. It seemed fitting that my final adolescent interaction with the Catholic Church, the other dominant factor of my first couple decades, should revolve around the same.

Who Happened to Be

THE FIRST CHRISTMAS after I finished graduate school—making this 1997—I was living on Michigan's west side with a group of undergraduate friends. On Christmas Eve, during lunch break at the bookstore where I was working, I received a card inside an unwrapped copy of the Irish writer James Stephens's out-of-print novel *The Crock of Gold*. The writing on the outside of the card was feminine, the sort of soft rounded script that I'd been deeply in love with since the fifth grade, when I first began to serve as courier for notes from one giggling girl in saddle shoes to the next giggling girl in saddle shoes, two seats up.

The gift's giver (and I mentally ran through the possibilities as I opened the card) was clearly someone who knew that I'd just gone to graduate school to study James Joyce, and also knew that Joyce and Stephens had been friends. Joyce, a superstitious man, shared a birthday and a first name with Stephens, another Irish expatriate on the continent; that Stephens's last name was Stephen Dedalus's first sealed the deal. The kinship ran so deep that, in a moment of despair, Joyce had once asked Stephens, a near midget resembling a leprechaun, to finish *Finnegans Wake* for him. The last seminar I took in graduate school was devoted exclusively to the *Wake*, which couldn't have been any more confusing, it seemed to me, had it had a hundred different authors.

For my final paper, I had been assigned to review a recently published critical study of the *Wake*, a shockingly au courant take on the book that posited, among other things, that Joyce was forwarding a decidedly progressive political position in his nearly impenetrable (and, to me, apolitical) epic, championing the various causes of the wretched of the earth. This critical stance was a rearguard action, a way to keep "relevant" a dead white male novelist by making his work a template onto which readers could project their own political agendas. As I would not be pursuing a Ph.D., and have never been one to leave a perfectly good bridge unburnt, I decided to blast the book, even though it had been written by a friend of my professor's, himself a respected Joyce scholar.

My evidence? Not overwhelming: a hand gesture of Joyce's, in fact, one that Richard Ellmann records in a footnote near the end of his biography of the novelist. In conversation with fellow Irishman Thomas McGreevy, Joyce once said: "I love my wife and my daughter and my son. For the rest of the world—" And here he held up his hands. How I loved that! And how, I asked in my paper, which I read aloud to the seminar room, does one square those words and that gesture—Joyce had expressed similar sentiments to others—with the man this critical study asks us to accept, concerned to his very core with the plight of the proletariat? Suffice it to say that no one was quite as impressed by my logic as I was. How could anyone have been? Could I have said to them that Joyce's holding up his hands meant as much to me as it did because it reminded me of my own father, the only man I respected more than Joyce, someone I had often seen use a slight hand motion or a shrug of the shoulders to signify (something that is anathema to the academy) his being socially and politically disengaged? A week after delivering that paper I'd packed my bags and, armed with an unusable M.A., traded Coral Gables for yet more Michigan winters.

I'd gone down to Miami on a graduate teaching assistantship, which I viewed as a good way to postpone adulthood for two additional years on someone else's dime. I had no intention of pursuing a Ph.D.; I wanted to be a novelist, and I'd use these two years to string the scenes I'd sketched out into a narrative. I had no idea how I'd do this, but I knew I needed primary characters besides my narrator. I decided to give him a couple of friends—a smart-ass intellectual who likes to steal statues of the Virgin Mary from old ladies' backyards; a deeply stupid tough guy given to beating the shit out of punching bags and black people—and I had an ending in mind. The three of them would buy some eggs and drive into Grosse Pointe, where their mothers were cleaning ladies, and exact a little class-conscious revenge. When this got boring, the smart-ass would have a better idea: Let's drive downtown, he'd say, and egg The Fist.

I'd decided, after leaving graduate school, not to settle in Detroit for several reasons, the main one being that no one I knew still lived there. My parents now lived outside the city limits, and the corner of Detroit that I'd called home was home no longer. Better, I thought, to leave the area altogether than live in a suburb. When people asked where I was from and my answer produced in them the usual uncertain smile and hesitant response—"Really? What was *that* like?"—I no longer took much pleasure in the exchange. It was like growing up anywhere else, I said, and it was, even though Detroit was like nowhere else.

I knew that I had to stay away from the city if I wanted to write about it; this was received literary wisdom, proven by generation after generation of expatriate genius. So when I read about Coleman Young's death a few days after Thanksgiving 1997, I was living at a couple-hundred-mile and two-year remove from the city. I gave it only glancing notice—no one around me knew, or cared, who Coleman Young was. Ever disobliging, Young, who suffered from a congenital respiratory condition, was almost four years out of office before he got around to doing what so many in our neighborhood had wished he would while he still occupied the Manoogian Mansion. Over the previous summer he had contracted pneumonia, a complication arising from emphysema, itself the result of a lifetime of heavy smoking. ("I had the pleasure of being teargassed at the 1968 Democratic Convention in Chicago," Young wrote, "and it drove me back to smoking.") Toward the end, there were reports of a heart attack. He was tended at home for a time by his cousin, Dr. Claud Young—later a board chairman of the Southern Christian Leadership Conference—and the privacy that surrounded the mayor meant that information had a tendency to leak out, as if he were dying the static-in-the-phone-lines death of a Third World dictator. To some, this was a fitting end.

I was a Catholic Detroiter—at least this was how I still thought of myself—who no longer lived in Detroit and whose connection to Catholicism was slipping by the day. I'd gone to Mass a few times in Coral Gables with an Irish girl from San Francisco, but this had had more to do with the old Catholic school strategy of sitting in the pew next to the cute girl, so that you could shake her hand during the sign of peace, than it did with actual piety. Accustomed as I was to answering questions about the manner in which I was conducting my life, it was a bit of a shock to find, at the age of twenty-four, that no one asked me anymore about my level of religious observance—that no one cared, that no one would inquire, and that, as an adult, I was free, on this and other fronts, to do as I damn well pleased. The Marist Fathers were no longer my teachers, and neither were the grade school nuns; and the aunts, uncles, and grandparents who'd asked after the state of my mortal soul simply weren't around anymore.

In the spring of 1994, my cousins and I served as pallbearers at Father Hec's funeral, at St. Paul in Grosse Pointe. After coming out of the church with his casket and sliding it into the hearse, I continued to walk down the grassy slope toward Lake St. Clair, where I read the historical marker on the lawn near Lakeshore Drive. One side concerned the rectory and parish house where Father Hec had lived: "St. Paul Rectory was built in 1911. The parish house was built around 1900 as the home of former (1876–77) Detroit Mayor Alexander Lewis. Stove manufacturer Edwin Barbour acquired the house in 1913. Barbour's heir sold the house to Saint Paul Parish in 1959." Even Detroit's nineteenth-century mayors, it seemed, moved out of the city just as soon as they had the chance. Father Hec was cremated, and his ashes placed behind the parish house.

Six months after bearing Father Hec's coffin, we did the same for our Grandpa Saulino, whose funeral service was out in the redneck section of Macomb County that he and my grandmother had moved to. After the funeral Mass, as we escorted his casket out of the church and into the cold November morning, a souped-up Camaro drove past, blasting AC/DC's "You Shook Me All Night Long," the sublimely lewd lyrics to which I'd been singing since the age of seven. Over our grandfather's casket my Macomb County cousins and I exchanged quick smiles, and one of them executed a barely noticeable headbang, which he made into an act of benediction. The old Catholics might be dying off, but heavy metal was forever.

The final direct link to an afterlife upstairs was severed in the fall of 1997, shortly before Coleman Young's death, when Sister Marcia died at the convent of the Sisters of St. Joseph of Nazareth, on the outskirts of Kalamazoo. I hadn't seen her since leaving Detroit for graduate school. Our last meeting, in fact, had been at Bon Secours Hospital in Grosse Pointe in the spring of 1994, during Father Hec's final days. "You should become a doctor," she told me as we stood in the hallway outside Hec's room. "You've got the right disposition for it." "I'm an English major, Sister." "That doesn't mean you can't go to medical school." "True." As she'd once been stationed at St. John Hospital, her words carried the authority of experience. "Just promise me you'll think about it." "I will," I said, knowing better than to disagree with a nun. There's no percentage in it.

"She always thought a lot of you, you know," my mother said when she called with news of Sister's death. "I know that, Ma." "She thought you were just as smart as could be—not to mention a nice boy." "You might have mentioned something about this before." "Your sister and I are going to the funeral. Dad's got some things to do, so he won't be able to make it. Everyone's busy, and no one will hold it against you if you can't come." I wasn't the least bit busy, and Kalamazoo was only an hour from my apartment; the trip from Detroit was twice as far. Still, I begged off.

"It was sad," my mother said afterward. "Almost ninety years old, and no family, no kids, nothing." Among the few possessions Sister had left behind were a wooden statue of Jesus and a rosary, both of which my mother claimed, as if we didn't already have enough of both. "It was *her* rosary," my mother said. "It was broken, and missing beads, but it was *hers*. She used it all the time—that's why it was pieced together like that." And then, as the Saulino girls tended to, my mother passed the rosary along to my Aunt Marianne, receiving I don't know what in return.

I'd settled in the kind of place, smaller than Detroit or Chicago, where people are proud of their minor league baseball stadium and their new opera house but still, each year—especially on the outskirts of town—are sure to pick up the *Farmers' Almanac* to see if the prediction for winter snowfalls corresponds to what is being prophesied by trick knees and migratory patterns. Though not Ann Arbor or Madison, it was still a kind of college town, with students from three or four smaller schools and a nearby community college moving, on average, two and a half times a year, leaving a trail of broken leases and best-forgotten boyfriends and girlfriends in their wake.

Apartments were plentiful, and cheap; that many were also exceptionally nice was usually lost on the guys, but the female students and alums, more closely attuned to the value of such things, could often be overheard discussing, with great excitement, the beveled windows, high ceilings, hardwood floors, and doorway detailing in their new place.

Not that they would admit to a nesting instinct. These were progressive young women, the planners of peace marches and "Take Back the Night" rallies, girls who did their shopping not at the supermarket but at the food co-op, from which they carried home their kidney beans and couscous in the backpack they had picked up the summer of their junior year, while on a trip through the Asian subcontinent in search of poverty-stricken oneness.

My future wife, painfully thin when I met her, had just returned from a semester in Ireland, where she'd read James Stephens and his *Crock of Gold*. A week after she'd given me the Stephens book, as I was getting ready to go out the door and drive to Chicago to celebrate New Year's Eve, my roommate said, "Oh, that girl called." "What girl?" "That girl you're seeing." "I'm not seeing anyone," I said, though I knew to whom he was referring. "You spent Christmas Eve with her, didn't you?" This was true. I had spent Christmas Eve with her, quite platonically, in the company of a mutual friend from the bookstore where we worked, a guy who never had anything better to do. A snowstorm had thwarted my plans to drive back to Detroit that night and kept me in town until Christmas morning. We stayed up late talking, and around eleven o'clock, while it continued to snow big, slow flakes, we began serious discussions regarding Midnight Mass—they wanted to go, had heard it was lovely, and hoped I could show them when to kneel, stand, cross themselves, etc. But I didn't know any Catholic churches in the area, so we just kept talking and lighting candles.

During the week between Christmas and the New Year it became clear that we were building toward something. Though I hadn't yet read the Stephens book, I couldn't stop reading the accompanying card: "May the splendors of Detroit be yours this holiday season." Still, we hadn't made plans to spend New Year's Eve together. My old high school locker partner was driving over from Detroit and picking me up on his way to Chicago, where there were some vague plans to meet friends. I really didn't care what happened. I'd brought a list of telephone numbers of people I knew in Chicago, figuring someone would be home and have a floor I could sleep on.

"Her apartment is on the way to the highway," I told Tom as we climbed into his Corolla. "We're running a little late," he said, but I reminded him that we gained an hour driving to Chicago, which was a time zone behind us. "Besides, it'll only take a second. I just want to see what she wants." Her roommate let us in and called her to the living room. Tom smiled when he saw her: so this was why we stopped.

She asked, shyly, what I was up to, and I said that we were driving to Chicago for the night. "When are you leaving?" "Now." "Oh," she said, "I open tomorrow morning at nine. Rats." She was a girl who said "rats." "Hold on a second," she said, and ran to the back of the apartment. She returned smiling, holding a toothbrush aloft. "Promise to get me back on time?"

The second we got to Chicago I tried to ditch Tom, who'd deftly driven us through a blizzard on I-94, but he accompanied us to an Irish pub in Lincoln Park called The River Shannon ("[snow] . . . was falling softly upon the Bog of Allen and, farther westward, softly falling into the dark mutinous Shannon waves"). He'd failed to find the people we'd come to meet, vague figures whose names I could no longer recall. He stayed at our table for a couple drinks before making a graceful exit, eventually finding his way to the apartment of a friend of mine where, after several increasingly frantic phone calls, I'd secured our use of the floor.

The walls of the pub were lined with the photos of cadets from the Chicago Police Academy from the turn of the last century, almost every one of whom had an Irish last name. We talked about her time in Ireland, which she'd spent in a small village north of Galway. The houses they'd lived in were poorly heated, and I was charmed by her description of how, before turning in for the night, they'd heat pans on the stove and then run them over the bedding to warm the sheets and blankets. Every sixty minutes, with another round of Jameson's to warm us, we noted that it was actually an hour later, our time; by eleven it was already the New Year according to our body clocks, but I was secretly happy to have another hour to plot my midnight strategy. When 1998 finally came to Chicago, I gave her a polite peck on the cheek. A pub wasn't the place. "Let's go," I said. We walked to my friend's apartment in the snow and wind, huddling around the corners of buildings when the breeze off Lake Michigan became too much. She smoked a cigarette, and I did, too, for the hell of it, and we made some progress from that initial peck.

"Get up," I said to Tom a couple hours later, giving him a kick. Everyone else in the apartment—nine of us were on the floor—was fast asleep. My new girlfriend and I had been forced to sleep head to toe in order to fit. "It's five o'clock." "We've got time, then," Tom said. "It's a three-hour drive back." "But it's already six in Michigan. We lose an hour going that way." "I thought we gained an hour." "That was eight hours ago. Get up. We promised to get her back on time." We made it back by five to nine, and she brushed her teeth in the bookstore's bathroom.

On nights when she didn't have class and neither of us had work she began to cook dinners. I hadn't enjoyed many home-cooked meals in graduate school, though the occasional female Ph.D. candidate had taken pity on me. Neither had I had many nutritious meals since. Books I couldn't live without, but if I'd had to be personally responsible for all that went into the making of a pleasant dinner—the shopping, preparation, serving, and disposal—I'd have quite happily starved. My days, like those of many another postgraduate male, were distinguished by their almost complete inattention to life's organizing principles.

Back in the seventh and eighth grades, I'd been attracted to the cute Italian girls whose upper lips had begun to darken around the time mine had. Now I had found a girl who was fair, non-Catholic, and completely, eerily calm most all the time. I'd never before realized that it was possible to live a life at such a low decibel level. There was no need, as in Detroit, to constantly assert oneself; silence could be pleasant, even productive. For our first formal date we attended a performance of Mozart's Requiem, and we talked only slightly less during the sixty-minute funeral mass than we did at other times. I appreciated her passivity, which seemed less like weakness than a source of power, after the manner of those martial arts in which you employ your opponent's aggressiveness against him. Her blood pressure, I thought, must be astonishingly low, a stark contrast with that of the people where I had come from, where the entire region had a vein pulsating on its collective forehead. She made me want to be other—better—than I was.

On the first night such information would have any relevance to me she took my hand—hers were shaking—and said, "There's something I have to tell you." I smoothed her hair back, smiled, and said I didn't care. Four months later she was pregnant.

"I just remind myself that worse injustices happen all over the world, all the time," she said. This was sincere: there was an Amnesty International sticker on her stereo speakers, directly above a picture of Kurt Cobain.

The very calm that had first attracted me now infuriated me; I felt that I had to seek retribution, on her behalf, for the rape she'd suffered two years before. Though the question was by no means constant, occurring with varying degrees of intensity and sometimes staying away for days, it was never terribly far from my thoughts, either: Which tree to hang this fucker from?

She hadn't, in fact, specified her attacker's race—she was too socially sensitive for that. But a mutual friend filled me in on this detail a few weeks later. She, too, was a delicate young woman, of a sort common among our group: vegetarian, single, her recipes taken from *The Moosewood Cookbook* and her toothpaste trucked in from an organic farm in Maine—the sort of girl, as Salinger puts it somewhere, with a head full of very touching crap. It was a surprise, then, that she would freely inform me that the attacker was black. I'd thought, in these circles, that it was holy writ that black men didn't commit such crimes, and that Gregory Peck could prove it.

But a black man didn't rape her, I told myself; a man who happened to be black did. In the interests of open-mindedness and a sense of fair play, I kept repeating this to myself: a man who happened to be black. Who happened to be. Happened to—how's that for a funny locution? What were the odds, I wondered, of that "happened to" happening?

When I learned of the landlord who owned the building in which the rape had occurred, and who could have been held legally liable for failing to equip the apartment building with a locking front door, my mood improved considerably. It warmed my heart to have a white guy to want to hang as well—wouldn't want to leave myself open to charges of racism. I could picture him: some sensitive dork in sandals—*sandals*—whose delicately exposed metatarsals constituted incontrovertible proof that he posed no possible threat to anyone—had never, in fact, harbored an ungenerous thought in all his life. What need was there for a locking front door? Sure, the building was in a black neighborhood, and the renters were mostly white college kids—what could go wrong?

Every jerkoff in town worth his ACLU card and condescending smirk wore those fucking sandals. The only grown man in Detroit I'd ever seen wearing sandals was John the Baptist, as we neighborhood kids called him: an eccentric dressed in flowing black garb who walked up and down our side street and strongly resembled Frank Zappa. He walked miles each day through the Detroit desert, surviving on a diet of insects. John the Baptist could be spotted, on any given Tuesday afternoon, at 7 Mile and Schoenherr, at 6 Mile and Hayes, at 8 Mile and Hoover, and just in front of your family's front porch. Memories of John the Baptist walking down the middle of the road, muttering to himself, seemed to me to present an image of powerful, penetrating sanity compared to the stupidity with which I was now contending.

I flashed back to that Christmas Eve night. At one point in the evening, there'd been a discussion of crime in the area (we'd heard what we hoped was a car backfiring outside), and someone brought up a spate of recent crimes against women, mentioning that a woman's body had just been found along a highway. "It's because of all these repressed conservative Christians around here," my soon-to-be girlfriend said jokingly, referring to the abundance of Dutch Reformists who lived in the area. There were still some dry counties on this side of the state. I sat silent, but in a way that sought to express solidarity with her sarcasm: yes, these repressed Dutch Reformists.

As if that's who'd attacked her. People in Detroit may have been racists, but this was *nuts*.

The black population on the west side of the state was relatively small, or seemed so to someone accustomed to Detroit. One of the distinguishing features of the place—impossible to miss—was that you could go all day and not see a black man with a black woman. You saw black women with black children; but you didn't see black men with black children, or with black women. You saw black men with white women—women pretty, as a friend put it, in an Ernest Borgnine sort of way.

Back in Detroit, during a summer home from college, a fat blond single mother and her dishwater blond children had moved in across the street and a few houses down from us, right across from the Lutheran family. "You know what follows white trash, don't you?" you could hear people asking each other across front porches. We did. The single blond mother can be found in any similarly depressed area, where the white trash women come equipped with stretch pants, pendulous breasts, and black boyfriends pleased as punch to have landed themselves a white (what's the word I'm looking for here?) *bitch*.

It's a term her boyfriend clearly took a shine to. You could hear it coming from him at four in the morning on warm summer nights when the windows were open. "Bitch, you shut that baby up!" "Bitch, I thought you got that tire fixed!" The gunshot blasts I'd long been able to sleep through, but this was something new, as was the music he blared when his car pulled up a little after three each morning.

Now what, exactly, would respectable whites have done here? Sightlessness? Hearing loss? Which of their senses would have had to go? This is black behavior that our social betters simply cannot countenance and therefore pretend not to notice. Just to show that they're not completely oblivious, and by way of warning, they might remind me that we live in a country that, *ostensibly* anyway, is dedicated to the proposition that all men are created equal. Which is fine. Which is fantastic. But what comfort is that when it's three in the morning and outside your window the bass is booming, the *bitches* flowing? Does the "I Have a Dream" speech really matter at such moments?

I recalled the conversation my mother and I had several years before, about my sister's boyfriend: Your dad just thinks, sooner or later, it'll be a problem.

For *whom?*

For me.

How should one live? This is the question, a critic once said, that underlies every major nineteenth-century Russian novel; there was an answer, I was certain, on my bookshelf somewhere. It was a matter of close reading, of paying attention. *"Think!"* I thought, tapping the side of my own head now that my father wasn't around to do it. There was nothing study and hard work couldn't solve. Apply yourself.

I tried, but I wasn't in the mood to read—I wanted a fight—so I fought with my favorite black authors, in much the same way that watching the nightly news had been a fistfight for the fathers in my old neighborhood, with them in one corner of the living room and Coleman Young, on TV, in the other. Instead of blood on the canvas, my books had red ink spilled all over the margins.

In his essay "A Fly in Buttermilk," about the integration fight in southern schools, Baldwin quotes the mother of a fifteen-year-old black boy—the first student to integrate a previously all-white high school—on the inevitable issue of what such integration might lead to: "I really don't know how I'd feel if I was to carry a white baby around who was calling me Grandma." Later, when Baldwin interviews the school's white principal, a man who says that he never dreamed of a mingling of the races, Baldwin manfully bites his tongue, refraining to mention "the lack of enthusiasm evinced by [the black student's] mother when musing on the prospect of a fair grandchild."

Bull's-eye, Baldwin. That's exactly right. It's always been the white belief that it's black *grandmothers* with a rooting interest in miscegenation. Even Ellison, perhaps the most gracious presence in all of twentieth-century American literature, was beginning to bug me. When, in one of his stories, a little boy observes to his friend that "white folks ain't got no sense," it was all I could do to finish it. Mm-hmm, I wanted to say. And to hell with you, too.

But white people *didn't* have any sense. I couldn't get over white people. White people! Not just stupid—a special kind of stupid. A credulousness that was simply remarkable. "Look, I'm not going to hand you some line," a panhandler had said one warm Miami evening as I walked the streets of Coconut Grove with a graduate school friend, who swallowed the line along with the hook and sinker, "but I'm trying to get some money together to take a group of sick kids to Disney World. Where y'all from?" My companion mentioned his hometown, outside of Chicago, and reached in his pocket for a fiver. "The east side of Detroit," I said, making no such move. "Really? No fooling? Finney High School!" the man hollered, naming the public school at the corner of Cadieux and East Warren. We were two Detroit boys from the east side, standing in an Atlantic breeze, Cuba off in the distance. Could you believe it?

An hour or so later, as we circled back, we saw the panhandler again, and for a second time he asked us for money. The story this time was that he was trying to take some retarded kids to Busch Gardens—something like that. "Hey, Shit-for-Brains," I said to my friend as he walked silently past, "aren't you going to give the nice man some money?" "I'm disappointed." "Disappointed? What does disappointed have to do with anything?"

What *does* disappointed have to do with anything? The white world, Baldwin says, is too powerful and too complacent to love easily. But above all, he says, it is "too ignorant and too innocent for that." I wasn't innocent enough to be disappointed, and I was beginning to doubt my earlier assumption about my ignorance—that my problem was a lack of knowing, something that my incessant reading sought to correct. What if there was nothing to know? What if, as an Oscar Wilde character remarked of women, blacks were sphinxes without secrets?

Negroes, Baldwin says in *The Fire Next Time,* know far more about white Americans than to believe the myths white America holds about itself. "It can almost be said, in fact, that [Negroes] know about white America what parents—or, anyway, mothers—know about their children." A recent black writer said simply: "We know white America better than white America knows us."

Whose fault is this? If I've spent this much time reading you, and you say that I still don't know you, then is it my comprehension that's lacking, or your level of expression?

Ellison had entitled his great novel *Invisible Man,* but blacks weren't invisible to me, never had been, not even in the limited sense that Ellison had meant. Baldwin entitled his second essay collection *Nobody Knows My Name.* I *always* remembered black people's names, though they didn't always remember mine. (My former grass-cutting partner, whom I sometimes saw back in Detroit, had taken to calling me Mark.) What if the men in Sal's barbershop had been right, and I'd known as much about black people as I ever would by the age of thirteen, simply from listening to their rants every three weeks when I got a haircut? A little lacking upstairs. Prone to violence. Repulsed by their own women. That pretty much covered it at Sal's.

In "A Letter from Harlem," the writer whose name I knew says: "*Negroes want to be treated like men:* a perfectly straightforward statement, containing only seven words. People who have mastered Kant,

Hegel, Shakespeare, Marx, Freud, and the Bible find this statement utterly impenetrable." It seemed to me I could do one better. I could read the canon, plus Baldwin on my reading of the canon, and *still* not understand this straightforward, seven-word statement.

Those seven words were perfectly penetrable, of course. What I didn't understand, would never understand, was what I was supposed to do about them. Was I supposed to RESPECT THE BLACK MAN, as the T-shirt of a former coworker of mine—not yet twenty, and the father of three—instructed me to do? What form, aside from a nodding acknowledgment of his presence each morning, would such respect take? And how could I tolerate, let alone respect—if I wanted to see *myself* as a man—the actions of the sonuvabitch whose continued ability to draw breath poisoned my every minute?

It became awfully hard to walk by my bookshelf and see *The Fire Next Time* standing there, spine out. "The fire *next* time? Why next time? Let's get it over with." My problem was that, every time I picked the book up, fully intending to throw it away, I ended up reading through it, feeding off the anger I felt on every page. (Eventually I did throw it out, only to replace it.) Near the end of the book, on the topic of interracial marriage, Baldwin writes: "Why, for example—especially knowing the family as I do—I should *want* to marry your sister is a great mystery to me."

Where to start? First of all it wouldn't, in Baldwin's case, be my sister I'd be worried about him wanting to marry. Second, no man, of any race, can understand why another man would want to marry his sister, knowing what every brother knows about his sister's pigtailed past. Third—and my family must have been an exception here, or the fellow must not have known us too well—one certainly seemed to want to marry my sister.

Or, worse, didn't. Though it's fashionable in some circles to mock the nuclear family, many of these same people persist in the mystifying practice of talking about interracial marriages. Look around: what does *marriage* have to do with anything? Doesn't this, too, feel a little shopworn, its portrait of black-white pairings as dated as the separate beds on a black-and-white sitcom? His parents, for instance—black father, Irish mother—weren't married. And though he and my sister had dated for quite a while, and had even begun to live together, there was still no engagement ring in sight.

Sooner or later it was bound to be a problem, and sooner or later arrived the night I told my mother and father about the attack and its perpetrator. It was a longish monologue, delivered while my mother shook her head, occasionally crying, and my father sat in silence. While both responses were expected, the latter bothered me; although a reverent silence can, in some cases, be the most powerful response to such news, it didn't seem, in this instance, to quite meet the moment. Did he hear what I was saying?

How could my father *allow* this, especially in light of what I'd just told him? Sixty-hour workweeks, Catholic school tuition payments, incredible hard work and struggle year after year after year—all, now, to be flushed down the toilet because some guy was *nice?* Life was a slippery slope—he was the man who'd taught me this, only too well—and yet here he was, allowing this stupid adolescent connection of my sister's, which could only end badly, to strengthen. If my mother was right, and my father didn't much care for this arrangement, how did he register his protest? He fixed the guy's truck. Whenever it broke down, and it often did, there was my father in the driveway, even in the middle of winter, changing the brake pads or fixing the clutch.

My fury only deepened after we'd moved in together and began to receive telephone calls from prison, a couple calls a week over the course of a few weeks. The first time the operator asked me if I'd accept the call—I could hear a voice in the background pleading—I said that I would, out of some mixture of curiosity and confusion. "You've got to help me," a black male voice said on the other end. "I shouldn't be here. I need you—" I hung up, shaking.

Back in Detroit, I'd fielded my share of wrong numbers. My favorite calls were those from callers who asked me who *I* was—to which, really, there was only one response: You called me; who the hell are *you?* In fairness, only half of these callers were actually rude; the rest were intoxicated, but polite enough. And they were all persistent: the message that Shakira didn't live here, that there was no Jamaal at this number, never seemed to sink in after one call.

The prison calls kept coming, though we couldn't be sure if it was always the same person (we hung up immediately). Neither could we be sure how, whoever he was, he had gotten our number. We had nothing but questions, all of them unsettling: Was this the attacker? Had he been caught, in connection with another rape? Had he seen her name beside the mailbox of her old apartment building that night, and was this how he'd been able to track down her new number? Could convicts call information? Or was this just some anonymous criminal, someone totally unconnected to our lives, calling us repeatedly because I'd accepted the call that once?

How did he know our phone number? What *was* our phone number? I myself hadn't a clue; I carried it around on a slip of paper in my pocket. I'd moved so much in the six and a half years since I'd left Detroit that the mailing addresses, apartment numbers, and phone numbers—nearly a dozen of each—were beginning to blur. The only reason I got my mail, much of the time, was because friends had taken over my old apartments, and brought it over in a bundle. If the calls kept up we'd have to move again, or at least change our number—again.

These calls, and the questions they raised, cut us to the quick, because it was only after such calls that we spoke of the rape in simple declarative sentences. Otherwise our references to her trauma were indirect, our sentences Jamesian. The "attack." Her "attacker." Such were the euphemisms we'd settled on. But one's internal thought processes, having little need for euphemism, tend to be more blunt, and I felt caught off-guard when—grocery shopping, for instance—I picked up a pear. *Pear:* a perfect anagram. My mind just automatically switched around the letters in certain words—*carpet, parade*—to form that other word. More than once I thought: Am I nuts? Should I see a therapist?

One evening she walked into the apartment beaming. "Good news—my test came back negative!" Why she got the yearly test went unremarked on, and her happiness at the result—she needn't worry about sickness anytime soon—struck me as one of the saddest things I had ever witnessed. Other references to the crime were completely unspoken. If we were walking down the street together, holding hands, and a black man approached, I'd sometimes feel a slight tug, directing me to cross with her to the other side of the road, where she'd feign momentary interest in something.

My questions always circled the subject. One night, after storing the query for months, I asked how she had got the scar on her upper arm. "Oh, that! That's a cat scratch. We had a kitty when I was growing up, and he liked to crawl around your neck and shoulders. Usually he was gentle, but one night something spooked him . . ."

Sure. Okay. Could have been caused by a cat. I can see that.

We were working together at a bookstore until she finished her history degree. She worked in Arts, and I was in the Used Books department (read the first five letters of that last word backwards), where I spent a portion of each shift, when not talking to friends or flirting with the female employees, writing phony jacket copy for books. To replenish our stock, skids of used books arrived upon request from Paramus, New Jersey, the place where books go to die. Dozens of boxes arrived on the truck every month or so, sorted by category. It was part of my job to unpack them, price them, and put them on the shelves.

Opening these boxes was a quick lesson in the brute realities of the literary business. While some of the books were in fact used copies of titles published decades before, others were new titles that, having sold poorly, were clearly the publisher's overstock, sent to us as a way to empty the warehouse. Sometimes a dozen untouched copies of the same book appeared in one box, occasionally even the book's proof copies, included in which there would be an editor's recommendation, extolling the unparalleled virtues of this particular novel or work of nonfiction. Bored, I began, mentally, to write blurbs for books that I invented on the spot.

After opening a box of Sociology/Current Affairs: "This is the story of a young black man, formerly angry, now simply bitter, who no longer wants to kill white folks—that's all behind him—but who still wonders when he's gonna get *his*, y'know what I'm sayin'? It follows him from the streets of Detroit, where he runs with the wrong crowd, to prison, where he receives a college education, to college, where a host of white professors and a handful of white girls *nearly* make him forget where he comes from. But only nearly. For in this honest and unflinching memoir, written in a lean, muscular prose . . ."

Still unpacking that same box: "In this moving work of urban reportage, a bearded man with tenure has set himself the difficult task of describing, in vivid detail and at long last, what it's like to be a member of the impoverished black underclass in America's fifth—sixth—no, seventh—wait, *tenth*-largest city. How does one combat such crushing hopelessness? Soul and a surprising strain of humor was his guess before beginning, but he decided to research this. Each and every weekday for the span of one year, he made the twenty-five-mile journey from northern Oakland County to Detroit's Cass Corridor, in order that he might show white America what she is doing to the most helpless of her children. When, in the coming weeks, he is interviewed on National Public Radio in connection with the project, he will testify to the inextinguishable sacredness of the human spirit and the deep sickness of a society that allows . . ."

Outside of these angry thoughts I continued to function as a perfectly sane individual, going out of my way to be respectful and friendly to black customers. I didn't understand those who said this wasn't possible; it's distinctly possible—simple, even, if from kindergarten on one has been schooled in the Catholic art of self-denial. Simply refuse to give in to your desires and force yourself instead into their opposites.

The strange part was that, even as I smiled politely, this friendliness didn't feel at all forced—didn't feel as if it were, in fact, the opposite of my deepest desires. Even as I threw out *The Fire Next Time* and fumed at the comments of Ellison's characters, I found myself unable to sustain that anger. (The book was replaced, the story reread.) Like many a failed misanthrope, I discovered that my abstract rage, when confronted by an actual human being who'd done me no wrong, simply dissolved. It was a disappointing thing to learn because empty sadness, which is what remains after hatred fades, isn't the same expansive force. Whereas profound hatred can feel transfiguring, sadness just sits there.

At night she did homework—it was her last semester—and I revised my novel. What I had previously considered a boon—the material provided by my Detroit upbringing—now seemed an albatross. I recalled driving along I-94 years before with Shane, my college roommate, who'd come to Detroit on a visit. I told him, after declining another of his invitations to write for the school paper, that I was starting to write a novel instead. "If I can't write a good book about Detroit," I said, "I can't write anything."

It was harder than I thought. In the book's original ending, the three kids, still armed to the teeth with dairy products after egging houses in wealthy Grosse Pointe, drive downtown and park near The Fist, intent upon egging the shit out of it. They fit nowhere—the suburbs, the city—and so are reduced to this impotent gesture. "We should have bought yolkless eggs," one of them remarks. Though it had made no difference in Grosse Pointe, the symbolism of the all-white egg would have been better downtown.

And so they begin, to the accompaniment of alphabetic swearing. "Asshole!" one of them hollers, letting the first egg fly. "Bitch!" And so on, until they get to the letter *n*, when the scene fades out.

They were picked up by the Detroit police, the narrator says in a postscript, on charges of drunk and disorderly and destruction of public property. But nothing had been destroyed—the eggs washed right off—and there's nothing disorderly, the narrator asserts, about civil disobedience executed in alphabetical order.

It was a sophomoric production, front to back. And I was losing touch with the material. The three "kids" were around twenty, the age I was when I began sketching my scenes. But I was now closer to thirty, and hadn't felt much like a kid at twenty. The novel was set in Detroit, where I no longer lived. It mocked suburbanites—which, in a small way, my family now was. And with shattered statues of the Blessed Virgin strewn across its pages, the book had courted blasphemy in the hope that a little leeway might be granted a practitioner of the faith, which I no longer was.

Worse, it lacked gravitas. I'd treated the material—Detroit, race, class, Catholicism—as things to "play around" with, just as my father tinkered harmlessly in the garage with his less important hot rods. But this stuff was not to be trifled with, and I was no longer in the tinkering mood. I wanted the thing to go fast—*now*.

Though I still argued with Ellison and Baldwin, my best times were spent in the company of Malcolm X. It was time to return to the direct, extraliterary seriousness that only Detroit Red could provide. My copy of his autobiography was a tattered Grove Press paperback with a black and red border and a photo, taken during a speech, of Malcolm X on the cover, biting his lower lip indignantly and pointing toward something in the distance: the White Man, or Mecca, or maybe his old hometown back in mid-Michigan. I'd bought it, years before, at a used bookstore on Cadieux and East Warren. By the time I began to reread it for what I hoped would be the final time, years of being flipped by my fingers had taken its toll. The pages, full of highlights, underlinings, and marginalia, were beginning to fall out from the center, where the spine was most badly broken. In some ways, the book resembled the Norton Critical Editions that I'd had to read in college—editions in which, in a footnote at the bottom of the page, you could find out what the hell *hypos* meant in the first paragraph of *Moby-Dick*. My copy of *The Autobi-*

ography of Malcolm X was similar: there was the main text, along with a running commentary of my own along the bottom, sides, and top of the page.

When I'd first read it years back, I'd felt a faint adolescent desire to clench my fist in solidarity; on subsequent readings I'd simply hung my head. Now the arguments began. Oh, the disagreements we got into! Neither of us emerged unscathed; it seemed, at times, that we might never emerge at all. More than any fire-and-brimstone homily delivered during my Catholic school days, Malcolm's book seemed to seal my eternal damnation, a fate I now began to rail against. White Hell, if I'd followed the book's line of thinking correctly, was going to be an underground Mexico City: smog, congestion, really bad rush hours. "To bear even the sting of an insect for all eternity would be a dreadful torment," says a priest in Joyce's *A Portrait of the Artist*. "What must it be, then, to bear the manifold tortures of hell for ever? For ever! For all eternity! Not for a year or for an age but for ever. Try to imagine the awful meaning of this." I had, many times.

What I discovered when I reread Detroit Red was that I couldn't read him at all, not anymore. I turned pages, saw letters, sounded out words, but no reading took place, in the sense of serious engagement with an author whose story I was willing to grant a sympathetic hearing. Passages that had charmed me in the past—his admission, at the beginning of Chapter 2, that he'd been beaten in a boxing match by a white boy, then pummeled again in the rematch—failed to make any impression. Whereas before I had been drawn to the good-humored modesty of the admission ("he knocked me down fifty times if he did once"), I now wanted to *be* that white boy, Bill Peterson. "I'll never forget him," Malcolm says.

My feelings about the book were bluntly antagonistic from the outset, or at least from the bottom of page two, where Malcolm discloses, with considerable distaste, that his maternal grandfather was a white man—a "white rapist." For a page and a half I was fine, reading *The Autobiography of Malcolm X* much as I'd read any other book. But at the bottom of page two, when I encountered the words "white rapist," the reading stopped and the fistfight started.

In the very same paragraph, while discussing his mother, he says, "Of this white father of hers, I know nothing." How, then, does he know the man was a rapist? Is this a metaphorical flight? Mere wishful thinking? No, it wasn't possible to read beyond this point. It was a fight now ("A fight! A fight! A nigger and a white!" as the song had gone back at 6 Mile and Gratiot), and I suffered all the classic schoolyard symptoms: my palms sweat, my heart raced, I muttered to myself.

And I was certain that, unlike Bill Peterson, I was going to lose.

The most interesting observation in the autobiography, it seemed to me, came on page 268: "The white man—give him his due—has an extraordinary intelligence, an extraordinary cleverness. His world is full of proof of it."

What's revealing about this statement is that for most of his book Malcolm refers to the white man as the devil. So when he says what he says here—give him his due—what he's really saying is, Give the devil his due. And from whom is he plagiarizing this phrase? From Shakespeare in the first part of *Henry IV,* wherein Prince Hal defends the character of Falstaff by saying that he "will give the devil his due." Malcolm X, then, while giving surface praise to the white man, throws in a backhanded condemnation of the white man—that intelligence, obviously, only increases our malevolence—a condemnation appropriated, wholesale, from a white man. You could get lost in the layers of irony.

And there could be no doubt that Malcolm X knew from whom he was stealing this phrase, because Malcolm Little had done his reading in prison. Nowhere did I feel more of an affinity for him than when he was discussing his love of reading. It's one of the great tensions in his book: his simultaneous love of learning and his hatred for bourgeois, educated blacks—one of them, a " 'token-integrated' black Ph.D. associate professor," who, Malcolm says, "got me so mad I couldn't see straight." And yet he ends the book by saying, "I would just like to *study.*

I mean ranging study, because I have a wide-open mind. I'm interested in almost any subject you can mention." Just before this: "My greatest lack has been, I believe, that I don't have the kind of academic education I wish I had been able to get. . . . You can believe me that if I had the time right now, I would not be one bit ashamed to go back into any New York City public school and start where I left off in the ninth grade." I come close to feelings of love when I read such lines.

This bookishness begins in Chapter 11 with his prison reading. "In either volume 43 or 44 of The Harvard Classics I read Milton's *Paradise Lost*," he says. "Schopenhauer, Kant, Nietzsche, naturally, I read all of those," he says. "Another hot debate I remember I was in had to do with the identity of Shakespeare," he says. "The King James translation of the Bible is considered the greatest piece of literature in English. . . . Well, Shakespeare's language and the Bible's language are one and the same. . . . In prison debates I argued for the theory that King James himself was the real poet who used the *nom de plume* Shakespeare."

Who gives a shit? Try as I might to focus on Malcolm's literary pursuits, I kept coming back to the "white rapist." Or, rather, he kept coming back to me, because he was everywhere in the book. In a sense this was consoling: however fixated I might have been, whatever mental disorder I might have been suffering from, it paled in comparison to Malcolm X's problems. Chapter 12: "Yes! Yes, that raping, red-headed devil was my *grandfather!* That close, yes! My *mother's* father! If I could drain away *his* blood that pollutes *my* body, and pollutes *my* complexion, I'd do it! Because I hate every drop of the rapist's blood that's in me!" Chapter 14: "For the white man to ask the black man if he hates him is just like the rapist asking the *raped,* 'Do you hate me?' " Same chapter: "But what is this slavemaster white, *rapist,* going about saying! He is saying *he* won't integrate because black blood will *mongrelize* his race! *He* says that—and look at *us!* Turn around in your seats and look at each other! This slavemaster white man has already '*integrated*' us." And so on.

In Chapter 17 Malcolm heads off to Mecca, and his warming toward whites begins. Stopping in Europe: "My brother Muslim and I both were struck by the cordial hospitality of the people in Frankfurt. . . . Europeans act more human, or humane, whichever the right word is." As he flies from Europe to Mecca: "Packed in the plane were white, black, brown, red, and yellow people, blue eyes and blond hair, and my kinky-red hair—all together, brothers!" The we-are-the-world lyricism continues in Mecca: "In the Muslim world, I had seen that men with white complexions were more genuinely brotherly than anyone else had ever been. That morning was the start of a radical alteration in my whole outlook about 'white' men." Reading this stuff is just death. In Chapter 18, Malcolm X (now El-Hajj Malik El-Shabazz) returns to Kennedy Airport in New York, where, to a group of reporters, he delivers this speech: "In the past, yes, I have made sweeping indictments of all white people. I will never be guilty of that again—as I know now that some white people are truly sincere, that some truly are capable of being brotherly toward a black man. The true Islam has shown me that a blanket indictment of all white people is as wrong as when whites make blanket indictments against blacks."

In the final chapter, Malcolm X thinks back to a discussion he'd had with a white American ambassador in Africa. "What you are telling me," he says to the ambassador, "is that it isn't the American white *man* who is a racist, but it's the American political, economic, and social *atmosphere* that automatically nourishes a racist psychology in the white man?" The ambassador agrees. Following this exchange, Malcolm X says that he had "a new insight—one which I like: that the white man is *not* inherently evil." His italics. Next to which I had written, in devilishly bright red ink: "Not true."

My novel was still garbage but I kept at it, incorporating more and more Malcolm X into its pages, hoping that the friction might spark something. My wife did better, graduating summa cum laude. Our first child was conceived, as close as we can tell, on the day of her college graduation.

Immaculate Heart of Mary

I CALLED FROM ACROSS THE STATE to my old high school and asked one of the priests who'd chaperoned the France trip if he'd be willing to perform the wedding ceremony. I explained the circumstances, and he asked that after we'd moved back to Detroit—Step One of our hastily put together master plan—we stop in and see him.

Under the circumstances, relocating to Detroit may seem odd—move back to a black city, knowing what I knew? Yet there was one overwhelming factor in Detroit's favor: my family was still there. It wasn't just that I loved my family—everyone loved his family, even those friends who did nothing but complain about their parents. I felt something rarer for mine: actual fondness. And behind these tender feelings was something else, something I'd come to think of as the background music to my days in Detroit, a tune I heard only in the company of my parents and sister. It was a comforting song, but I'd grown tired of it for a time; now I wanted to hear it again, and was frustrated when I couldn't hum it. I hoped, going home, to hear it again.

We applied for our marriage license downtown at the City-County Building. Nine months later, this structure would be renamed the Coleman A. Young Municipal Center—"Coleman's Place," as it came to be called. There were no questions asked of us at Coleman's Place; Coleman knew the score. Near the end of his tenure as mayor, despite previous denials, a paternity test had proven conclusively that Young, himself a former Catholic schoolboy, had fathered a child out of wedlock with a woman some forty years his junior.

Though our baby had been conceived before marriage, we weren't about to let it be born out of wedlock like the Young love child. I was going to do the right thing, and in this the Catholic Church was going to help me. My wife-to-be, terribly nervous, was three months' pregnant when we sat down across from Father in the priests' house. She was not only non-Catholic but non-baptized, which Father said required special dispensation from the archdiocese. "It can take months to come through," he told us.

I informed him that we didn't have months. My wife wanted to be married in her mother's wedding dress, so at best we had three weeks. The chapel had been rented, the organist hired, the dress altered, the restaurant was ready: all we needed was the permission of the Church.

A form had to be filled out, naturally, before the archdiocese would consider our request, and so my mother—a piece of work, by anyone's standards—called upon the powers that be, in the space provided at the bottom of the form, to consider just how much she and my father had spent on twenty-six years of Catholic schooling for their two children, and just how little they, the archdiocese, had paid the groom-to-be's great uncle, Father Hector Saulino, over the course of his more than fifty years of faithful service to the Detroit Archdiocese. "I've never seen anything like it," Father said four days later when he called, approval letter in hand.

That was the tune I'd missed.

When we discovered the pregnancy I sold my mountain bike—the replacement for the one stolen in Boston—along with a first edition of

Samuel Beckett's first book, his deeply depressing monograph on Marcel Proust simply entitled *Proust* (London, 1931). There was some minor chipping at the top of the dust jacket, but otherwise it was in excellent condition. My mother had bought it for a quarter at a Grosse Pointe estate sale. "I thought I'd heard you mention him before," she said, handing me the book. She'd done this sort of thing previously, bringing back from Grosse Pointe estate and garage sales editions of books by famous authors about which there was little to be said other than that they were extremely old and worth more or less the quarter that she had paid for them. But the Beckett was a real find, even if the text itself was tough sledding. Sample sentence: "We are not merely more weary because of yesterday, we are other, no longer what we were before the calamity of yesterday." Still, it was worth some money.

And I was frantic for the stuff. More than once did we sit down with my mother, who'd pull out a pen and a legal pad, and discuss our "finances." "You're going to be *fine*," she said at the end of each session. It was her usual message, one I depended on: Relax. Don't worry. Things have a way of working out. "We were worse off than you guys when we started out, believe me," she often said, telling us how, after I was brought home from the hospital in that ice storm, the boiler blew up in the basement; how my father had been a delivery-truck driver for the *Detroit News*, had stirred vats of syrup at the A&W root beer plant—oh, he'd had all sorts of odd jobs before he began work at Diamond Racing, where he got his foot in the door of Detroit's auto industry. "The first dinner I made for your father after we got married—hot dogs," she said, smiling.

At such moments I was overcome by a distinct sense of things unraveling. Only the constant application of common sense could keep disorder at bay, and because somewhere along the line my constancy had failed, chaos was now closing in. That I'd found a job was beside the point. Indeed, it was absolutely irrelevant, at least as it related to my mother's scheme for righting our finances after the baby had been born. "You know, based on your last year's earnings, you guys probably qualify for some kind of public assistance." "Ma, we were working at the bookstore. Those were just student jobs." "I'm just saying," she said.

As had been the case when I was applying to college, our financial need was being calculated on an unrepresentative year; but whereas the change back then was negative—my father had gone from earning good money to earning none—in this case it was positive: I had already begun working at a job that precluded our receiving such help in the future. The help we were to receive from the Women, Infants, and Children (WIC) program, which provides redeemable coupons for food staples—baby formula, peanut butter, milk—would be for one year and one year only. My wife, standing on principle, said she wouldn't use the coupons that were meant for her, redeemable for milk and peanut butter—just formula, just things for the baby. All I could think of was the taunt Kurt and I had hurled at our grade school classmate: "Is that welfare cheese?"

Though I felt as if I might keel over, my mother asserted, again and again, that it was the right thing to do. This little bit of assistance, which we would repay countless times over in income tax during the rest of our lives, would be of great help to us *now*, freeing up money for car insurance, rent, student loan payments—all sorts of things.

"Yeah, don't worry about the baby formula," my father said in a reassuring tone, not bothering to look away from the television set. "You can always get the government to buy you more."

The job I'd landed was with a Catholic college, and since its offices were located downtown in a city building, I made the same drive along the Ford Freeway that I had over summers home from school. Everyone else in the building worked for the City of Detroit, but because our work had been subcontracted out to the college there was no residency requirement to abide by—a good thing, too, since we'd rented an apartment that, though still south of 8 Mile, was a few blocks outside the city limits. In an office of ten, I was one of two white people, and the only male.

As I got on the freeway one morning that fall I saw signs in the embankment urging passersby to VOTE THE BLACK SLATE in upcoming elections. Twenty-five years earlier, in the fall of 1973, the Shrine of the Black Madonna, the west side church that organized these campaigns, had put out a similar call:

Safe Streets For <u>All</u>

End STRESS
On Nov. 6

Elect
Coleman
Young
and the
Black Slate

Vote a Straight
Black Slate

"Stop The Robberies, Enjoy Safe Streets" (STRESS) was the Detroit Police undercover unit that sent cops, dressed as easy marks, out onto the streets to lure criminals. When he beat Police Chief John Nichols in 1973, Young made STRESS a major campaign issue, holding the squad responsible for numerous deaths caused by white officers who, he said, used STRESS as a pretext for brutalizing Detroit's black population. After Young's victory, the unit was disbanded.

By 1998 everything in the city had long since come under black control, so white foes had to be found outstate. In this respect Michigan's governor, John Engler, was a godsend. Like most Republican politicians since Lincoln, he was widely disliked in the black community, particularly in Detroit, where he had begun to orchestrate the state's takeover of the failing Detroit Public School system.

And yet many of us in the City of Detroit building owed our employment to him, and to the Republican Party's welfare-to-work reforms of the mid-1990s. MICHIGAN WORKS! said the sign on the outside of the building, and it was our job to test the aptitude of our clientele, many of whom were on public assistance, and to link them with training programs where they would gain the skills necessary to find employment as heating and cooling specialists or licensed practical nurses. It was mindless work, and there was a lot of downtime in which to write.

Many of our clients were already talking about their future careers and what they would do with the money they earned when they walked in the door. Others, as I made my way up and down the aisles, handing out the multiple-choice tests and giving verbal instructions, would look up and say: "You know what job I want? Yours." Such statements were poison darts. I had no doubt that they could do my job, and worried that someday soon I might be jobless and, like them, in need of assistance to get off assistance. I'd already taken a step, however small, in that general direction.

My boss, Dorothea, had given me advice on how to deal with such comments. "Just don't let them make you lose your cool. These people are unemployed, they're angry. They lash out. They'll complain, 'That white guy made me whatever,' you know? Just do your job and you'll be fine." Trim and classically chic, she seemed at times to have stepped out of a black-and-white photo from decades before, when things like posture and elocution mattered—an era when people paid attention to how they comported themselves. She was in her early forties and childless. Many of the women in the office, particularly the more educated, were either unmarried or childless or both. Some of them lived twenty miles out in the subuns, but Dorothea stayed in the city. One morning, after driving by a very small brother and sister out walking the streets alone, she came into the office furious. "People don't have any sense. These kids are what—four, five?—and they're out walking to school, or *somewhere,* all by themselves. It makes you just want to take people's children away from them." Like many in Detroit, she was adept at a sort of racial self-deprecation; in the presence of whites, she'd point out black actions by which she'd been annoyed, and I'd reciprocate by mocking some white politician or celebrity.

The women I worked with, like all the women I'd known, suffered a severe addiction to fashion magazines and clothes catalogs. They could recall any article in any issue of any wide-circulation magazine within the last year; they could remember which outfit was in which catalog—Spring/Summer, Fall/Winter, Winter Closeout, Spring Clearance—and they could read any magazine article, no matter how superficial, at least twice. They would examine the catalog photographs of outfits they'd already bought, to gauge how the reality corresponded to their expectation. They had a memory for the minutiae of the lives of models and celebrities that, if applied in other areas, would have resulted in the memorization of Shakespeare's major tragedies. A good portion of each workday was spent passing magazines and catalogs back and forth over cubicle walls.

They could be cutthroat in their observations, particularly with white models and celebrities. "Sure, she's got the boobs, but where's her butt? I don't see any butt." When a failed white candidate for governor began to hint that he might want to run for mayor of Detroit, there was a good deal of discussion of his wife, who had been visible on the campaign trail. One of the younger women suggested that the candidate's better half—his blonder half—may not have been the brighest bulb. "Don't say that. No, don't say that," one of the older women said. "You're just saying that because she's blond, and that's not right." Though the photo I'd taped up in my cubicle, taken in the Boston subway, was done in black-and-white, it was clear that my wife was blond.

Our office staff made periodic trips to the campus of our employer, the Catholic college on the city's west side, where we took part in training sessions and orientations. It was pleasant to get away from the City of Detroit building for a day and to walk on the grounds of the school's wooded campus—which, if you walked in deep enough, could give you the impression of not being in Detroit at all. The buildings were made of stone and weathered to perfection; everything looked like a chapel. Occasionally, walking around, you'd even see a nun.

But a church, as we'd been taught in Catholic school, was not a building; it was its *people* (here's the church, here's its steeple), and the people I saw on campus didn't strike me as being particularly Catholic. Though this wasn't entirely unexpected, I was surprised to learn that the school's new president, who'd come from a historically black college down South, was a Baptist.

The training sessions themselves were the usual blur of bagels and name tags. By the end of the afternoon, when we'd broken out into focus groups, the name tag would begin to curl in on itself, and it was possible to expend a good deal of mental energy in wondering how much sweater lint the adhesive backing might remove. In one such session, concerning the future of the college, it was agreed that the school would actively seek to retain its Catholic character. "Whatever that means," a young black woman in the seat next to me said, laughing.

Back in our City of Detroit building the next day, the boss asked me to read over a narrative history of the college. From this, I was to write multiple-choice questions for the clients who came into our office, in order to test their reading comprehension. The narrative started with the founding, in Europe, of the order of nuns who ran the school, and went on to discuss the order's move to the Americas; its subsequent move to Detroit; and its pride in the past, its commitment to the present, and its faith in the future.

The section on the 1960s spoke of the college's commitment to integrating its surrounding area. The college president, an Immaculate Heart of Mary sister, asserted in a press conference that the school would not want a "lily-white neighborhood." And I thought: You wouldn't get it, Sister. No, instead of lily white you got the opposite—and, by the time I began working here, a Baptist president for your Catholic school.

Weather permitting, I would spend my lunch hour outside, reading in a small square across the street from the General Motors building on the corner of Cass Avenue and West Grand Boulevard. A couple miles down the boulevard was the General Motors Poletown plant, built back in the early 1980s from the remains of an old Hamtramck Dodge plant. To accommodate the new plant, which Mayor Young desperately wanted, some four thousand Detroit residents—many of them Polish, like the residents of adjacent Hamtramck—were forced from their homes. At the beginning of a decade in Detroit that, by its end, would see some three dozen Catholic parishes disappear, Cardinal Dearden immediately okayed the closing of two churches in the condemned area—one of them dedicated to the proposition that the mother of our lord had been conceived immaculately, and led by a priest, Father Karasiewicz, who openly fought his superior's decision. Eventually Ralph Nader came to town, siding with those residents of the area against the plan put forward by Coleman Young and General Motors. Nader, on Young: a "petty dictator." Young, on Nader: a "carpetbagger from Washington." Again: "This man has a phobia. Whenever you mention General Motors Corporation, he foams at the mouth."

As I sat reading *Paradise Lost* one day in the square, enjoying the sunshine and a sandwich, I attracted company. "You the original white man, ain't ya?" a black man asked me, stopping as he walked by. He was not a degenerate, and, deep into middle age, he seemed still to have his wits about him; why he'd chosen me to pick on I had no idea. White I certainly was, but also unshaven, swarthy, sloppily Mediterranean in appearance—no one's idea of Aryan purity, in other words. There were plenty of white men walking out of the GM building across the way who fit the bill better than I did. It was, I suspected, the book that did it: the white man *reads*.

I had, over the years, developed certain safeguards when it came to this sort of thing. For comments of the "white motherfucker" variety, which were not at all infrequent, I chose a proud silence, coupled with an internal recitation of some lines from late Auden: "Even Hate should be precise / Very few White Folks / Have fucked their mothers." For something like this, I drew on the lessons I'd learned as a Denby Bulldog wideout; namely, that the genius of black teasing was not that it made sense, but that it didn't. Searching such questions for signs of actual substance showed not how stupid the questions were but how dumb I was. The pointlessness of the give-and-take was its point, the way it rocked your opponent back on his heels. I'd learned, over the years, to respond in kind.

The original white man. "Now why would you say that," I asked, "being that you're Jewish yourself?"

I could see him racking his brain, trying to place what "Jewish" might mean. Weren't they—weren't those the people—hadn't Farrakhan, in a speech . . . "What's that mean, 'Jewish'? I'm a black man." "Come off it," I said.

He walked away, and I turned back to Milton's poem. In the opening of Book 2 of *Paradise Lost*, the fallen angels have gathered in Pandemonium, Satan's palace in Hell, "with hope yet of regaining Heaven." To this end, Satan presents those cast "into the great Deep" with their two options as he sees it: battle or trickery—"open war or covert guile." After asking for counsel, he sits back on his throne and the floor is opened for debate:

> [Satan] ceased, and next him Moloch, sceptred king,
> Stood up, the strongest and the fiercest spirit
> That fought in Heaven, now fiercer by despair.
> His trust was with the Eternal to be deemed
> Equal in strength, and rather than be less
> Cared not to be at all; with that care lost
> Went all his fear: of God, or Hell, or worse
> He recked not, and these words thereafter spake:
> "My sentence is for open war."

If there was a better passage in English poetry I didn't know it. I recalled that in Chapter 11 of *The Autobiography of Malcolm X*, when Malcolm Little's prison time turns scholarly, he provides the following synopsis of Milton's poem: "The devil, kicked out of Paradise, was trying to regain possession. He was using the forces of Europe, personified by the popes, Charlemagne, Richard the Lionhearted, and other knights. I interpreted this to show that the Europeans were motivated and led by the devil, or the personification of the devil. So Milton and Mr. Elijah Muhammad were actually saying the same thing."

Uh-huh.

The Honourable
Circuit Court of
Yoknapatawpha County

O UR APARTMENT was just across Alter Road, a divider between Detroit and Grosse Pointe, situated by the slimmest of margins on the right side of those tracks. Alter is perhaps the most appropriately named street in America—cross it, and boy does the scenery ever. Driving back into the city along Jefferson Avenue, one notes that the colonials, Tudors, and Cape Cods of Grosse Pointe give way, in the space of a few blocks, to a perfectly representative area of the City of Detroit, where many homes have bars on their windows, though few seem worth the bother of breaking into. It's not unknown for newcomers to the area to crane their necks to get a last look at Grosse Pointe after crossing Alter, as if to verify that the transition had indeed been that abrupt.

The first several blocks in Grosse Pointe north of Jefferson, before you get to the big houses with big yards, serve as a buffer between the extremes they border. Former servants' quarters from the days of the automotive mansions, the single-family homes in these blocks are mostly small bungalows, many of which have been subdivided into apartments; the rest of the area is composed of two-and four-family residences populated by college students and postgrads, a smattering of blacks, and a recent wave of Russian and Albanian immigrants.

To those from the east side, Alter is just another border crossing, like 8 Mile, and its juxtapositions no longer startle. It's a quirk, actually, that both sides of Alter Road are in fact Detroit proper. The city-suburb divider is not the roadway itself, as is typical, but the fence line separating the backyards of the Detroit homes on the east side of Alter Road from those of the Grosse Pointe homes in the block directly behind them. It was on the side of Alter Road abutting Grosse Pointe that my father's cousins, Uncle Johnny's six boys, had grown up during the fifties and sixties, when they attended St. Ambrose, at the foot of Alter and Jefferson. My father would frequently bike to his cousins' from his house by St. Jude, a six- or seven-mile ride.

Though later just a grade school, St. Ambrose also had a high school back then—"a couple hundred kids," according to my father—and a football program that was strong out of all proportion to the school's size. In the 1961 Goodfellows Game—the yearly contest between the champions of the Detroit Catholic League and the Public School League, played at Tiger Stadium—St. Ambrose beat Detroit Pershing, a school of many thousand students, by a score of 20–0 before a crowd of thirty-seven thousand. The next year St. Ambrose beat Detroit Cooley 19–0. The following year the Catholic League champ, my future alma mater, would lose to Detroit Denby 7–0. St. Ambrose would restore Catholic pride in 1964, shutting out Detroit Southeastern 20–0. In 1965 Denby and my alma mater would play to a 14–14 tie. St. Ambrose would beat Denby yet again the next year, and the year after that—1967—would mark the end of the three-decades-long tradition of St. Somebody playing Detroit Somebody in the Goodfellows Game. By the time I started high school, contests between the two leagues—meaning, in many cases, games between an all-white and an all-black squad—were called Operation Friendship.

More than three decades after the Goodfellows Games had come to an end I drove up and down Alter Road, passing St. Ambrose from both directions, thinking long and hard about a certain passage from Faulkner. Back at the apartment, I'd been rereading Chapter 6 of *Light in August*, thirty of the greatest pages in American literature, and the chapter's first line had become my mantra: "Memory believes before knowing remembers." Five words, if properly understood, that could help me unlock the door to something—of that, if not the meaning of the words themselves, I was certain. Memory believes before knowing remembers. Before knowing remembers, memory believes. Memory's beliefs precede knowing's remembrances.

I was trying to solve another problem while mumbling to myself behind the wheel, and for help in finding a solution I drove to the home of a retired Detroit cop of my acquaintance, a widower who had been stationed for many years at the Fifth Precinct, at the corner of Jefferson and St. Jean. During the '67 riots, the Fifth Precinct had been home base for the Eighty-second Airborne, called in to help patrol the east side. We had talked many times—though never about what was most on my mind these days—and like all Detroit cops he was an extraordinary storyteller, in the tradition of the nineteenth-century realists. His best story, however, defied belief entirely, sounding like pure fantasy. In it, he told of a somewhat idealistic young cop who had voted for Coleman Young back in 1973 ("I thought it was time the city had a black mayor"), an act he would remember, like Scott's return from the South Pole, for its costly miscalculations.

A realist, not a racist: there was a distinction there, though one likely to be lost on the list of usual suspects upon whom such things were typically lost, the professional point-missers. In the world as such cops saw it, everyone fit a profile: the European ethnicities had been captured perfectly by the centuries-old stereotypes that they'd carried with them across the Atlantic, and black Americans enjoyed the benefits of full citizenship in the republic, as guaranteed by the Fourteenth Amendment, by being just as fallen as their fellow citizens, just as corrupted by the power they now held in the City of Detroit as every previous group that had had the misfortune to hold the reins in what was, without question, the worst city in American history.

There were those who found such a realistic worldview refreshing, and preferable to liberal cant. "I will pull off that liberal's halo that he spends so much time cultivating!" Malcolm X declares. Coleman Young, who considered himself a radical, not a liberal, spends much of his autobiography expressing a similar dislike. He was frequently apoplectic over the "tireless effort of knee-jerk liberals on City Council. Together with assorted bleeding-heart newspaper types, they have managed, or at least attempted, to sabotage just about every proposal for economic growth that has come out of my office. They've made it clear what they oppose—the motherfuckers are against everything—but I've yet to figure out what they propose." Many Detroit cops felt similarly about liberals, particularly suburban ones: The motherfuckers are against everything, but what do they propose? *You* try patrolling these streets.

It wasn't beyond either Coleman Young or Malcolm X to express admiration, or at least grudging respect, for people whose realism clearly crossed the line into racism. Upon the death of Orville Hubbard, who for more than three decades was the mayor of Dearborn, that citadel of racism, and remained fiercely opposed to any policies that would facilitate integration, Coleman Young said: "Orville Hubbard was quite a man. Believe it or not, he was a person I admired. He and I disagreed on some things, but he was a hell of a mayor. I regarded him as one of the best mayors in the United States. He took care of business. He knew how to meet the needs of his people." Contrast this with Young's statement about a progressive former New York City mayor: "I think Ed Koch is full of shit."

A racist, perhaps, but probably not full of shit: such was my image of myself as I drove to the foot of Alter Road, crossing over into the city via a small bridge that took me onto one of the tiny islands that dot the banks of the Detroit River. On one such island my father's great-aunt had lived, and may have yet: she was the sort of distant relative we all have, and forget about, and who lives to be a hundred and six. I'd visited her house a few times as a kid—I recalled clutter and floating dust motes—but couldn't for the life of me have found it now. Somewhere in here, too, according to family legend, was where my Grandpa Clemens had been a bootlegger during Prohibition, when these little islands in the river served as drop sites for cases of whiskey smuggled from Canada.

On the Grosse Pointe side of this bridge, in the middle of a boulevard bounded by Windmill Pointe mansions, was a historical marker that I often stopped and read. It told the story of the Fox Indian Massacre: "Encouraged by a potential alliance with the English, the Fox Indians besieged Fort Pontchartrain, Detroit, in 1712. Repulsed by the French and their Huron and Ottawa Indian allies, the Fox retreated and entrenched themselves in this area known as Presque Isle. The French pursued and defeated the Fox in the only battle fought in the Grosse Pointes. More than a thousand Fox Indians were killed in a fierce five-day struggle. Soon afterward French settlers began to develop the Grosse Pointes." Reading this always cheered me, as did the thought, plagiarized from a novel set in the area, that the French settlers proceeded to name this waterlocked spit of land the "Fat Tip" in a three-hundred-year-old dirty joke no one ever got.

Such was the stalling I engaged in as I thought things through. My problem was that I hadn't a clue how to begin. I had no idea where to find—whom? Whoever he was, he knew who my wife was. Why shouldn't I know who he was? How was this fair? Knowledge is power, and I wanted to *know*. What I would do with such knowledge was something I'd decide once I had it.

Like a high school boy with a crush, I sometimes drove past the retired cop's house, even when his lights were on and his car in the drive, my nervousness preventing me from knocking. Other times I stopped, only to talk about nothing in particular. And then one day, feeling neither more nor less prepared than any other, I told him what was weighing on me. What I wanted to hear was his considered solution to my troubles. I should leave it to him: he'd take care of everything. After all, I had a family to raise.

Instead he smiled, said he understood, and gave me the number of another retired cop, a guy he knew from his days on the force who had turned to private detective work to supplement his pension. A week later, when I had the apartment to myself, I let this man in the door.

"What can you tell me?" he asked, sitting down in one of our garage sale chairs. I sat on our Salvation Army couch. He was older than I expected, in his midsixties, but still solid and handsome. An Italian, he looked like one of Sal's customers, and his salt-and-pepper hair was feathered and layered in a way reminiscent of Sal. He was all business, but not in the least abrupt. He could have been a contractor giving me a quote on a new driveway.

One question, and already I was out of my depth. I had almost nothing to tell him, and I sensed he knew it the moment he walked in the door. He'd sized me up, and only politeness had kept him from walking back out. I knew a few broad details—the attacker's race, the approximate date, the location—and nothing more. What I could tell him wouldn't take ten seconds.

I felt the same deflation I experienced when I sat down to write a story that I'd been contemplating forever, only to find, when I finally started to put it down on paper, that I had three sentences that didn't add up to a thing. In my imagination, these stories had been immense; but when I began telling them I had a half-furnished scene and the beginnings of a character sketch.

"I don't know what your economic circumstances are," he said, looking around the small apartment, "but I'd need a five-thousand-dollar retainer to take on a case like this." This was said perfunctorily, as part of the spiel.

"I can get it," I said, having no idea how. My paternal grandmother, perhaps: she had the money, along with certain opinions about black criminals.

"If you don't want the man brought to trial"—I'd made this clear—"what do you want him found for?"

"You'd simply be paid for finding him," I said, as if this payment were a hurdle already cleared—the first step in a plan each stage of which would be as easily executed.

He thought about this. "And then what—doorknobs in a pillow-case? Is that what you're saying? Sorry, I can't. I understand, believe me, and in your shoes I'd probably be doing the same. But I can't. I was a Detroit cop for thirty years. Trust me, this guy will get his. You don't even need to get involved."

We hadn't talked for five minutes before saying goodbye. Though I appreciated his belief in my capacity for vengeance—my sentence is for open war—he was giving me more credit than I deserved. I really didn't know what I would do with such information, if and when I should get it. Doorknobs in a pillowcase was one option; so was doing nothing. And even if I were capable of decisive action, simple prudence might prevent me from going forward. Or maybe I'd split the differ-ence, and do nothing—for now. After we'd had more kids, put them through college, married them off, and held a few grandchildren aloft, maybe then—I'd have carried the slip of paper with his name and specs in my coat pocket all this time—maybe then I'd say to myself, *Now*, and speed the sonuvabitch's progress to hell.

It was a comforting plan, susceptible to infinite postponement. I began, in my darker moments, to despair of my good citizenship. I had no tickets or accidents on my driving record. I had a perfect credit rat-ing. I showed up for jury duty, reported my earnings honestly, and aside from one time when I was three and a half had never been picked up by the cops. I couldn't even steal a goddamn hood ornament, try as I might.

I abandoned thoughts of revenge, and went back to books.

The novel was going badly, though some of it could be salvaged. There would still be a lot of driving around—my device for connecting the disparate scenes—but the drive downtown would now bypass The Fist entirely. My narrator remained, but his friends had morphed: the dumb bully had become a sensitive boy, the love interest of the narrator's sister; and the smart-ass was still a smart-ass, and still a racist, though his racism now had a stronger rationale: his mother had been raped. The plot, such as it was, concerned their search for the perpetrator. The narrator had supplied a cabbie who hung around the neighborhood barbershop with the police composite sketch, and told him to keep an eye out. Some time later, the cabbie spots the guy down in the Cass Corridor, just a few blocks behind the machine shop where the narrator works. As a way to make sense of things before exacting his revenge, the smart-ass—an intellectual killer like Raskolnikov—becomes obsessed with the writings of Malcolm X and William Faulkner.

At the urging of a college girlfriend, I'd begun my reading of Faulkner with *As I Lay Dying*, the story of poor, struggling, and ever-so-slightly stupid whites—which seemed applicable. In an American literature class I'd read *The Sound and the Fury*, and later I read *Light in August* and *Absalom, Absalom!* on my own, along with other novels, stories, and letters. But it was these four books, written over a span of seven years, that I fixated on. It was a line from another Faulkner novel of that period, however, that gave me a tingle down my spine. It came from the trial scene at the end of *Sanctuary,* when the bailiff intones: "The honourable Circuit Court of Yoknapatawpha County is now open according to law." No other line in Faulkner had this effect on me; it was the line's simple message concerning the meting out of justice that did it. Someone, you couldn't help but sense as you read that line, is about to *die* here.

I began again at the beginning, with the monologue of Benjy, the retarded Compson son who narrates the opening section of *The Sound and the Fury*. I recalled Hugh Kenner's line: "A work conceived as Faulkner conceived his art could hardly not have generated an idiot."

In the second section of the novel, narrated by Quentin Compson on the day of his death, June 2, 1910, Quentin recalls conversations he'd had with his father before moving north to begin his freshman year at Harvard. These recollections are, to my mind, the best thing in the book, maybe the best thing in Faulkner: the dialogue between the earnest, talented, suicidal son and the cynical, witty, apathetic father, a man who has so lost his ability to be shocked that, at Quentin's suggestion that he has slept with his sister, Caddy, Mr. Jason Compson III, drink in hand, does little more than scoff. "You are too serious," he says to his son's false revelation of incest, "to give me any cause for alarm."

Even Quentin's suggestion (and I've added the punctuation to these lines, conveyed in the book in Quentin's stream of consciousness) that suicide may be on his mind is met by his father with nothing more forceful than moral relativism. "We must just stay awake," Mr. Compson says in his greatest, bleakest pronouncement, "and see evil done for a little while." "It doesn't have to be that long," Quentin replies, "for a man of courage." "Do you consider that courage?" "Yes sir. Don't you?" "Every man is the arbiter of his own virtues," Mr. Compson says. "Whether or not you consider it courageous is of more importance than the act itself."

We must just stay awake and see evil done for a little while—could that possibly be bettered? But if Mr. Compson truly felt this way—why, then, send your son to Harvard, especially when you had to sell off your family's land to finance that education? Why the pessimism on the one hand, and the steep investment in the future on the other?

Faulkner could be confusing this way. If you want to read him at his least convincing, look at the transcript of a speech delivered in Stockholm on December 10, 1950, wherein the Nobel laureate, surveying the human landscape from his newfound literary heights, says: "Man will not merely endure; he will prevail." Do the novels that earned him that Nobel Prize—the books that brought him to Sweden and earned him the right to speak those very words—bear out this claim?

In *The Sound and the Fury*, Quentin Compson's suicide sets off a chain of disasters—deaths, departures, acts of drunken despair—that, by book's end, leave the once-proud Compson clan to be represented only by their black cook, Dilsey, and their overgrown, retarded, castrated son, Benjamin.

In *As I Lay Dying*, the Bundren family overcomes fire, flood, and the circling of buzzards overhead and succeeds, barely, in burying the corpse of their steadily decaying mother, Addie, forty miles from their home, after which their most sensitive son, Darl, gets carted off to a mental institution.

In *Light in August*, Lena Grove, in her ninth month of pregnancy, begins the book by walking from Alabama to Mississippi in search of the father of her unborn child, and ends it in the back of a pickup truck in Tennessee, husbandless, looking at the scenery with her new son in her arms while, in the book's other narrative line, Joe Christmas, the tragic mulatto, ends his days martyred and, like Benjamin Compson, with his balls cut off.

In *Absalom, Absalom!*, Thomas Sutpen, founder of Sutpen's Hundred, Yoknapatawpha County's largest plantation, sees his grand design begin to crumble along with the rest of the Old South when, at the outset of the Civil War, his half-breed son from his first marriage gets romantically entangled with his daughter from his second marriage—the half-breed's white half sister, in other words—setting in motion the most disastrous plotline in all of Faulkner, culminating with pretty much everyone dead, or near dead, and the teller of this ghost-haunted tale, who is reciting it from his freezing Harvard dorm room—Quentin Compson—about to be dead by his own hand, thus bringing Faulkner's seven most productive years as an artist full circle.

Man will *prevail?* This was preposterous. Everything worthwhile Faulkner had written said otherwise. As a way to counterbalance such insipid optimism, I kept the book's basic premise—the novel would still end with a death—except instead of killing the guy who raped his mother—a scene I'd never write—the smart-ass would kill himself. A suicide, like Quentin Compson.

At the end of the novel, everyone leaves Detroit. Some things I couldn't change.

I eventually found what I was looking for in Chapter 10 of *Light in August*, which opens with echoes of the first line of Chapter 6: "Knowing not grieving remembers a thousand savage and lonely streets." The chapter then goes on, in typically circuitous Faulknerian fashion, to follow Joe Christmas as he attempts to run from his past and his mixed ancestry following a beating he receives at age eighteen. The beating is at the hands of whites who, on the basis of Joe's trace or two of black blood, have identified him as a nigger and have dealt with him accordingly. "From that night," Faulkner writes of Joe's fifteen years on the road, "the thousand streets ran as one street, with imperceptible corners and changes of scene, broken by intervals of begged and stolen rides, on trains and trucks, and on country wagons with he at twenty and twenty-five and thirty sitting on the seat with his still, hard face and the clothes of a city man and the driver of the wagon not knowing who or what the passenger was and not daring to ask." Who or what Joe is, of course, is at the heart of the novel, and who gets to define who or what Joe is defines his tragedy, which culminates with his death at the Christlike age of thirty-three, when Joe allows himself to be shot by the redneck National Guardsman Percy Grimm.

"They ran my father out of Alabama for being an uppity nigger," Coleman Young said of his early years in the South. The Young family moved to Detroit when he was five years old, in 1924, the year Faulkner published his first book, a collection of poems ("most of them worthless," according to Malcolm Cowley) entitled *The Marble Faun*. The Young family settled on Detroit's east side, in the area known as Black Bottom, and Coleman, after being denied entrance to De La Salle by the

Christian Brothers, went on to graduate from Eastern High School, work for Ford, serve with the Tuskegee Airmen, testify before HUAC, get elected state senator—and, eventually, become the goddamn Mayor of Detroit.

After being run out of Mississippi, Joe Christmas, in Faulkner's telling, reaches Detroit twice. "The street," Faulkner writes, "ran into Oklahoma and Missouri and as far south as Mexico and then back north to Chicago and Detroit and then back south again to Mississippi." Later, after Joe, while still in the South, has "tricked or teased white men into calling him a Negro in order to fight them," and has fought a "Negro who called him white," he again reaches the North, making it back to Chicago and then to Detroit, where "he lived with Negroes, shunning white people." In Detroit in the early 1930s, living with Negroes would have meant living in Black Bottom, and there Joe Christmas "lived as man and wife with a woman who resembled an ebony carving."

In a *Detroit Free Press* interview from the fall of 1990, Young said, "I was telling some of Louis Farrakhan's people the other day that the original founder of the Muslims was a door-to-door silk merchant, who lived near us in Black Bottom on the lower east side. I'd see him all the time. He used to call on my mother, selling her silks and perfumes."

In 1923, Elijah Muhammad (then Elijah Poole) moved his family from Georgia to Detroit, for fear of a white employer who had cursed him. Eight years later, in 1931—at the very moment that Faulkner was creating Joe Christmas and writing of his trips to Detroit—Elijah Muhammad met, on the streets of this city, a light-skinned transient of mixed ancestry who went door-to-door selling silks and telling all who would listen about the Lost-Found Nation of Islam. Could it, in fact, have been Joe Christmas that Elijah Muhammad met, posing as a seller of silks? There were those who claimed that the original founder of the Muslims was a character no less fictitious than Faulkner's creation. So if one were to assert that it was in fact Joe Christmas who had knocked on Elijah Muhammad's door that day in 1931, that it was Joe Christmas from whom Coleman Young's mother had bought perfume, would we be any further from the truth? What more appropriate instrument than the pen of William Faulkner—the man who said that he'd fight for Mississippi against the United States even if it meant going out into the street and shooting Negroes—to have brought the Nation of Islam into being, and to have made Black Power possible?

Dear reader, I was losing my mind.

Initial Here

W HAT'S WITH THE GLASSES?" I asked my father a few years back, on the second day of his wearing an old pair with a dark tint. It was evening, and I'd stopped by my parents' house, where I have a standing invitation—from my mother, anyway— for dinner. My father removed the glasses slowly, revealing a horribly blackened eye. "And you got that how?" I asked. He motioned for me to walk with him out to his car.

He opened the door and reached down under the driver's seat; his hand emerged holding a knife with a twelve-inch blade. "A guy tried to carjack me the other morning as I pulled into work," he said. My father still works downtown. "He came at me with this"—he pushed the knife my way in slow motion—"and I grabbed it with both hands. I hung on, he let go, and because I was exposed he got me with a right cross." "Can you describe the suspect for me?" I asked. He smiled, declining to do so. Such easy antipathy was not his style. Though he'd never read Baldwin—has never willingly read a book in his life, as far as I know—he seemed to grasp instinctively Baldwin's statement at the end of "Notes of a Native Son." "Hatred," Baldwin writes, "which could destroy so much, never failed to destroy the man who hated and this was an immutable law." My father would have appreciated the sentiment's praiseworthy selfishness: Stay clear of hatred, not to make the world a better place, but so as not to destroy yourself.

That's what his silence said to me when I'd tried to egg him on, asking him to describe the suspect—the same thing it'd said when I told him of the attack, trying to connect it to my sister's relationship, which by this time had run its course: Let it go. Gut it out. Suck it up. Ride it out. These were the thought rhythms—his—more familiar to me than those of Baldwin and Ellison, O'Connor and Faulkner combined.

Think.

Last summer, I accompanied my daughter to the birthday party of one of her classmates, a black girl who'd chosen a Macomb County fun center as the site of festivities for her and her four- and five-year-old friends. I was the only father there, with the exception of the birthday girl's dad. Besides us it was all women, and the girl's mother insisted that I sit by her husband. "The men *need* to sit together," she said, handing us each a plate of pizza and smiling. "Here—eat, eat." It was a comfortable sort of insistence, gender solidarity trumping racial distinctions. The two of us discussed schools, how our summers were progressing, the lovable snottiness of little girls, and our basic helplessness before female assertiveness, whether it be from wives or daughters. It all felt very simple. We watched the little kids, evenly balanced between black and white, jumping around on the indoor playscape, spinning themselves sick and screaming themselves hoarse with that obliviousness to consequence that is one of the great blessings of childhood.

When we were moving into our current house, my mother and father stopped at a garage sale in the block behind us, in search of a tool kit for me. To my father, this was lunacy: that a grown man, a *homeowner,* should be without a set of tools. The family holding the sale—a small surprise—was black. "I didn't know if I should say anything to you," my mother said. The house was barely outside the limits of the blackest big city in American history, and she didn't know if she should say anything. I was reminded of the funniest line in Coleman Young's autobiography, which comes not from the mayor, though he repeats it with relish, but from a white state senator with whom Young, then a senator himself, had lived in Lansing during the 1960s. Four senators from the east side of Detroit—two black, two white—lived together in a house in the capital, and though they tended to vote together on most issues, one of the white senators, out of deference to his Polish-Catholic constituency, broke ranks on an open-housing bill. Questioned about this apparent contradiction—voting against open housing while living with two black men himself—the representative said: "Oh, I can live *with* them. I just don't want to live *next* to them."

Of the black family hawking their wares, my father said, "No, no, they were good. They had a lot of nice stuff. I asked if they had a tool kit, and the mother said to the kid there, 'Go get your father's toolbox and bring it up front.' The kid ran right back and got it. Here," he said, handing the thing over. It was surprisingly heavy. "You owe me twenty bucks."

I drive to work downtown each morning listening to NPR. We subscribe to magazines and journals that tilt our mailbox a touch to the left. I've become, to some extent, what I beheld growing up: a suburban liberal. When my daughter's best friend from the year before, a black girl, switched to an expensive private school, my daughter kept asking why she didn't see Jasmine anymore. I told her it was because Jasmine was going to a new school. Could she go to that school too? No. Why? Because I didn't have the money to send her there. How could Jasmine's parents send her to that school? "Because," I said, "they have a lot more money than we do." I felt not the slightest pang. Instead, I felt a pleasant lessening of what I had never thought myself capable of feeling: liberal guilt.

At times, I feel like a failure in several directions simultaneously:

that, with my education and reading, I should be more broad-minded than I am; and that, with the education I received from my father and Sal, I should be angrier about what the broad-minded morons have wrought. I can hear the men in the barbershop: "Liberal guilt? They destroy your city, rape your wife, try to carjack your father—and what you feel is *guilt?*" A while back, when my father was discussing some expensive, harebrained scheme the city leadership had hatched, he said, after failing to get a rise out of me: "You realize, don't you, that even though you don't live in the city, you pay a one and a half percent city tax just for working in it?" I didn't realize. Why can't I get worked up about this stuff? I'll never lecture my kids about wasted tax dollars, about the need to come home when the streetlights come on, about the demand of some nun that a sweater be kelly green instead of hunter green. I'm no longer working class enough, no longer urban enough, no longer Catholic enough. And I'm insufficiently indignant, to those to the left and the right of me. Detroit, which drives people to extremes, has left me stranded in the middle.

I dug through box after box in my parents' basement while writing this book, sorting through the effluvia of an existence that felt like someone else's, someone who was a Cub Scout, a crossing guard, a National Honor Society president, a proud Catholic schoolboy, a toothless first-grader. At the bottom of one box that was beginning to mildew, I found a note from an old grade-school classmate. Though not someone I was particularly close to, he refers to me, in a chummy way, as "a fellow nigger hater." The note goes on to list other hatreds we shared in common—a science teacher, a certain song—and closes with the sincere wish that I enjoy my summer.

My first instinct, upon reading this, was to throw up. My second was to throw the note away—burn it, destroy the evidence, bury it in the garbage. Then I thought: why? Who among us, if judged by opinions we held when we were twelve and thirteen years old—less opinions, really, than poses—would escape whipping? We also wrote "666" in our notebooks and carved pentagrams into our desktops, like any self-respecting heavy metal fans; that didn't make us Satan worshippers, then or now. Anyway, I didn't recall this opinion being one I had held with any conviction, and if it was a pose I struck occasionally, well, such was life. A hell of a lot had happened since then.

Still, rather than throwing the note away, I put it in my wallet as a reminder. Of what? I wasn't entirely sure. Of the need to fight such tendencies, I suppose, because my grasp on open-mindedness is tenuous, however pleased I might be at donating to Amnesty International.

From a few months back, by way of example:

"Hello, sir—no need for concern. I'm not the neighborhood bad guy, I assure you. I've just got some magazines for sale." It was dinnertime, dark, and I didn't know the guy at the door, and neither did I want what he was selling. I'd just worked a long day. Scram. "Where are my manners?" He held out his hand, which I took. "My name is Stephen, and I live in a halfway house. You know what that is, right?" I told him I did. Stephen was black, in his midthirties, and in a hooded sweatshirt. I was in a tie, pressed pants, and Italian shoes—my office attire.

"A number of your neighbors, as you can see here"—he held out a sign-up sheet on a clipboard—"have seen fit to make a donation. It's not about the magazines, it's about supporting what I'm all about, which is trying to improve myself by accumulating points. As you can see on the sheet, I get a hundred points for each subscription I sell. When I make it to fifty thousand points, I become an assistant manager, overseeing other guys who go out and make sales. I also get an additional thousand dollars toward improving myself. I'm sure you get a lot of magazines coming to the house, so as I say, it's not about the magazines. A twenty-dollar donation earns me the same number of points as a subscription sale. Most of your neighbors have made a donation. May I ask what you do for a living?"

I said he could, and proceeded to lie about what I did and where I did it. He liked the give-and-take; we were two working men, having a chat. "Can I see the list?" I asked. He offered me the donor list. "No—

the list of magazines." "Sorry, sorry." I flipped through it, to stall for time—*Good Housekeeping, Field & Stream,* a bunch of car magazines my father kept in business—before seeing a magazine my wife bought off the newsstand each month at impoverishing expense. A former hipster magazine for adolescent girls, it had matured along with its readership and undergone a name change. A subscription would save us some cash. "How much is that one?" I asked. He pulled out a pricing sheet, and I noticed that it said "KILLER," in crayon, at the top of his clipboard. Was this his nickname, a little halfway house humor? Or did the other salesmen have "ARMED ROBBER" and "RAPIST" at the tops of theirs, by way of identification?

"It's forty-four dollars for two years, sixty-six dollars for three years," he said, folding back the sheet. "How much is it for one year, then? Twenty-two bucks?" "You can't get it for one year." "Why not?" "It doesn't come in a one-year subscription. None of them do. They're all at least two years." "I guess it looks like a donation, then. Let me get my wallet and see what I've got on me." I went into the dining room.

"Who is it?" my wife asked. "No one," I said, and went back to the door. "Here's all I got," I said to the guy, handing him a five. "This doesn't earn me any points," he said, looking down at what I'd put in his palm. "It's all I have." "I take checks. You can write a check." And you can take a flying fuck at the moon, I thought. "It's what I've got. Take it or leave it." "Okay," he said, looking me in the eye. I returned his stare and started to smile. Were we about to come to blows? "I need you to sign here," he said. I did. "And I need you to initial here." "Why do I need to initial what I've just signed?" What did I care! Was I trying to antagonize this guy, an ex-con of whatever sort? And was I the only person in whom liberal guilt and racial hostility were connected by the world's shortest bridge? "Any donation less than twenty dollars needs initials. It's so that when I report it to my supervisor . . ." More shit about points, and how he wasn't getting any out of me. "There you are," I said, putting "PC" alongside my signature.

I wasn't in the best mood, admittedly. A week before this we'd received a phone call informing us, nearly nine years after the fact, that the Michigan State Police had a DNA match from my wife's attack. It was an astonishing call to get out of the blue—frightening, disorienting, and somehow inevitable: *finally*. There was no soul-searching, no consulting of sacred texts, no grand literary or historical theorizing. Just a day off work and a couple-hour drive to the courthouse on a cloudy morning for the pretrial hearing.

I've often wondered, watching courtroom scenes, how the families of those who've been raped or murdered can refrain from jumping the banister and beating the assailant to a bloody pulp. What I learned, as I sat in that honorable circuit court, two rows behind the man who had raped my wife a year and a half before I met her (not his first assault: he appeared in court in his prison uniform), is that the whole legalistic setup acts as a deterrent. It's so plodding, so procedural, so antiseptic— "Next witness," "Your witness," "The court calls"—that one is lulled into a stupor in which the only recurring thought, as at the secretary of state's office or the Department of Motor Vehicles, is that of escape. I'd dreamt of this moment for years, and yet my emotions never rose above the level of frustrated resignation—oh well, may he rot in hell. The first thing the lead detective asked me, as we walked out after the hearing, was if I wanted to go with him to get my parking validated.

As we left the courthouse, my wife and I were approached by a black kid asking for directions. He had on a baseball hat cocked sideways and pants that needed to be pulled up, and he spoke with an intentionally slurred speech that was almost inaudible—shit for which I have no patience. Never was this truer than then. *Enunciate*, motherfucker. "You know where Westphalia Street is?" he asked, or so I deciphered. "I've no idea," I said. It was two blocks over. My wife, solicitous as ever—she is, by several orders of magnitude, a better person than I am—began to formulate an answer. "If you go straight—" "You're on your own, pal." I took my wife by the elbow. "Let's go."

Did I hate this kid? And what did I consider him? I had that cautionary note in my wallet by this point, along with my validated parking pass. Swirling around my head was a confusing mess: It's a not very nice word. Who paints a house purple? The powers that be. Solemn-faced and quoting the Bible. Have a beary merry Christmas. Suffered, died, and was buried. I wish I'd picked the damn cotton myself.

I didn't know if I wanted to grab my baseball bat or break down and cry.

But there's no disputing what parents—or, anyway, mothers—know about their children. And my mother claimed to know with ab-solute certainty which course I'd have chosen, if only I could. Which brings me back to the aftermath of that attempted carjacking:

After my father had set the knife, once again, safely under the driver's seat, we went back to the house. I walked into the kitchen, where my mother was still making dinner. "Can you believe that black eye?" she asked. "It's something, all right." "I'm so glad that your father was attacked and not you," she said, without looking up from her preparations. At first, this sounded flatly insulting to my father. His wife was happy that *he* was attacked as opposed to his younger, more vigor-ous son? But my mother has a talent for beginning her prepared speeches with line three as opposed to line one. I knew there was a thought process behind this. "What do you mean, you're glad it was him?" "I *mean*," she said, annoyed that I was too dense to understand straightaway, "if it had been *you*, and you'd gotten the knife off the guy, you would've killed him."

A Good, Moral Boy of at Least Average Talent

I WENT TO MIDNIGHT MASS alone last Christmas, driving west along 7 Mile to St. Jude, the steeple of which can be seen during clear daylight from a good distance. Decades before, my mother would wake my sister and me around eleven o'clock Christmas Eve night, after having put us down for a couple-hour nap, and bring us cinnamon toast and milk while we sat in pajamas in our sparkling living room, where all the lights were off except those on the Christmas tree. We'd stare with sleepy half smiles at the sight of the unopened presents, all of which were accounted for except those from Santa, which would be brought out later, and long after we'd ceased to believe. Sitting alongside the wrapped presents were the already opened gifts we'd brought back from the Saulino family gathering in the suburbs, presents my sister and I had stored under our respective sides of the tree when we got back to the city. After we'd finished our toast, our mother would hurriedly dress us—a little-man suit for me, party dress and party shoes for my sister—before walking the both of us, still half asleep, out to the car, which our father was scraping and warming up.

On the way to Mass, if the conditions were right and the way was clear, he'd expertly execute a 360 in an intersection, making us all laugh. A few minutes later, a little more awake now, we'd get out of the warm car and walk back through the cold night into church, where the organ music tumbled down from the balcony in back and the whole place, decorated in red and green and gold, smelled of incense and pine. Everyone within—the frustrated fathers, the frumpy mothers—looked lovely, utterly transformed. The moment felt like nothing but what it was: Midnight Mass, which came once a year, creating an atmosphere so dreamlike that its spell couldn't be recalled until 365 days later, when the same sensations returned. Whenever they played "O Holy Night" my mother would lean over and say, "This is my *favorite*." Her voice wavered with emotion as she sang. It was "Away in a Manger," however, that did her in: "The thought of that little baby, without a crib," she said.

I was an adult now, past thirty, with a pregnant wife and a child—neither of them Catholic—sound asleep at home. My parents had attended Midnight Mass at St. Jude the year before, and because the priest had provided some statistics on the parish for the benefit of the "visitors" who attended services once a year, which my mother had passed on to me, I had some idea of what to expect. The parish now had two hundred families—"instead of two thousand," my mother said, "when your father went there." "They used to have eight masses every Sunday," my father, a former altar boy, added, "and every one of them was standing room only. Now they can't even fill the place for Midnight Mass." The school population, too, was small, and predominantly non-Catholic, with only one white student. "Forty years ago," my father said, "they used to have to bring in portable trailers to make space for all the kids." The space inside the church was smaller now, too; my mother said that they'd taken out about half the pews. My father considered, making mental calculations. "Yeah," he said. "About half."

Along with Assumption Grotto, at 6 Mile and Gratiot, St. Jude was the prettiest of the east side's Catholic churches. One of the least attractive, certainly, was our actual parish on 8 Mile, where we rarely went for Mass. St. Peter was typical of the churches built after the Second Vatican Council—which, along with doing away with the Latin Mass, had called for churches to be more utilitarian in design. In Detroit, the post-Vatican II period coincided with the era of suburban church building: the last Catholic church within the city limits was built in the late 1950s. South of 8 Mile, then, were the churches that aspired to be the neighborhood cathedral at Chartres; north of 8 Mile—even those just on the north side of 8 Mile, like our parish—were churches resembling hospital wards and Mexican restaurants. But because it was our home parish we had to pay dues whether we went there or not, on top of putting money in the basket wherever we happened to go that weekend: to St. Brendan, St. Matthew, St. Raymond, St. Clare, St. Ambrose, or any of a number of other churches, all of which expected attendees to ante up. It was enough to make one give thanks for time and a half on the weekends. "We *are* the poor," my mother would say, opening the cupboards, whenever my sister and I told her that we had to bring canned goods to school for a food drive. Every Catholic mother on the east side, opening her cupboards, said the same.

There was a new priest at St. Jude saying Midnight Mass, a young man fresh out of Sacred Heart Seminary, as Father Hector Saulino had been sixty-five years before. I have a photo of a newly ordained Father Hec, wearing his priest's collar, posing with his brothers Herbie, Mario, and Antonio and their father, Umberto, all of them suave and handsome in their 1930s suits, looking like hired goons from a gangster flick. Sister Marcia, in her veil, is not to be seen in the photo. As someone said of Mary Magdalene's role at the Last Supper, she was probably doing the dishes.

At the top of Father Hec's application to Sacred Heart Seminary—from 1926, when he was fourteen and had just left the St. Francis Home for Boys—is the following: "An applicant for the Seminary must be a good, moral boy of at least average talent. He must be of legitimate birth, free from deafness, blindness, impediments of speech, and taint of insanity in his family or among blood relatives." This good boy of legitimate birth was all of the above. His mother was dead. He had four surviving siblings—three brothers, all younger, and one older sister. His father's first name he Americanizes to Humbert. Father's Occupation or Business: painter and decorator. Racial Descent: Italian. To the question, "Besides furnishing your books and stationery will you be able to pay each year Fifty Dollars for Tuition and Two Hundred Dollars for Board and Laundry?" the teenage boy, provided a long dotted line on which to respond to the question, answers simply: "No." There is a follow-up: "In case you are unable to pay and the Diocese defrays your expenses wholly or in part, will your parents or guardian agree to refund all moneys paid out for your education in the Preparatory Seminary in case you are dismissed, or leave of your own accord?" Answer: "Unable." Next: "In the event they cannot do this will you yourself later on see that it is done?" "Yes."

The young priest at St. Jude wore a headset microphone that, like a pop star, he fiddled with throughout Mass. The former altar, at the front of the church, was now closed off, and a smaller altar jutted forward, creating a theater-in-the-round effect, forcing the priest to move this way and that during his homily, playing to those seated to the left and right. During the homily, for reasons unclear to me, he occasionally made quotation marks in the air. As I'd been told, the pews at the front of the church had been removed since my last visit, to make room for the new altar, and many of the pews in the back had also been taken out. Whereas before you could enter the church's back doors, cross yourself with holy water, genuflect, and sit down, you now had to walk a good twenty yards before coming to the last row of pews. It seemed to me that two-thirds of the seating had been taken out.

The life-size crucifix that had hung behind the old altar now hung in the church's eastern alcove, replaced on the new altar by a small wooden cross in a stand. No Christ, no nails, no crown of thorns, no stab wound from a Roman spear: just stained wood, about eighteen inches high. In the western alcove, where our family once sat, was a life-size statue of Mary, arms still outspread, still looking down upon her children with tenderness—though too big, this one, to be dragged into the middle of 7 Mile. Because the pews on both sides of the church now faced in toward the altar, no one faced the Blessed Virgin any longer. Her centrality—the old joke: "I don't believe in God, but I believe that Mary was His mother"—was clearly in decline.

I could have tolerated this (very Protestant) demotion of the Blessed Mother were it not for the fact that, in her and her son's stead, there was now a prominent stained-glass partition that ran along the back of the altar. It contained the likenesses of a number of religious figures, two per panel, the panels lightly folded upon one another, creating a zigzag effect. Among those I could clearly identify were Pope John Paul II, who was in one half of the central panel, and Father Solanus Casey, a Capuchin friar. Many American Catholics were working for canonization on behalf of Casey—who, if the campaign on his behalf should succeed, would be the first American-born male sainted. In 1995, the pope pronounced Casey "venerable"—two steps east of sainthood. Before making my confirmation in eighth grade, I had had to volunteer at a Capuchin food kitchen in the Cass Corridor.

I should have been able to do better, but while I waited for Mass to begin, listening to the carols while down on my knees, that was about the best I could do, at least as far as Catholics went. Others whose likenesses I thought I could identify behind the altar, in stunned disbelief that I was identifying them at all, were Mahatma Gandhi, Confucius, and Dr. Martin Luther King Jr.—a Hindu, a Confucian, and a Baptist. Had Catholicism, in the time I'd been away, become "inclusive," or were such gestures limited to the inner-city precincts? Had religious relativism crept into the thinking coming out of Rome? Did certain absolutes—the belief in Jesus Christ as Savior, say—no longer hold sway?

I was only a couple of miles from the old De La Salle, but this all felt light-years from those stories I'd heard from my father and Uncle Tony about the fierceness of the Christian Brothers. I was a couple of miles, too, from St. David, where my mother, aunts, and uncle had been instructed in the Baltimore Catechism. "Who is God?" "God is the Supreme Being." (Or as a young boy had once recited it back to Father Hec, in a story he often repeated: "God is a string bean.") Had this sort of rigor, easily mocked as it may be, been replaced by cultural sensitivity? I finished my preliminary prayers, crossed myself, and pushed up the kneeler in front of me as I sat back down. Another Baptist, I wanted to inform the parish staff—Martin Luther King Sr.—had initially called for the defeat of Kennedy in 1960 on account of the candidate's Catholicism.

In part I understood. The school was black, and the desire for black representation in the church, even if the students themselves were non-Catholic, was a commonsense nod to current demographics. Anyway, I'd already worked for a Catholic university with a Baptist president. But Gandhi? Confucius? The Hindu and Confucian populations on Detroit's east side remained small. Were they brought in, along with other non-Western religious figures whom I was having difficulty identifying, simply to balance the ticket, to make Dr. King's presence seem less like tokenism than a part of the broad patchwork of humankind's religious striving?

I didn't much care. My primary focus was on the person in the central panel with Pope John Paul II, a figure who looked familiar but was difficult for me to place. Pope John XXIII? St. Peter? St. Jude? Around the time of the Gospel reading, another possibility presented itself. Could it be—no, it couldn't—Martin Luther?

The Gospel, Luke 2:1–14, was one I had by heart. "In those days a decree went out from Caesar Augustus that the whole world should be enrolled," it begins in the New American Bible, which is what was being read at Midnight Mass. I didn't much care for this version's vagueness—*enrolled?* The New International Version was better: "In those days Caesar Augustus issued a decree that a census should be taken of the entire Roman world." *Census* was a clear improvement on *enrolled;* but the King James Version, as ever, was best: "And it came to pass in those days, that there went out a decree from Caesar Augustus, that all the world should be taxed." That was more like it. You take a census—would Detroit stay above a million people? if not, would federal support dwindle?—and this helped determine how Coleman Augustus would *tax* his population.

I only half heard the reading, translating what I was hearing into the cadences of King James's English. Joseph and Mary go to Bethlehem. Jesus is born. Swaddling clothes. Manger. No room at the inn. Frightened shepherds receive a visitation: "Fear not: for, behold, I bring you good tidings of great joy. For unto you is born this day in the city of David a Saviour, which is Christ the Lord. And this shall be a sign unto you; Ye shall find the babe wrapped in swaddling clothes, lying in a manger." I looked down the pew, to see if my mother was crying. She was at home, fast asleep.

After Mass had concluded I went out the church's western doors, accepting a parish flyer from an usher. "Excuse me," I asked, and pointed up at the altar, "but who is that next to the pope? I haven't been here in a while, and I've been wondering all Mass."

"To which side of him?"

"In the same panel."

"You know, I don't know."

"Do you know who might?"

"Ask Jim," he said, pointing to an enormous usher who was talking to a woman a couple pews up.

I walked over and cut in on their conversation. It was one-fifteen in the morning, and I still had a My Little Pony castle to assemble and put under the tree before turning in. "Pardon me," I said, "but can you tell me who that is in the panel with the pope? The usher by the door said you might know." Jim looked down at me as if he reserved the right to kick my ass for asking. "I thought it might be Martin Luther," I said, laughing a little. If so, I nearly added—if being inclusive meant including the constipated Luther—me and Catholicism were calling it a day.

Big Jim told me it was Father Gabriel Richard.

"Thank you," I said, and walked back out the church doors, declining the offer of a second flyer. My faith in Catholicism restored, I started to drive north, in the direction of our old house.

Our second bungalow was well decorated for Christmas, with colored lights framing the living room and kitchen windows and candy canes stuck to the glass. The place looked pretty much the same, aside from a privacy fence in the backyard. Even my paint job, peeling badly in spots, was still on the garage. Afraid that I'd spook someone if I idled in front of the house much longer—my father would have been out after me already—I drove off.

And then, fearing I'd missed something, I looped back around the block. I wanted, above all, to get another look at the trees that had been given to us as housewarming presents by Mr. and Mrs. Shannon when we moved from our old bungalow at 6 Mile and Gratiot to this one, more than two decades back. One of the trees was mine, the other my sister's, and a coin toss had determined which went where. I won, and so mine stood in the front of the house while my sister's was along the side, where it was beginning to grow into the living room's side window. When the trees were planted they had been smaller than my sister and I; they were now the height of the house, which seemed to me indestructible. There was a great deal of evidence, not too many blocks away, to contradict this, but the brick bungalow in which I'd been raised struck me then as being possessed of the permanence of the pyramids, as indestructible in reality as it is in my memory, where it can be rebuilt, brick by brick, at a moment's notice.

Eventually, a white woman in dress clothes opened the front door, fiddled with something around the mailbox—a pretext to see what I was up to, presumably—and went back inside. I didn't wait around to see if that front door was going to open again.

Shortly after I began work on this book—a testament to the novel I hadn't the talent to write—I excused myself from a Sunday dinner at my parents' house, saying that I wanted to go home and get some writing done. My mother said fine, that she'd be glad to babysit. My father followed me out to the car. "Still chasing that rainbow, are ya?" he asked, laughing a little at my literary pretensions. "Yeah, Pop," I said. "Still chasing it." Except instead of working on a novel about parentless adolescents in Detroit—instead of distorting the experience, to no clear end—I now wanted to write honestly, using as my primary literary influence my life's main influence.

My father stood in the middle of the driveway, arms folded; up ahead in the garage was his latest hot rod, which he'd raced at Milan Dragway the weekend before. He wasn't too happy with how things had gone; the miles per hour clockings were all right, but the elapsed time lagged, indicating problems with the start—a poor launch. His heart wasn't really in drag racing anymore—the sport had been corporatized, with huge infusions of money that had loosed it from its white trash roots—and he was planning to sell the car, though not before he got it running right.

Behind the garage, in the house one block back, there had been a drug bust not long before. Several blocks over, a drifter doing odd jobs in the neighborhood killed an elderly woman. More and more bass booms from the cars that drive by, rattling the front windows. "I've never lived more than four miles from where I was born," my father said, somewhat defeatedly, at the dinner following my Grandma Saulino's funeral—a remark made to relatives living at 17 Mile, and 21 Mile, and 23 Mile roads. Still south of 8 Mile, a few houses onto the suburban side of the Ford Freeway—it'll be time, very soon, for my folks to get out of here.

My father was wearing a yellow T-shirt from his garbage bag collection, bearing the words WOLVERINE 200, after the twenty-four-hour bicycle race held on Belle Isle each spring from eight on Saturday morning to eight on Sunday, making the intervening night the only one of the year that visitors are allowed to stay over on the island, the elegantly laid-out interior of which was designed by Frederick Law Olmsted, the architect of Central Park. A five-mile course is plotted around the island's perimeter, and the object is to make forty circuits—two hundred miles. The race is sponsored by the Wolverine Bicycle Club, which gathers every Wednesday evening at the Cadieux Café.

My father and I entered the race twice, when I was in seventh and eighth grades. We both rode two hundred miles the first year, reaching the milestone by eight o'clock on Sunday morning, but the second year I finished alone, twenty-one hours after starting out. My father, a few hours into that year's race, had fallen off his bike, dislocating his right shoulder. My mother took him to Detroit Receiving Hospital as I continued to pedal around the island. He came back to Belle Isle after several hours in the emergency room with his right arm in a sling and a noticeable bump on his right shoulder. It looked, under his T-shirt, as if he'd suffered a compound fracture and had a bone sticking out of the skin.

We'd taken two cars to Belle Isle, and I drove back home with my father in the Renault. Driving a Renault in Detroit wasn't quite the sacrilege it might seem, the American Motor Company, whose suburban headquarters had so angered Coleman Young, having been bought out by the French manufacturer. Because my paternal grandfather had worked for AMC, and briefly for the bigger fish by which it had been swallowed, he got a discount on the already cheap Renaults. By the time he sold the compacts to my father, their odometers were pushing six figures and the cars were pretty close to free. "You're going to have to shift for me," my father said as we got in, nodding toward his sling. He could still steer with his left arm.

I put his keys in the ignition for him, turning them when he told me to start it. The car was already in first gear, which got us going. Around ten or fifteen miles per hour he put in the clutch: "All right, try second. Pull it straight back." Success. Around twenty-five miles per hour, the two of us out on the Belle Isle Bridge now, he again let up on the accelerator and put in the clutch: "Now up and over, for third." Again, success. "Just tell me when for fourth," I said. "I think third is all we'll need for surface streets," he said. "I'll just wind out the gear a bit. You'll have to downshift for me, though, when we slow down." "Just tell me when," I repeated, to show my readiness. And then, joking: "I think I know how to drive a stick now."

Well, he didn't know about that. Shifting was important, and I seemed to have that down, but there was still the footwork—gas, clutch—and I'd need to learn to coordinate the shifting with what went on with the pedals. But I still had two years before I turned sixteen; I'd get the hang of it. "Now, when you get *real* good," he said, holding out for me an impossible standard of achievement, like a perfect score on the SAT, "you can shift without even using the clutch."

I felt my confidence grow as we got off the bridge and turned right onto Jefferson Avenue. Behind us was the site of the old Uniroyal Tire plant, where my mother had worked while pregnant with me. After the plant's closing in 1980, the land was sold to the City of Detroit, and the site was cleared a few years later. Though riverfront property that the City had hoped to develop, the land is now fenced off, with a sign pronouncing the site contaminated.

I might, that Sunday morning in 1987, have taken this emptiness as a harbinger of things to come. All of my father's old shops in the city would soon close, if they hadn't already. The Catholic grade schools from which my friends and I were then graduating—St. Peter, St. Brendan—would fold before long, reopening under incense-free names like Heart Academy and the Detroit School for the Industrial Arts. The former parish house of the School of the Guardian Angels would become the St. Jude's Home for Boys, and the building that had formerly housed the St. Francis Home for Boys would serve as the first-year home for a Jesuit academy for at-risk black males. Fifty-five years after its founding, St. Bernadette—once the spiritual home for thousands of wops with wet feet—would become the headquarters for an Arab community service organization, the road it sits on now called Saulino Court. Around the same time, Sal's barbershop would close up, replaced by a nail salon.

Nothing was sacred. The residency requirement for City of Detroit employees would be rescinded, with nearly half of all Detroit cops estimated to be living outside the city limits—legally. Most telling of all, perhaps, would be the closing of the last rest stop on the outskirts of metropolitan Detroit, one I used to pass on my drives to and from college, its bathrooms, candy machines, and You Are Here map of Michigan's highway system no longer necessary now that the suburbs—some of them thirty, forty, and fifty miles outside the city center—had surrounded it. The only thing I might have predicted back in 1987 was that, sooner or later, the State of Michigan would elect a governor who was Canadian by birth. Such a turn of events was inevitable in a state whose largest city is Detroit. Because I still don't have cable, on Saturday nights during cold-weather months I continue to twist my television's antennae this way and that, trying to tune in *Hockey Night in Canada*.

"I grew up in a part of Detroit that doesn't exist anymore," Coleman Young writes on the first page of his autobiography in reference to Black Bottom, leveled to make way for the Chrysler Freeway and urban renewal. Still on page one: "Detroit will never again be the city it once was." It's the feeling of every Detroiter, black and white alike, and not only a feeling—it's a fact, more often than not. A. J. Liebling, writing in the 1950s of Chicago, called it less a big city than merely a large place. This was even truer of late-twentieth-century Detroit; some of its residents couldn't have found the city's downtown if they had to. They had their neighborhoods, and that was that. Coleman Young was less the mayor of a major city than the overseer of a large place—much of it empty space—collected under the name Detroit, the border of which stretched along 8 Mile to what felt like the ends of a flat Earth. At auction a few years back the nameplate that Coleman Young kept atop his mayor's desk sold for six hundred dollars. It said "MFIC."

In *The American Earthquake,* Edmund Wilson, sounding a little like Mayor Young fifty years later, writes disapprovingly of Henry Ford's "removal of his factories to Dearborn outside the city limits, in order to escape city taxes." Elsewhere, sounding like the soul of common sense, Wilson observes: "You can see here, as it is impossible to do in a more varied and complex city, the whole structure of an industrial society; almost everybody who lives in Detroit is dependent on the motor industry and in more or less obvious relation to everybody else who lives here. When the industry is crippled, everybody is hit."

Whatever. Back then, as we were leaving behind Belle Isle and the blank space where the Uniroyal Tire plant had been, heading toward the Chrysler Jefferson plant that, a decade hence, would become the DaimlerChrysler Jefferson plant, it was just me and my father in a car. We came to a red light on Jefferson—"Slip it in neutral"—and coasted to a stop. I put the car back into first as we idled, and we took off again, using the gear progression to which I'd grown accustomed. But my father started to get fancy. "You can skip gears, you know. Go ahead—put it in fourth if you're so good." He accelerated hard in second, so that the car wouldn't chug in the higher gear, and put in the clutch. I made the shift, but went up and over to third before pulling back and finding fourth. "That's cheating. Now back to second," he said, hitting the brakes. I found the lower gear, bypassing third entirely this time. "Not bad. The hardest downshift is from fifth to second." "Let's try that," I said. "We can't get going fast enough for fifth on Jefferson," he said. "We can go to third, though, without the clutch, if you want to." He was quiet, listening to the engine, trying to find the sweet spot. "Okay," he said after a time, letting the car coast, "go on. Slow." Concentrating hard, I pushed the shifter up and over while staring at my father's feet, both of which were firmly on the floor mat. The gears didn't grind— his doing, not mine—and we drove on in third. It was the closest we ever came to discussing the facts of life. "You did it right," he said, smiling.

Do the thing right. Goddamnit, do it *right*—how many times had I heard this growing up? No, no, not like that—there, like *that*. See the difference? Want me to show you again? Yes, I think these days: show me again. Let me see it again. Because it's going, all of it, and the only way to preserve it is to put it down on paper and to hope that I managed, at long last, to get some things right.

Acknowledgments

Many thanks to my agent at Russell & Volkening, Timothy Seldes, and to my editor at Doubleday, Adam Bellow. Thanks as well to those who commented upon various versions of the manuscript, particularly Rob Franciosi and Stanley Shapiro, talented readers both. To my immediate family, I owe a debt it will take lifetimes to repay.

Thanks to Roman Godzak, archivist for the Archdiocese of Detroit, who shared with me Father Hec's records. Mr. Godzak's books *Catholic Churches of Detroit* (Arcadia, 2004) and *Make Straight the Path: A 300-Year Pilgrimage: Archdiocese of Detroit* (Editions du Signe: Strasbourg, France, 2000) were just as considerable a help. For similar assistance with facts related to Sister Marcia, I must thank Sister Marilyn Sullivan at the Sisters of St. Joseph of Nazareth convent outside Kalamazoo.

The books that I kept beside me throughout were: *The Quotations of Mayor Coleman A. Young* (Droog Press, 1992), compiled by reporters for the *Detroit News* and *Detroit Free Press; Detroit and Its World Setting: A Three Hundred Year Chronology, 1701–2001,* edited by David Lee

Poremba (Wayne State UP, 2001); *The Detroit Almanac: Three Hundred Years of Life in the Motor City,* edited by Peter Gavrilovich and Bill Mc-Graw (Detroit: Detroit Free Press, 2001); Ze'ev Chafets's *Devil's Night: And Other True Tales of Detroit* (Random House, 1990); and *Hard Stuff: The Autobiography of Mayor Coleman Young* (Viking, 1994), by Young and Lonnie Wheeler. Both these latter books belong back in print. The sections dealing with the residency requirement and STRESS, in particular, draw from *Hard Stuff.*

The best academic treatment of contemporary Detroit that I have read is *Racial Situations: Class Predicaments of Whiteness in Detroit* (Princeton UP, 1999), by John Hartigan Jr. The section dealing with the opening of the Malcolm X Academy is indebted to his fine book, from which details and quotes have been drawn.

The quotes from Tocqueville in the opening chapter come from his *Journey to America* (Yale UP, 1960), translated by George Lawrence and edited by J. P. Mayer. The "Vote the Black Slate" sign from the fall of 1973 appeared in the Detroit Public Library's 2004 exhibit on the Reverend Albert Cleage and the Shrine of the Black Madonna.